KNOSSOS . . . MYCENAE . . .
TROY . . . ATHENS . . . ALEXANDRIA

The indebtedness of Western civilization to Greece far exceeds the well-known glories of Periclean Athens. For, as modern archaeology has revealed, before Periclean Athens there was the Lyric Age— and before that, the Dorians and Mycenae, "rich in gold," . . . and the Bronze Age culture of the Minoans.

Penetrating the mists of prehistory to the battlements of New Stone Age settlements, archaeologists have assembled a fascinating picture of the continuity of mankind's culture on the mainland and across the islands of the ancient Greek world. Paul MacKendrick presents that picture in all its rich detail, weaving the suspenseful "detective story" methods of the archaeologist with the enduring values of the cultural historian. The result is a magnificent re-creation of the ways of life, religious practices, agriculture, trade, and—above **all**— the arts as they flourished over three millennia in the Aegean.

Here are doomed Minoan knights marching off to do battle against iron-armed "barbarian" invaders, ancestors of the Classical Greeks . . . wealthy trading cities racked by earthquake, fire, and sword . . . Homer's Greece and its emergence in literature, sculpture, painting, and architecture. Here too is the perfection of the Athenian Acropolis; the Delphic precinct of Apollo, monumental Agrigento, and the Hellenistic cities of Asia Minor and Egypt.

"A thrilling tale. . . . For those who want an authoritative exposition of what archaeologists are accomplishing in Greek lands, whether along the Euphrates or in Sicily or somewhere in between, for such was the extent of Hellenism itself."—C.A. Robinson, *The New York Times Book Review*

Other MENTOR Books on Ancient Greece and Rome

THE MUTE STONES SPEAK by Paul MacKendrick. The story of the dramatic archaeological finds in Italy which have revealed the fabric of ancient Roman civilization. Lavishly illustrated. (#MQ673—95¢)

THE CIVILIZATION OF ROME by Donald R. Dudley. A cultural and social history of Rome from the earliest times to the fall of the Empire. (#MT472—75¢)

GREEK CIVILIZATION AND CHARACTER edited by Arnold J. Toynbee. Brilliant translations of expressions of Hellenic experience and life that shed light on contemporary problems. (#MP501—60¢)

MYTHOLOGY by Edith Hamilton. A brilliant retelling of the classic Greek, Roman, and Norse legends of love and adventure. (#MP665—60¢)

THE GREEK STONES SPEAK

The Story of
Archaeology in Greek Lands

PAUL MacKENDRICK

A MENTOR BOOK

Published by The New American Library, New York and Toronto

Published as a MENTOR BOOK
by arrangement with St Martin's Press, Inc.,
who have authorized this softcover edition.
A hardcover edition is available from St Martin's Press, Inc.

First Printing, April, 1966

MENTOR BOOKS are published in the United States by
The New American Library, Inc.,
1301 Avenue of the Americas, New York, New York 10019,
in Canada by The New American Library of Canada Limited,
295 King Street East, Toronto 2, Ontario

PRINTED IN THE UNITED STATES OF AMERICA

For

WALTER R. AGARD

FOREWORD

This book is a companion to *The Mute Stones Speak: the Story of Archaeology in Italy* (New York, St Martin's, 1960). In both books, my aims have been twofold: to write cultural history based on a selection of archaeological evidence, and to illustrate archaeological inference at work. My choice of sites has been based on these aims, and this book is a matter ultimately of personal choice. But I have felt bound to include more sites in the Greek than in the Roman book, because of the wider area covered—from Sicily to Syria—and because excavation is going on so actively in Greece and Greek lands; so actively that I have had to eliminate any discussion of results announced after August 23, 1961, the terminal date of my last visit to Greece.

I have found it a significant commentary on a profound cultural difference between Greece and Rome that while it was possible to write a book about archaeology in Italy with minimal reference to sculpture and painting, such omission has proved both impossible and undesirable in a book on excavation in Greece. But criticism of art is not primarily my aim, and exceeds my competence; I have tried rather to emphasize the history of architecture. I have deliberately extended my scope to include a selective account of what happened to Greek architectural forms under the Roman Empire, a neglected field, the treatment of which here fills a gap noticed by a few reviewers of *The Mute Stones Speak*.

My obligations are many, and it is a pleasure to record them, with warmest thanks. I first visited Greece and Greek lands in 1936, on a traveling fellowship from Harvard. Subsequent visits were made possible by the Fulbright Commission in 1950, the Trustees of the American Academy in Rome in 1956, the Guggenheim Foundation in 1958, and the Research Committee of the University of Wisconsin Graduate School in 1961. I am grateful for the hospitality of the libraries of the American Academy in Rome and the American School of Classical Studies in Athens, whose librarians, Mrs. Inez Longobardi and Mrs. Mary Zelia Philippides, exceed in helpfulness the most exacting scholar's ideal; and for the friendly efficiency of the staff of the Agora Excavations. I am grateful also to the dozens of archaeologists who have patiently answered my questions as we ate together in Loring Hall in Athens, that worthy successor, as a *phrontisterion*, to the Museum at Alexandria. I have not always accepted their advice; I may not have interpreted them accurately: for these sins of omission and commission they are of course not responsible. Three friends and colleagues, Walter R. Agard, Emmett L. Bennett, Jr., and Francis R. Walton, have read the manuscript in whole or in part; where I have heeded their criticisms, the book has benefited. Professor Bennett and another colleague, Professor John Paul Heironimus, have been kind enough to read the proofs. The dedication to the first of these four friends is partial and inadequate thanks for sixteen years of patient, friendly, and inspiring counsel.

Pharos Aiginis
August, 1961

CONTENTS

ILLUSTRATIONS

xiii

NOTE

The legends under each illustration give references to sources, either in full or by short title. The key to the short titles is in the list of *Books and Articles Consulted*. Where no reference is given, the source is assumed to be in the public domain. For permissions to reproduce photographs, warmest thanks are due to the holders of copyright.

Fig. 1.1 Troy II, "Priam's treasure." Two gold cups and a gold "sauce-boat," actually 1000 years older than Priam. Formerly in Museum für Vor- und Fruhgeschichte, Berlin; abstracted by Russians, present whereabouts uncertain. (F. Matz, *KMT*, Pl. 5)

1 The Aegean in Prehistory (to 1900 B. C.)

On May 31, 1873 Heinrich Schliemann, far on the lofty plains of windy Troy, wrote in his journal, "Eight or nine meters down I laid bare the stretch of the circuit wall of Troy by the Scaean Gate and discovered, in a room of the House of Priam adjoining this wall, a copper container . . . filled with great silver vases and with silver and gold cups (Fig. 1.1). To keep these from the workmen's greed, I had to extract them, hide them [in his wife's shawl], and send them off in such haste that I neither know their number nor am in a position to describe their form."

The excavations that uncovered this treasure, begun three years before, opened a new and fascinating chapter in ancient history. Later investigation showed that the treasure, the house, and the wall were not Priam's, but a thousand years older; that the findspot was not a room in a Trojan house, but a hiding place in the wall itself. But for all his error and amateurishness, Schliemann was a pioneer, the founder of the new science of archaeology, which by now has revolutionized our ideas of the origins of Greek civilization. He began in a new spirit. His enthusiasm was not simply for treasure in gold and silver, but for evidence: evidence, now universally accepted, that the Trojan war as described in Homer was historic fact. To establish this thesis, he learned

21

to depend on what have been the archaeologist's most re-
liable indicators ever since, potsherds (Fig. 1.2) which, he
wrote in 1876 to his friend Gladstone, "are far more in-
destructible than all the city or fortress walls in the world.
The strongest wall in the world can easily be removed, but
no mortal man can remove the potsherds with which the
site of every ancient city is covered."

In an age when Greek scholars scorned everything pre-
classical Schliemann devoted his efforts entirely to prehistory,
and most of what we know about the Aegean since the third
millennium B.C. we owe to beginnings made by him. When
in 1882 he persuaded the twenty-nine-year-old William
Dörpfeld, a trained architect who had already dug at
Olympia, to join him at Troy, the combination of Schliemann's enthusiasm and wealth (derived from judicious prof-
iteering in the Crimean War) with Dörpfeld's precision,
clarity, sound method, and sobriety made possible a genuinely
scientific contribution to the understanding of the history of
Troy. This understanding was still further refined by the
University of Cincinnati excavations under C. W. Blegen
(1932-38). The whole dramatic story of prehistoric archaeology in the Aegean area, bound up as it is with strong
personalities, is as full of human as it is of scientific interest.

Schliemann's earliest report on his excavations at Troy is
dated April 21, 1870, and is addressed to the president of the
Institut de France. In it he expresses his conviction that
the eighty-five-foot mound of Hissarlik, some three and a half
miles back from the sea, is Homer's Troy. He describes with
impatience his difficulties in getting authorization to dig from
the Turkish government, records his decision to dig without
permission, and tells how within an hour of first striking
spade into Trojan earth, he came upon ancient walls. Already he has some of what we now recognize as the in-
stincts of the archaeologist. He notes the depths of finds,
records strata (including evidence of burning and earthquake) and fortification walls, mentions finds of coins, potsherds, and unidentified clay objects (they were spindle
whorls, of which Troy has yielded an astonishing number).
He identifies as a temple a building of rectangular plan that
later turned out to be a megaron, the standard Early Bronze
Age upper-class dwelling. Schliemann's megaron at Troy had
when it was new a long narrow hall with a weighty roof of

Fig. 1.2 Troy I-II, pottery shapes (Nos. 17-31) compared to those of eastern Anatolia (1-16), and early mainland Greece (32-45), to show how archaeologists determine cultural relations between sites. (Schachermeyr, 1955, p. 155, by permission of the publishers, W. Kohlhammer, Stuttgart)

cypress beams, a central hearth thirteen feet wide, an open porch, and a single door. Some scholars claim it to be the ancestor of the classical Greek temple.

In this first dig Schliemann often drew inferences as if by instinct from the very objects that have since proved most useful to archaeologists in their work of reconstructing a culture from mute stones and clay. But in 1872, in his impatience to get at the Homeric city, he dug the great north-south trench that ruined so much—almost a quarter —of the precious stratification of his beloved city. The damage was not irreparable, however, for he left "islands" in the midst of his trench from which Dörpfeld and Blegen were later able to recover the history of the site. By 1879 he knew his business and was able to distinguish seven superimposed citadels on the hill of Hissarlik. His findings would have been more precise had not the Turks, for military reasons, forbidden all measuring and drawing on the site. In 1881, after two years of desk-work at fourteen hours a day, he published his findings in *Ilios*, a landmark in the history of Greek archaeology.

Of all his finds, the most thrilling and spectacular was "Priam's treasure" (see Fig. 1.1). Besides vessels and weapons in bronze and copper, which proved the hoard to belong to a civilization that has already emerged from the Neolithic age, the treasure included vessels and jewelry in precious metals: a golden flask and a "sauce-boat," a golden diadem, earrings, and necklaces, in which he arrayed his lovely Greek wife, Sophie, and had her picture taken; six golden armbands, bar silver, many vessels in silver, and in the alloy of gold and silver called electrum, and 8700 miscellaneous golden objects: granulated gold earrings, buttons, and beads. The earrings mostly were not matched pairs, and were therefore probably the spoils of Trojan raids; if they had matched, there would have been more reason to believe that they came from a Trojan princess' jewel box.

Though this was only one of nineteen such hoards found by successive excavators on the site, it was the one that captured the public imagination and established Schliemann's fame overnight. Apart from its intrinsic value and the romantic circumstances of its discovery, the treasure has another, deeper interest. After Dörpfeld's careful work had established that the treasure belonged not to Priam's Troy, but to Troy II, over a thousand years earlier, it became clear that this early Troy's wealth was princely, derived from

Fig. 1.3 Troy, Dorpfeld's plan, distinguishing three subdivisions of Troy II. The darker the wall-line, the earlier the level. Blegen added four subphases, but Dörpfeld's pioneer work has stood up well. (Dörpfeld, 1902, fac. p. 16)

war, but perhaps also from profitable trade with inner Anatolia, the Aegean Islands, and the Balkans, for all these regions have yielded to the archaeologist's spade objects comparable to those which make up the treasure. The "sauceboat" is Aegean, the granulated gold technique is Mesopotamian (there is a Mesopotamian cylinder seal among the finds to reinforce the connection), and the handsome "parade ax" in lapis lazuli which forms part of another treasure of the same date has parallels in Bessarabia. Finds of Baltic amber, too, point to connections with the north.

When Schliemann died in 1890, he had dug at Mycenae, Ithaca, Orchomenos, and Tiryns, and had negotiated, unsuccessfully, for excavation rights in Crete, but the plan and dating of the various levels at Troy were still not entirely clear. That Dörpfeld was able to draw and date a plan was due largely to funds generously provided by Schliemann's widow, and later by Kaiser Wilhelm II, to whom Dörpfeld's two great volumes on Troy are dedicated. His trained architect's eye was able to distinguish nine superimposed levels on the citadel, and his plans of 1902 are still au-

Fig. 1.4   Troy VI, fortification wall. Built in segments, with a pronounced batter (receding slope) to support mud-brick superstructure. (F. Matz, KMT, Pl. 114)

thoritative (Fig. 1.3). Among his 120 workmen were many named after Homeric heroes, who proudly answered, "Here!" as the names Agamemnon, Odysseus, Achilles were called at muster. On the evidence of the technique of the walls (Fig. 1.4), and of the pottery, which resembled that found at Mycenae, he identified the sixth level from the bottom, which had not been completely excavated at Schliemann's death, as that of Homeric Troy. This conclusion remained unchallenged until Blegen's more meticulous techniques modified it in 1937. Dörpfeld and his colleagues distinguished building materials of different dates, dated fortification walls, recorded the pottery carefully level by level, catalogued the thousands of small finds in metal, stone, bone, and clay, described the sculpture, inscriptions, and coins of the post-Homeric levels, and drew masterly conclusions about the history of the pre-Homeric and Homeric cities. In 1902 it seemed as though the definitive archaeological history of Troy had already been written.

But in the next thirty years new excavation on the Greek mainland, in the Cyclades, and in Crete (see map, Fig. 1.5) had raised new problems about the history, culture, and trade relations of prehistoric settlements in the Aegean basin, so that when in 1932 the Taft family made funds available to Professor Carl W. Blegen of the University of Cincinnati, he eagerly reopened the excavations at Troy. His aim was to use the information collected since Dörpfeld's book to fix a chronology and clarify Troy's cultural relations by means of artifacts from which he could draw dependable inferences because their precise findspots in the complicated levels were known. The terms of the Taft grant placed him under no compulsion to be startling or sensational, or to court publicity, and indeed the contents of his four massive volumes (1950-58) are more scientific than glamorous. In the first of his seven campaigns he dug over three miles of trenches in a fruitless search for pre-classical tombs; in 1935 he dug in eleven areas and removed with his light railway 3000 carloads of debris; in 1937 he moved over 10,000 carloads of earth. His finds, chiefly pottery, he deposited in the Archaeological Museum in Istanbul, reserving a sample collection—400 boxes of certified potsherds—for the local museum in Troy's port town, Chanakkale, while a still more select sampling was kept for exhibition in the Excavation House on the site.

Fig. 1.5   Neolithic, Bronze, and Iron Age sites in Greek lands, numbered in the order of their presentation in the text. To illustrate Chs. 1-3.

1. Troy	17. Malthi	33. H. Triada
2. Thermi	18. Chalandriani	34. Athens
3. Poliochni	19. H. Andreas	35. Salamis
4. Sesklo	20. Phylakopi	36. Perati
5. Dimini	21. Knossos	37. Miletus
6. Iolkos	22. Mochlos	38. Ialysos
7. Orchomenos	23. Mycenae	39. Enkomi
8. Eutresis	24. Dendra	40. Assarlik
9. Tiryns	25. Pylos	41. Old Smyrna
10. Korakou	26. Amnisos	42. Karphi
11. Zygouries	27. Gla	43. Vrokastro
12. Prosymna	28. Eleusis	44. Dreros
13. Asine	29. Mallia	45. Perachora
14. Lerna	30. Tylissos	46. Thebes
15. H. Kosmas	31. Gournia	47. Thermon
16. Asea	32. Phaistos	48. Sparta
		49. Samos

ANATOLIA

LYDIA

CYPRUS
(SAME SCALE)

Blegen's methods, a model of scientific archaeology at work, are the envy of his fellow archaeologists. They involve patience, persistence, and controlled imagination. He had to remove the enormous dump of earth from Schliemann's excavations, first making sure that the site chosen for the new dump was archaeologically sterile. He had to assure the continuity of his staff, so that the same scholar could be in charge of the same area for season after season. He had to train his workmen; to issue them, for example, only small picks, so that the delicate pottery would not be damaged. He had to make sure that the excavation daybooks were meticulously kept. He dug trial trenches to determine strata, being careful to dig always at right angles to walls, not parallel to them, so as to record the contiguous strata. He took levels carefully with a surveyor's transit. He saw to it that the expedition's architect kept up with the dig, drawing stone-for-stone plans. Every find, however insignificant, had a wooden label attached, recording the area, section, and level in which it was found, assigning it a number and a date, with a cross-reference to the notebook where its detailed description was recorded. The earth was sieved, as though the excavators were panning for gold; and indeed from the historical point of view their conclusions were more precious than gold. The smallest finds were placed in pillboxes, cushioned with cotton wool. Sherds were cleaned in a dilute solution of hydrochloric acid, pots were mended with shellac, gaps in them filled with plaster. Inventories were kept, the finds numbered by categories, thousands of photographs taken.

Dörpfeld's nine settlements stood up well under Blegen's more refined analysis, but each was broken down into subphases, so that in the end forty-six subdivisions were distinguished. The criteria used for setting up the nine phases were sweeping shifts in orientation (Fig. 1.6), changes in implements, artifacts, and pottery. Careful type-charts drew distinctions, vital for dating, in pot shapes and decoration (the pots of Troy I were handmade and incised), and in types of pins, idols, bone awls, and spindle whorls. Blegen found copper in the lowest level: Troy I was already on the way to the Bronze Age in 2600 B.C. Molds in stone and terracotta show that the artifacts were made on the spot. None of the pottery in this earliest level could be matched elsewhere: this settlement was not yet sophisticated or important enough to have much of an import trade. A sur-

Fig. 1.6a Troy I. b. Troy II, to illustrate criteria for
distinguishing phases. Note difference in orientation, and, in
II, more sophisticated plan: larger megaron, portico, double gates. (Schachermeyr, 1955, Figs. 42 and 144)

prising and unique find was a sandstone slab or stele with a representation of a human face, the earliest such monument known from the Aegean area.

And Troy I was fortified. What was excavated was a citadel, a place reserved for the king and his nobles, with no evidence throughout its ten subphases of any of the humble dwellings or artifacts which would have indicated the presence of a lower class. Yet the finds revealed that there were Trojan farmers, fishermen, potters, stonemasons, and builders. These must have lived in the lower town, as yet unexcavated, below the hill of Hissarlik. Between this lowest level and Troy II was the evidence, in a burnt layer, of the destruction of the earliest settlement by fire.

In Troy II Blegen, carefully observing the pottery, and with the help of the stratification in the "islands" left by Schliemann and Dörpfeld, was able to distinguish seven subphases, compressed into two meters vertically. Most of these subphases in most places belonged to the final phase. Within this level the culture developed rapidly: wheel-made pottery now first replaced handmade ware; excavation of the fortification walls showed that the citadel was expanded and remodeled on a grand scale, with massive double-roomed gateways and a double megaron surrounded by a colonnade. Late in this level falls Schliemann's "treasure"; the finds, in gold, silver, and crystal, and abundant pottery show, as we have seen, contacts with and imitations of neighboring cultures, to the north, in the hinterland of Asia Minor, and in the Aegean islands, and the ratio of imported to local ceramics increases from phase to phase.

Troy II ended in cataclysm, as Schliemann's treasure shows: no survivor returned to recover it. In one room of a private house, the excavators report, the "orderly rows of loomweights, and the 189 small gold beads found scattered on the floor, suggest a wife busy at the loom, summoned to flee for her life; in her haste to escape, we may suppose she abandoned her bracelet or necklace, perhaps caught in the fabric she was weaving, or taken off and hung up while she was performing her task."

The next three levels, while they yielded less impressive finds, were more than mere villages; Troy VI, richer still than Troy II, and apparently destroyed by an earthquake, brings us to the threshold of Priam's city, discussion of which is best postponed to the next chapter. Since the lowest five levels yielded no frescoes or inscriptions, the prehistoric twilight remains nearly impenetrable, but the evidence is clear of aristocratic prosperity, derived from trade; of distinction between class and mass; of life lived with a certain elegance: drinking vessels in precious metals, shaded porticoes to walk in, heated houses, but with a certain insecurity too; the Trojan princes felt the need to protect themselves behind walls over thirty feet thick.

The relative chronology of artifacts found on a site can be established if careful attention is paid to the levels in which objects are found. Stone artifacts are, normally, earlier than copper, copper than bronze, bronze than iron. Incised pottery is usually earlier than painted ware. Similar objects found at different sites establish synchronism between the corresponding levels. But in prehistoric archaeology, where most sites were inhabited by a population ignorant of writing, absolute chronology, expressed in years B.C., is harder to arrive at. Usually it depends on equations established between finds on such a site as Troy, where no early written records exist, and finds from more sophisticated places such as the Hittite country in inner Asia Minor, or Egypt, where dated written records were kept from very early times. Where there is no writing, pottery is very important. Thus sherds from Troy II resemble closely in fabric and decoration a sherd from Asine, on the Greek mainland, in the Argolid (see map, Fig. 1.5), which is stamped with a swastika seal identical with some found in Egypt in a context dated to the Vth Dynasty. Written records date the Vth Dynasty between 2500 and 2350 B.C. Such is the complicated set of equations by which a fixed point can be established within Troy II (see table, Fig. 1.7). Once this date is firmly established, all stratified objects found at Troy below the level of our eloquent potsherds are obviously earlier, and all stratified objects found above it are later than this date. Some notion of the duration in time of a given level results from the thickness of the strata. Thus the date accepted by most scholars nowadays for Troy I is 2600-2400 B.C.; for Troy II, 2400-2200; for Troy III-V, 2200-1900; and for Troy VI, a deep stratum, 1900-1300. This still does not bring us down to the date assigned by Greek literary sources to the fall of Priam's Troy, which is 1184 B.C.; Blegen found reason to date it some fifty years earlier.

The net result of ninety years of archaeological study of Troy, from Schliemann to Blegen, has been to change it from a romantic and puzzling source of golden treasures and

Homeric adventure tales into a thoroughly known series of organized settlements. History has replaced false glamor, and this in the long run is a good thing.

	Crete	Cyclades	Mainland		Troy	
3000 plus						3000 plus
2900	NEOLITHIC					2900
2800	Neolithic		Neolithic A			2800
2700						2700
2600						2600
2500	Early Minoan I				Troy I	2500
2400				Neolithic B Macedonia and Thessaly	Troy II	2400
2300		Early Cycladic	Early			2300
2200	Early Minoan II					2200
2100	Early Minoan III		Helladic			2100
2000					Troy III–V	2000
1900	Middle Minoan I and II	Middle Cycladic				1900
1800			Middle Helladic		Troy VI	1800
1700	Middle Minoan III					1700
1600						1600
1500	Late Minoan I & II*	Late Cycladic	Late Helladic I			1500
1400			Late Helladic II			1400
1300	Late Minoan III		Late Helladic III		Troy VII A	1300
1200						1200
1125	Sub-Minoan		Athens Sub-Myc.	Corinth	Laconia	1125
1075	IRON AGE		Proto-Geometric			1075
1000	Proto-Geometric	Proto-Geometric		Proto-Geometric	Proto-Geometric	1000
900						900
850			Geometric	Geometric		850

(The left margin reads "BRONZE AGE" vertically spanning from roughly 2600 to 1200, and "IRON AGE" from 1125 to 850.)

* Late Minoan II is a subdivision of Late Minoan I; it is peculiar to Cnossus and contemporary with the last 50 years of L.M I.

Fig. 1.7   Synchronisms: Crete, Cyclades, mainland, Troy. (Hammond, p. 21)

While the Americans under Blegen were digging at Troy, a British expedition led by Miss Winifred Lamb was excavating at Thermi, six miles northwest of the picturesque town of Mytilene on the rocky olive- and vine-clad island of Lesbos, some sixty miles south of Troy. Here the sea had eroded the cliff face to expose walls, pebble floors, and sherds "as thick as plums in a cake." In the mountainous, thin-soiled Greek islands, land is at a premium, and peasants are understandably reluctant to sacrifice arable land to the archaeologist's spade. They drive hard bargains, as Schliemann found when he tried to excavate in Crete. But Miss Lamb had difficulty only with one landowner, and managed to dig at Thermi for five seasons, unearthing five superimposed towns, each distinguished by different houses, differently oriented, and separated by sterile strata indicating gaps in the occupation of the site. Miss Lamb's work was in the best tradition of modern scientific archaeology. A gun emplacement on the site supplied a bench-mark from which levels could be taken; she drew stone-for-stone maps of each of her five towns, dividing them into areas lettered in Greek so that the workmen could read the labels attached to the finds, and understand the importance of recording the find-spot of each artifact exactly.

Her most important conclusion was negative. Of the 604 pots she catalogued from all five towns, not one was wheel-made. All can be matched in shape and decoration from Troy I or other Anatolian sites known to be contemporary with Troy I. This means that the history of all five towns at Thermi is embraced within the 200 years (about 2600-2400 B.C.) assigned to Troy I.

Among artifacts, weapons are rare, and Thermi I was unwalled: this suggests a peaceful agricultural community without fear of aggression. Bones found in the houses show that animals—goat, pig, and ox—were domesticated, and Miss Lamb was able to report that there had been a local breed of prehistoric dog "about the size of a fox-terrier." The earliest settlers of Thermi were fishermen, too, as their descendants still are. Bone fishhooks and terracotta net-sinkers were found, and shells of limpets, oysters, sea urchins, and cuttlefish show that seafood was part of the diet. The site yielded vegetable seeds, but no grain; yet, since the houses have ovens, grain must have been raised and used for bread. Spindle whorls, loom weights, and spools found beside the hearth present a pleasant if dullish pic-

Fig. 1.8   Thermi V, showing double or triple circuit wall and long narrow houses with common party walls. (Schachermeyr, 1955, p. 167)

ture of the domestic occupation of women.

Beginning with Thermi II, Miss Lamb found molds, some containing a cupreous deposit, which on assay proved to contain an amount of arsenic appropriate to Anatolian copper; she also found whetstones of emery, the nearest deposits of which occur on the mainland coast opposite Lesbos, but not on the island itself; from these facts the inference is warranted that Thermi's earliest trade relations were with Asia Minor. But over 100 teracotta figurines or idols, crudely representing big-breasted, fat-bottomed women—the "Mother Goddess"?—have hybrid parallels, ranging from Thessaly to the Cyclades and south and central Anatolia.

Thermi's developed town plan (Fig. 1.8) presents long narrow houses of the megaron type familiar from Troy. They are equipped with built-in benches, sleeping alcoves, an altar, an oven, and a well. The lower courses of their walls are built in the herringbone fashion also found in Troy I. The houses are close together and were probably flat-roofed. They radiate from an open space which is the ancestor of the classical agora or market place. Beginning with Thermi II, the streets are paved—with beach pebbles —and Thermi V has a double or triple circuit wall, the innermost of which is thick and equipped with towers. The walls, like early Troy's, must have been built to meet a threat from the Hittites or some other rising power in central Anatolia. Miss Lamb found no evidence of violent destruction: the site appears simply to have been abandoned for a thousand years. When it revived, its pottery shows the influence of Mycenean Greece. A final cataclysm destroyed the site about 1200 B.C. What destroyed late Thermi is what destroyed Troy VII*a*: the Achaean expedition immortalized by Homer. Achilles sleeps with one woman of Lesbos, spoils of a raid; and is promised others, similarly acquired, by Agamemnon, when he tries to persuade him to renounce his wrath and rejoin the battle.

American and British activity at Troy and Thermi was matched between 1930 and 1936, and has been matched again since 1951, despite the imminent danger of being blown up by land mines, by Italian excavation at Poliochni, on the east coast of the island of Lemnos: in mythology, the seat of the forge of the lame smith-god Hephaestus. The early work at Poliochni trained a generation of young Italian archaeologists, but the original excavator died without having produced a final publication. Recent work has been complicated by the vandalism of German troops quartered on the island in World War II. They robbed the walls of building stone, dug trenches through the main street of the prehistoric settlement, and dumped into meaningless heaps the pottery finds from 150 carefully labeled cases. Old

Fig. 1.9 Poliochni, Yellow level, house blocks. Note oven, and wells marking two public squares. (Bernabo Brea, 1955, p. 150, by permission of Prehistoric Society of England and Wales)

notebooks proved incomplete: there were no drawings, sections, or restorations, and no complete site plan. This is a pity, for Poliochni was a vast Bronze Age town, one of the most important in the Aegean. It had (Fig. 1.9) a circuit wall, regular wide streets and squares, sometimes paved; blocks of houses bounded by alleys; public wells, storm sewers, warehouses backed against the circuit wall—all giving evidence of a strong central authority and a high degree of civic organization and social progress. Separate rooms for artisans show division of labor, and one large chamber is identified by the excavators as an assembly room for the town elders. The Italians distinguish seven levels, which they designate by colors. (This is a sensible way of meeting a difficulty; namely, that at the outset of a dig an excavator cannot be sure that the lowest level in his first trench is really Level I, the next above Level II, and so on; another trench may reveal an earlier level.) The oldest or Black level is thirty feet down; since it contains oval huts, known elsewhere to be older than houses of rectangular plan, this level is presumed older than Troy I, but it has emerged from the Neolithic, since bronze was found in it. The three levels above this, Blue, Green, and Red, are dated by pottery to the time of Troy I and early Troy II. The three upper levels, Yellow, Orange, and Brown, have the same time span as Troy II-V (2400-1900 B.C.). The Yellow level, which corresponds in its earliest part to the height of Troy II, yielded the most impressive buildings; no princely houses, but complexes of twenty rooms or more are evidence for a prosperous bourgeoisie. In one of these, in the summer of 1956, workmen clearing away roots pulled to the surface a buried jug containing a gold treasure comparable to "Priam's," and of the same date. It included a soldered filigree gold pin with two animal figures, gold earrings, buttons, torques, and necklaces; the technique is Anatolian. Pots knocked to smithereens from falling walls, but with the fragments still fairly well united, give evidence of a violent and unexpected destruction of this level, about 2000 B.C. or a little after. This ended Poliochni's prosperity, for this is the best period of conspicuous architectural remains. This destruction may have been the work of invaders not from Anatolia, but from mainland Greece, themselves refugees from intruders from the Balkans who were probably, as we shall see, the first true Greeks, in the linguistic sense, to enter European history.

Though the earliest modern work on the prehistoric
Greek world was not done on the mainland, it inspired work
there, especially by Greek, German, and American archaeologists, and what they found proved to be earlier than Troy
I; in fact, Neolithic. (Thus far palaeolithic discoveries in
Greece have been few, but they are well attested and fairly
widespread. Fourteen graves containing stone implements
of the Mousterian period [ca. 130,000 B.C.] were reported in
1959 from the Peneus valley in Thessaly. A small cave in
Boeotia [Seidi near Haliartos] has also produced palaeolithic implements.) Among the earliest and best work was
that published in 1908 by the pioneering Greek archaeologist
Chrestos Tsountas at Sesklό and Dimίni in the rich farm-
ing land of Thessaly (see map, Fig. 1.5). Sesklo—the name
means "beet" in modern Greek—lies two and a half hours'
walk northwest of Volos, now the second port of Greece;
in antiquity it was called Iolkos, and was the port from
which sailed Jason and the Argonauts after the Golden
Fleece; an important palace of Mycenaean date has recently been discovered there. Sesklo is of unique interest
because Tsountas found there a stratum nearly ten feet deep,
far, far below the levels of pottery that matched Troy
I. This stratum contained sherds in context with stone weapons, in jadeite, granite, and jasper. These must belong to a
developed Neolithic age: Tsountas called it Neolithic A. This
period, to judge by the thickness of the deposit, must antedate the founding of Troy by a good 200 years. Nowadays
over 150 Neolithic sites are known in Thessaly, but of these
Sesklo and Dimini are still among the best recorded.
Tsountas' great virtue was an analytic mind combined with
a sharp eye. He laid down over fifty years ago categories of
Neolithic pottery which, though expanded in the youthful
work (1912) of the great English archaeologist A. J. B. Wace,
have never been superseded, and which have proved valuable
for producing order out of chaos wherever Neolithic ware has
appeared in northern Greece, and for providing certified
parallels with Neolithic pottery elsewhere. The most interesting Neolithic A ware is painted, not incised, with geometric
patterns. With the next level above, Neolithic B, restraint
disappears, and the pottery (Fig. 1.10), while still not
naturalistic in motif, is of a truly barbaric lavishness and
undisciplined exuberance, in two or three colors, involving
meanders, checkerboards (sometimes in different fields on
the same pot), spirals, chevrons, ripples, zigzags, hatched

Fig. 1.10 Dimini, Neolithic B, two patterns on the same bowl. The patterns recur on Geometric ware 1600 years later. (Wace, Prehistoric *Thessaly*, p. 76, by permission of Cambridge University Press)

circles, bowed curves, executed with the greatest freedom and variety, at its best anticipating and outdoing in stylistic technique the Geometric ware that was to be the fashion in Greece 1600 years later.

This pottery was found mostly on the acropolis of Sesklo (Fig. 1.11), which lies strategically located, with water for man and beast, in a secluded mountain glen between two rivers, 650 feet above sea level. Traces are preserved of what is perhaps a double circuit of Neolithic B walls in the southwest. The largest house has a porch, a main room with three postholes and a fixed hearth, an inner room with two ovens, and a back apartment, divided into three small rooms, which Tsountas thought was made over for the eldest son of the house when he married. (There was some provision for privacy: one house had a device for locking the bedroom door from the inside.) There is some evidence that the houses were built to a standard measure, the unit being 0.30 m. (about a foot). Chunks of dried mud, with an imprint of reeds, preserve the traces of a pitched roof; Tsountas saw in the houses, with their porches and inner rooms, the prototype of the classical Greek temple.

In the houses Tsountas found fifty-nine idols in clay, stone, and bone, mostly exceptionally well-padded females, with

Fig. 1.11 Sesklo, plan. The lighter level is the earlier. Rooms 1-5 make up the made-over house described in the text. (Schachermeyr, 1955, p. 70

■ Sesklo-Stufe

▨ Dimini-Stufe

their hands on their breasts, and with rolls of fat at the hips. There was one Neolithic madonna and child, and one male statuette two and a half inches high, grasping his private parts with both hands. Obviously fertility was an abiding interest, if not an obsession, with the Neolithic inhabitants of Sesklo. Among other artifacts might be singled out knives of flint (imported from Albania and Epirus), and obsidian (imported from the island of Melos). Neolithic B foodstuffs included wheat, barley, peas, acorns, almonds, and figs.

Prehistoric Dimini (Fig. 1.12), an hour seaward (east) of Sesklo, was first discovered in 1901 during excavation of

Fig. 1.12 Dimini, plan, showing parts of six circuit walls, with megaron built against the inner northeast face of the innermost. (Bengtson, *Grosser historischer Weltatlas*, 44a, by permission of Bayerischer Schulbuch-Verlag)

Maßstab 1 : 1500

0   5   10   20   30 m

tholos or beehive tombs of later, Mycenaean times nearby. The acropolis is noteworthy for at least six concentric circuit walls in stone, much spoiled by the plow; pottery dates them to Neolithic B, about 2650 B.C. They enclose an area of over 10,000 square yards. Since the innermost area, with a hearth or altar in the middle, is not all built over, it is clear that the outer walls were not added to enlarge living space, but to act like watertight bulkheads, providing protection in emergencies for refugees from the countryside. The building technique shows great skill and much experience of sieges. The various entrances or gates in successive circuit walls are in a straight line; the series on the southwest, on the axis of the impressive megaron and against the innermost circuit wall on the northeast, is impressive enough to have seemed to Tsountas a prehistoric ancestor to the Periclean Propylaea or monumental entrance to the Acropolis at Athens. All the gates but one are planned to be too narrow to permit two invaders to charge abreast; the one in the outermost circuit on the northwest was perhaps left purposely wide to let refugees bring in their chattels. The walls are too narrow (two to four and a half feet thick) to stand on and still leave room for battlements; the defenders must have stood behind them, but the ground level must have been lower outside the walls than inside; otherwise they would have been too easy for the invader to climb. The third wall, counting from within, must be contemporary with the inner two, since the second was never a complete circuit: it is finished with squared ends on east and west, while houses, which would have needed protection, lie outside it to the north. The open space around the megaron, in the middle of the acropolis, was probably surrounded by a portico or stoa; at all events a manger-like structure on the west has walls too thin to have been left unprotected from the weather. The whole plan suggests monarchy, control literally central. This has been described as the first major fact in the political history of Europe.

Multiple circuit walls like Dimini's were known in Tsountas' time from Herzogovina and Transylvania, so that the results from Dimini were used to infer direct Danubian or Illyrian influence on Neolithic Greece, but Tsountas had excavated others on the island of Syros in the Cyclades; and he knew of still others from Phylakopí on Melos. Others have been excavated since, as we saw, at Thermi on Lesbos and Poliochni on Lemnos, so the question of origins remains open, with Anatolia a distinct possibility. The megaron house, too, is known in the Danube area, and is suitable for a cold climate, but whether the influence runs from Anatolia to central Europe, or the other way about, is also an unsettled question.

But the relation to mythology and the Argonauts is interesting. Why, Tsountas argued, should not the later beehive tombs of Dimini be the graves of real Argonauts, as Troy VIIa is the city of a real Priam, and Mycenae, rich in gold, the stronghold of a real Agamemnon? These tomb builders, the "Minyans," would be invaders—from Asia Minor, on the evidence of Anatolian parallels with "Minyan" pottery found in Greece—who drove out the inhabitants of Sesklo and Dimini; the refugees will have moved south and taught their southern neighbors to build fortification walls, megara, stoas, and public hearths. These notions seem less fantastic now than they did when Tsountas first published them in 1908, especially since the newly discovered palace at Iolkos has been dated to a time contemporary with Achilles' father Peleus.

A beehive tomb of the Mycenaean period led to the discovery of pre-Mycenaean remains elsewhere than at Dimini. In 1870 the villagers of Skripoú, the ancient Orchomenós, in Boeotia, in central Greece, heard the hollow echo of something like an explosion from inside a nearby hill. They ran and found that the ceiling of a chamber adjacent to a beehive tomb, which had held for over 3000 years, had finally yielded to the weight of the earth above it. Schliemann excavated the tomb in 1881, and restored on paper the handsome rosettes, spirals, and lotus blossoms of the ceiling decoration, but it was left to his compatriot H. Bulle, in 1903, looking for a palace to go with the tomb, to find the round buildings that are apparently the oldest evidence of habitation on the excavated part of the site of Orchomenos. Bulle worked under difficulties: when he began, the only communication with Athens, less than ninety airline miles away, was by wagon, two days over deplorable roads; when the railroad was put through in 1905, he congratulated himself that the journey took only five hours. A scientific staff of two was inadequate to supervise eighty to a hundred workmen, who, left for a short time unwatched, triumphantly dismantled the entire walls of two unique prehistoric round buildings. The workmen never learned—it is not easy—to distinguish prehistoric mud-brick walls from the surrounding earth. An iron nail and a Turkish shoe in a deep stratum proved how thoroughly Schliemann's deep trenches had upset the levels. The villagers refused, quite reasonably from their point of view, to sacrifice their vegetable gardens to let the excavators extend their trenches, and the village cemetery lay directly in the midst of what proved to be the most promising area for excavation. Under these circumstances, it is no wonder Bulle's results were equivocal.

He discovered three superimposed building levels (Fig. 1.13). The lowest buildings, on bedrock, were round, with lower courses in stone. While he was digging, a winter colony of nomadic Vlachs (from Rumania) had settled on a nearby hillside, and he triumphantly compares their round huts with what he was excavating. The Vlach huts had a frame of pliant boughs, overlaid diagonally with twigs and then interwoven with reeds. They were rain- and windproof, but let smoke escape. On St. George's Day (May 6) the Vlachs would dismantle their huts, store the reusable wood, burn the reeds, and strew the ashes where the floors had been. This is a nice analogy, but it is damaged by the fact that some of the round buildings excavated by Bulle were too small for even two people, and in none of them was any trace of a doorway found: hence they are more likely to have been granaries or silos than dwellings.

In the level next above them, the typical building plan (the two lower courses, in stone, alone survived) was horseshoe-shaped, with pits (*bothroi*) in the floor, sometimes more than one to a room. These were filled with ashes, animal bones, sherds, and plant fibers. Between this and the next higher level were the traces of burning that indicate the overthrow of a settlement by violence; above the burned stratum, the house plans are rectangular.

Orchomenos is a prime example of a site whose intelligibility is much reduced because no proper track was kept of the pottery. Over twenty years and a major war intervened between the publication of the site and the publication of the pottery: in the interval, the scanty reports of levels had been lost. The pottery could still, by analogy with that from other sites, be grouped and distinguished as Neolithic, Early Bronze, and later, but no connection was any longer possible between the pottery and its precise findspot. However, one of Bulle's trenches (K), reopened, yielded at bedrock a type of burnished ware everywhere typi-

Fig. 1.13 Orchomenos, Bulle's trenches. Note plans of mysterious round buildings in K, N, and P, apsidal buildings in A and N. L is the later beehive tomb. The site would repay further digging, especially under the cemetery (Friedhof) and in the swamp (Sumpf) to the north. (Bulle, Pl. II)

cal of the Early Bronze Age, of the period called Early Helladic I, corresponding on the mainland south of Thessaly to Troy I-V and datable 2600-1900 B.C. This means that neither of Bulle's two lower levels, neither the round nor the horseshoe-shaped buildings, is Neolithic; rather they are both Early Helladic (see Fig. 1.7), and pre-Greek. The burnt layer is the mute evidence of the same invasion of Greek speakers that we met in Thessaly, and the rectangular (megaron-type) houses are like theirs. The fact remains, however, that though the excavated buildings are Early Helladic, Bulle found plenty of Neolithic pottery, in enough variety to suggest a long development. Unfortunately, no one knows exactly where it came from. Some of it may have been thrown into the round buildings when they were covered up to make level ground for the village of horseshoe-shaped houses, some of it may have come from Schliemann's dump. But the Neolithic settlement at Orchomenos, as such, has never been found; perhaps it is to be sought to the north of the area excavated by Bulle, closer to the swamp indicated on his plan.

Twenty miles southeast of Orchomenos, and about seven miles southwest of Thebes, at Eutresis, a site much visited in antiquity because on it the Thebans beat the Spartans in the Battle of Leuctra (371 B.C.), Miss Hetty Goldman excavated under American auspices, in four campaigns (1924-27). She was attracted to the site because the very surface of the rolling plateau was strewn with sherds she recognized as prehistoric; the visible traces of an extensive circuit wall (Fig. 1.14) proved on excavation to be Late Helladic, 400 years younger than the early Bronze Age. In the lowest level of twenty-one feet of deposit, she found traces of what she describes as "round tepees or huts," which sound not unlike Bulle's mysterious round buildings in the lowest level at Orchomenos, but she was not able to tell whether these formed a sequence with later settlements at higher levels, or whether they had been deserted by previous inhabitants. Later American work, reported in 1959, established that the site was occupied in Neolithic times; Neolithic pottery was found effectively sealed off under tight pebble pavements of Early Helladic I. In the level above, the houses were close built, as at other pre-Greek sites, such as Thermi; a house containing a broken copper—not bronze —chisel, and therefore belonging to a period transitional between the Neolithic and the Bronze Age, contained spiral-decorated pottery with relations both to Sesklo and to the island of Amorgos in the Cyclades, where the favorite motif was the spiral. (Eutresis lies only six miles from a port in the Gulf of Corinth, so import would be comparatively easy.) Miss Goldman judged the date to be Early

Fig. 1.14 Eutresis, plan, showing excavator's trenches. There are Early and Middle Helladic houses at 1 (lower right quadrant), and south of the medieval tower. The eastern part of the circuit wall, probed properly by trenches perpendicular to it, is Mycenaean. (Goldman, Pl. I, by permission of Harvard University Press)

EVTRESIS
PLAN ᴏꜰ EXCAVATIONS
1924–1927

SCALE

DISTANCE BETWEEN CONTOUR LINES 1 METER

Helladic. But excavation had shown that Early Helladic could be divided into three subperiods. In the second of these, in the level next above the house of the broken chisel, belongs a house (Miss Goldman calls it L) of roughly megaron type. It bore evidence—stacked bowls crushed by fallen walls—of having been destroyed by violence, but this time natural, not man-made: what did the damage was an earthquake. In the level above this again, which would be Early Helladic III, containing for the first time at Eutresis some wheel-made pottery, an equation with very late Troy II, House H had the roof of its large room supported by a brick column, the oldest known from mainland Greece. The Early Helladic III phase of House H was destroyed by burning: the third

piece of evidence we have noted of the cataclysm that overwhelmed Greece about 1900 B.C., when the Greek-speaking
invaders came. A later phase of House H contained so many
high-stemmed goblets that the excavators nicknamed it the
House of the Tippler. An outbuilding, belonging to the Early
Helladic III phase, was horseshoe-shaped and clearly served
for stabling animals; perhaps this is a way to explain Bulle's
horseshoe-shaped structures at Orchomenos. Many of the
small finds from Eutresis are typical of Early Helladic sites:
clay loom weights, spools, figurines, buttons, spindle whorls;
bronze of an Anatolian alloy; tool handles of red-deer horn;
obsidian (always a sign of trade connections with Melos
in the Cyclades, the prehistoric source for this dark volcanic
glass, used for sharp-edged tools and weapons); boars' tusks
pierced for sewing to leather helmets. By custom, or from
poverty, the graves contained few objects; in those of the
levels after the invasion as at other sites of the same date,
the bodies were buried in a cramped position, with the
head pillowed on the hand.

Eutresis is one site in which the ubiquitous Schliemann
never set spade. On the acropolis of Tiryns in the Argolid,

Fig. 1.15 Tiryns air view, from south, showing
northern loop added in Phase III (see Ch. 2) as place
of refuge. (University of Wisconsin Geography De-
partment)

on the other hand, (traditionally Heracles' city, and the surviving walls (Fig. 1.15) are certainly Herculean), he dug first
in the late summer of 1876, noticing prehistoric pottery,
which he carried away to Athens without recording just
where it was found. He found house walls, too, but, as at
Troy and Orchomenos, he destroyed some evidence with one
of his enormous trenches. He dug again, more carefully,
with Dörpfeld in 1884 and 1885; the resulting book (1886)
treats the architectural remains with Dörpfeld's characteristic and marvelous clarity. After the turn of the century, as
more and more was learned from Evans at Knossos, from
Tsountas in Thessaly, from the British in the Cyclades (at
Phylakopi on Melos) about earlier levels of culture, Dörpfeld encouraged promising young German archaeologists to
dig again, and their final results appeared in publications
that were models of constructive scientific archaeological
method, the volume on architecture in 1930, that on pottery
in 1938. The sherds from earlier digs stored in nearby
Nauplia, partly in a mosque, partly in a windowless cellar,
proved very difficult to work with, and their findspots had
mostly not been recorded. The massive citadel proved to be
Late Helladic; it falls beyond the limits of this chapter.
The search for older levels proved to be difficult, since the
important and impressive Late Helladic (Mycenaean) remains had to be preserved, but to the east of the megaron,
beneath the citadel's first phase, the excavators re-examined
deep strata that Dörpfeld in 1884 had called "chaos," out
of which by 1930 they had made sense. They distinguished
twelve levels: in the lowest some sparse Neolithic pottery,
and an idol. More striking were the footings of houses, oval,
apsidal (horseshoe-shaped), and rectangular, in three levels,
dated by the potsherds they contained to the Early Helladic
period. The pottery included narrow-spouted ware, almost
certainly used as babies' nursing bottles; a double-walled wine-
cooler; and a vase with an impression made in the wet clay
with an engraved cylinder, showing a dog in full cry after
a hare. The pottery, thin-walled and with sophisticated décor,
is clearly the tableware of an aristocratic class. Its settlement must once have extended over the whole area later
occupied by the citadel, and perhaps over the level ground
around it, though excavation here is limited and the levels
disturbed by the installations of a government agricultural
experiment station. Still more important are the stone-built
remains, footed on bedrock, of a massive round building
(Fig. 1.16), 286 feet in circumference, which underlies the

Fig. 1.16 Tiryns, round building, plan, showing concentric foundation walls, buttresses, and burnt tile
(Lehmziegel) from pavement or roof. (Matz, *Hdbh*, p.
198 by permission of C. Beck, Munich)

center of the later palace. It must have been a lofty structure,
for traces of buttresses remain. If its height matched its
diameter, it was over eighty-six feet tall, a most impressive

tower, very like the Sardinian watchtowers called *nuraghi* (described in *The Mute Stones Speak,* pp. 15-18), but much older; the excavators deduce that it was destroyed by fire (possible evidence, unique in Tiryns, of the Greek-speaking invaders) before the beginning of the Middle Helladic period about 1900 B.C. Burnt tile found in its remains comes either from its pavement or its roof. This is the first monumental building on Greek soil; the excavators, with pardonable exaggeration, compare it with the Pyramids.

Sesklo and Dimini, Orchomenos, Eutresis, and Tiryns are typical Neolithic and Early Helladic sites on the Greek mainland. They are not the only ones; new, important, and interesting excavations go on every year. Brief mention of a few key sites will suggest what all of them have added to our knowledge. Many of them are interesting precisely because they are humble, the villages of nameless prehistoric men, whose exploitation made possible the later brave displays of Mycenae, rich in gold, and Agamemnon, king of men.

Among them are Korákou and Zygouries near Corinth (see map, Fig. 1.5). Here Blegen excavated in the twenties. At Korakou he dealt with 100,000 sherds. They enabled him to propose an over-all chronology for the Bronze Age and a terminology for the various types of pottery. These are still generally used. At Zygouries he discovered a potter's shop (later than the period with which this chapter deals) with a stock of over 1330 stacked pieces, unused. At Prosymna, near Argos, he excavated tombs, some rich, some plundered, some poor, ranging in date from Neolithic to Late Helladic. They yielded fine animal figurines and bronze daggers (of Mycenaean date) with a gold and silver inlay of dolphins and birds.

Off the mainland, at Vounous on Cyprus, an Early Cypriote III tomb (of about 2300 B.C.) produced evidence of Bronze Age ritual: a spirited clay model (Fig. 1.17) of a sacred enclosure, containing bulls in pens, a figure enthroned, and another carrying an infant. Still others, wearing bull's heads, stand holding hands, from which snakes hang down. Six more stand or sit on benches, while one, apparently excluded, tries to climb over the wall.

At Asine on the coast of the Argolid a Swedish expedition, with Crown Prince (now King) Gustav as a member, worked from 1920 to 1924. The Swedes unearthed thirty tons of sherds (two to three million of them), Early Helladic apsidal

Fig. 1.7 Synchronisms: Crete, Cyclades, mainland, Troy. (Hammond, p. 21)

houses, the Egyptian seal that helped to date Troy, and evidence (fire) of the violent break frequently found between Early and Middle Helladic.

At nearby Lerna, a series of American campaigns uncovered the complex plan of the rich and sophisticated House of the Tiles (published 1954-58), and, even more important, a towered Early Helladic double ring wall; with the House of the Tiles, it is an impressive monument of the period in Greek prehistory when Anatolian influence dominated. The excavator, J. L. Caskey, uses the evidence from Lerna to suggest that the violent cultural break in the Bronze Age occurred between Early Helladic II and III, while the transition from Early to Middle Helladic may have occurred in many places without extreme violence.

At Hagios Kosmas on the Attic coast, Mylonas excavated (1930-31, 1951) an Early Bronze Age settlement, possibly of islanders from Melos trading in obsidian. It died out, according to the excavator, in the Middle Bronze Age, but if Caskey's analysis of the pottery from Lerna is sound, the matching pottery from Hagios Kosmas must be dated earlier, so that the destruction will have occurred at the close of Early Helladic II. At all events the settlement revived in Mycenaean times.

At Asea in Arcadia another Swedish expedition (1936-38) unearthed Neolithic and Early Helladic remains, followed, after the customary evidence of conflagration, by later levels. On the rocky hilltop of Asea the accumulations of pottery are thin and subject to confusion by erosion and human activity, so that the evidence is equivocal, and Asea may (or may not) have been sacked after Early Helladic II, as were Lerna and Hagios Kosmas. The important thing is that Caskey's conclusions from Lerna will require a complete rethinking of the accepted chronology of the Early Helladic period in the Argolid and Arcadia. His results, published in 1960, sixteen years after Asea, will illustrate the tentative nature of all attempts at chronology and the need for caution in drawing categorical conclusions from them. About Neolithic pottery from Asea there is no doubt; it shows close cultural connections with Thessaly, the Early Helladic with Anatolia. At Malthi, the ancient Dorion, in Messenia, still another group of Swedes dug (1933-35) five superimposed town-levels, the bottom two unwalled (and destroyed at the end of Early Helladic), the top three walled, and centering around a palace which has been held to reflect the strong will of an invading ruler. No classical Greek city plan is so centralized, so schematically neat. The 320 houses have common party walls, as at Thermi and Poliochni; the total impression of all these sites is of a unity of culture in Neolithic and Early Helladic times that Greece was not to know again until Roman days.

To that prehistoric cultural unity a major contribution was made by the Cyclades, the group of Aegean islands clustered around the sacred isle of Delos. The Cyclades are lovely: blue sea, tawny sand, mountains bare or clad in gray-green olive, harbor towns where the spotless white of the houses vies with the spotless white of the windmill sails. They are lovely, and they are remote. Consequently, the archaeological richness has hardly been tapped, though Greek excavations on Naxos since World War II have revealed a site as rich as anything hitherto known in the Cyclades. A dozen others, Middle Cycladic (equals Middle Helladic in date) or earlier, await the spade. Greeks better than barbarians bear the rigors of travel by small sailboat to the outlying islands. It is not surprising, therefore, that some of the earliest and best work in Cycladic archaeology was done before the turn of the century by Tsountas. He excavated hundreds of tombs on Amorgos, Paros, and neighboring islets; tombs and citadels on Syros and Siphnos. The 190 graves on Paros yielded bronze, but so scant as to indicate a date very early in the Bronze Age, corresponding to Early Helladic on the mainland: for this culture Tsountas coined the name Early Cycladic. The scanty remains of houses with apsidal and megaron plans, containing incised and painted pottery of the same type as that found in the tombs, some of it wheel-made, showed that the Cyclades had reached the same stage of development as Troy II. The equation EC=EH=Troy II=2400-2200 B.C. is therefore possible and even probable. Tsountas' richest site was Chalandrianí on Syros, where he found some 500 graves, and an acropolis with a double wall of which the inner was towered. At Hagios Andreas on Siphnos he excavated 250 yards of another acropolis wall, later in date, but also double, cunningly contrived, the gates few and narrow, and access to them made ingeniously difficult. The graves on Syros yielded two kinds of objects of unique interest. The first is a series of clay artifacts shaped like a frying pan (Fig. 1.18), incised with spirals, a triangular symbol probably representing the female sex organ, and a likeness of a ship with a fish figurehead. Tsountas conjectured that they were intended to be filled with water and used as mirrors. The second is a series of violin-shaped marble idols, whose cool severity appeals strongly to modern taste. In the same style, though not from Tsountas' dig, are some handsome marble statuettes of musicians (Fig. 1.19) rivaling the best of the archaic Greek sculpture of 1600 years later; the one illustrated here is from Amorgos, and stands about nine inches high.

Fig. 1.18 Syros, Cycladic "frying pan," clay, incised with running spirals, a ship with high prow and figurehead, and possible fertility symbol. Laid this side down, and filled with water, it might serve as a mirror. Athens, National Museum. (Matz, KMT, Pl. 12)

But the best known and best published site in the Cyclades is Phylakopi on Melos, excavated by a British team between 1896 and 1899, the first important prehistoric dig since Schliemann, and again by another British group in 1911. The prehistoric town owed its prosperity to an obsidian factory, from which were shipped, all over the Aegean world,

Fig. 1.19 Amorgos, Cycladic marble statuette (ht. 8¾ inches) of lyre player. The simplicity of line appeals strongly to modern sculptors. Athens, National Museum. (Emile Seraf)

cores and blades of the glass-like stone which flakes to so sharp an edge that knives, razors, arrowheads, harrow teeth, and sickles made with it were prized beyond metal well down into the Bronze Age. Out of this site came, for four seasons, until excavation was suspended in favor of Evans' epoch-making dig at Knossos in Crete, 10,000 to 20,000 fragments a day, providing a unique, orderly pottery sequence extending over the whole Bronze Age. The excavators distinguished three phases of the city, of which the first (Fig. 1.20; typically Anatolian in being small, unwalled, self-contained, with minimal commerce) was overwhelmed, about the same time as the cities of mainland Greece, by the same kind of catastrophe, caused no doubt not by the Greek-speaking invaders but by refugees from them, who fled to Melos and ousted the original settlers of Phylakopi. After the catastrophe the city was rebuilt on much the same plan, with double fortification walls as at Chalandriani, stepped rectilinear streets with drains, close-packed houses, numerous private baths, and a palace quarter with a megaron like those of Troy VI, Tiryns, Mycenae, and, as we shall see, Pylos. The spirited wall-painting of flying fish (see Fig. 2.17) is in the Minoan tradition; it belongs to a later period. The increasing use of metal for spear points, arrowheads, and tools caused a fall-off of the obsidian trade, and the third city gradually declined, finally falling prey to invasion from the mainland. In its time of prosperity its aesthetic taste and the passion for cleanliness evinced by the baths and drains show that its main cultural connections were with one place, Knossos, the metropolis of Crete.

If Knossos shares with Troy the glamor among prehistoric sites in the Aegean basin, it is because it, like Troy, was excavated by a rich and flamboyant character, Sir Arthur Evans. He succeeded, where Schliemann had failed, in breaking through the local landowners' "almost inexhaustible powers of obstruction," and bought outright the site he was to name the "Palace of Minos." From 1900 until his death in 1941, Knossos was his whole life, and upon it he lavished the considerable resources of his energy, his imagination, and his fortune. As his half-sister Joan wrote, he "had come to the site in hope of finding a seal impression and a clay tablet, and Time and Chance had led him to discover a civilization." As early as 1900 he had identified Neolithic levels there, as well as three subsequent strata, which he christened Early, Middle, and Late Minoan. His reconstruc-

Fig. 1.20 Phylakopi I and II, plan. The darker walls are later. Note resemblance to Poliochni (Fig. 1.9). The massive circuit wall, lower left, belongs to Phylakopi III. (Atkinson, Pl. II)

tion, largely at his own expense, of the Palace of Minos, while not always accurate in detail, makes the site the easiest to recreate in the imagination of any in the prehistoric world. It is vivid to the modern traveler because it was vivid to Evans: "out of an inchoate mass of pottery and stone, metal and faience, clay tablets and seals, walls and pavements," writes his half-sister, "he had to achieve a synthesis." And he did, in four massive and sumptuous volumes (1921-36), which have become the Bible of prehistoric Greek archaeology, and, like the Bible, the prey also of the Higher Criticism.

Of the thirty-eight feet (Fig. 1.21) of deposit which Evans records under the west court of the Palace at Knossos, the bottom twenty-four feet belonged, on the evidence of pottery, to a Neolithic settlement, one of the largest and most important known in Europe or the Near East. The coarse, undecorated, handmade earthenware is more primitive and therefore older than Neolithic A at Sesklo; it probably goes back to 3000 B.C. Higher up in the Neolithic level comes incised ware like that of Troy I, figurines and obsidian from the Cyclades. The houses are rectangular, their lower courses of stone, their floors of pebbles; their plan involves a number of small rooms clustering around a main one: already in miniature the labyrinthine plan that the Palace was to make famous as the home of the Minotaur, the fabulous monster, half-bull, half-man, slain in his lair by the heroic young Theseus, prince of Athens.

The Early Minoan levels, distinguished by the first appearance of copper, and by kiln-fired and painted pottery, were much destroyed when the site was leveled off for the Middle Minoan I Palace. Characteristic of this early level is mottled ware, produced by uneven firing. There is also a number of stone vases—the best come not from Knossos but from an American dig at Mochlos—where the striations of alabaster or steatite make patterns extraordinarily pleasing because of the tension between the rectilinear décor and the curve of the pot. Such vases have parallels in Egypt, and make possible the dating of Early Minoan (somewhat shakily, for stoneware may endure long after the period of its making) from 2600 to 2000 B.C., but Evans identified the craftsmanship as local. At the end of Early Minoan, the art of engraving on gems and seals flourished: a lens found in a Knossos grave may have been a magnifying glass used by a craftsman in intaglio. The most impressive architectural

← N   S →

ORIGINAL SURFACE OF GROUND

LATE MINÔAN STRATUM

2.50

5.35

PAVEMENT OF WEST COURT

FLOOR LEVEL MIDDLE MINÔAN III   1.0

MIDDLE MINÔAN   1.50

FLOOR LEVEL MIDDLE MINÔAN II

STRATUM BELONGING TO EARLY MINÔAN III

STRATUM BELONGING TO EARLY MINÔAN II   EARLY MINÔAN

FLOOR LEVEL EARLY MINÔAN I
(SUB-NEOLITHIC)

NEOLITHIC STRATUM   6.43

VIRGIN ROCK

Fig. 1.21 Knossos, Palace of Minos, levels below West Court, schematic drawing. The extraordinary depth of the Neolithic stratum shows long inhabitation. (Evans, BSA 10 [1904] p. 17)

survival of this age is the great *hypogaeum* or underground
vault under the south porch of the Palace. It is twenty-six
feet wide and twice as high, curving up to a beehive vault.
Access to it was by a winding stair round the outside, with
windows at intervals opening into the vault, or alternatively
by an elaborate tunnel. All this implies something worth
guarding, and hints already at the prosperity enjoyed by the
rulers of Knossos, and attested by the contents of the storerooms of the later Palace.

The transition from Early to Middle Minoan (about 2000
B.C.) is marked by wheel-made polychrome pottery with
charming plant motifs ("Kamares ware"), by the emergence
of an as yet undeciphered hieroglyphic script, and by the
consolidation of the house-blocks of the Early Minoan settlement into the earliest palace (Fig. 1.22). This is the period
also of the earliest palace levels discovered by the French
at Mállia east of Knossos and by the Italians at Phaistós
near the south coast. At Knossos the debris of the Early
Minoan settlement was used to make a terrace for the palace,
which was approached on the west by a ramp and causeways,
from the north by an entrance protected by a keep, one of

Fig. 1.22 Knossos, Palace of Minos, Middle I phase, simplified
plan showing relation to earlier and later phases. (Pendlebury,
1939, p. 96, by permission of Messrs. Methuen, London)

Fig. 1.23 Knossos, Palace of Minos, late MM II phase, plan, showing how older house-blocks were consolidated. The wealth of the palace was stored in the long, narrow magazines on the west. (Evans, 1921, Fig. 152, by permission of Messrs. Macmillan, London, and the Trustees of the Sir Arthur Evans Estate)

the fortified blocks which made up the first palace. The provisions for drainage were elaborate. At this time too (Middle Minoan I, *ca* 1950 B.C.) the old trade route from the south was improved by the construction of a great viaduct: it was by this route that Egyptian artifacts arrived. The inscribed statue of an Egyptian ambassador or purchasing agent in XIIth Dynasty style (1990-1780 B.C.), found in a Middle Minoan II level, belongs to the next phase of the palace (Fig. 1.23), when the fortified blocks were consolidated into a homogeneous whole. In the process, three deep round pits, called locally *koulouras* (Fig. 1.24) were sunk under the west court to contain the broken pottery from the palace rubbish heaps. A series of fifteen long, narrow storerooms was constructed on the west to contain the tribute receipts from vassal cities, in oil, wine, grain, copper, bronze, silver, and gold. A new ramp gave access to the central court from the south; to the northeast rose the royal pottery store and a roomful of giant *pithoi,* storage jars taller than a man. To the east the hillside was later cut away to make a great Domestic Quarter, the private apartments of the king and queen. The whole complex was elaborately drained, with stone-built, cement-lined conduits, and a latrine with gypsum-lined walls, wooden seats, and provision to prevent the escape into the room of noxious odors. To this period is dated the first real

Fig. 1.24 Knossos, Palace of Minos, circular, lined rubbish pits, and remains of earlier houses, under West Court. (Pendlebury, 1954, Pl. I.2, by permission of Max Parrish, London)

piece of mural decoration, the feature that, as restored, makes later phases of the palace colorful today. This is the "Saffron Gatherer" (Fig. 1.25), a grayish-blue figure picking crocuses and putting them in vases set among rocks, against a red background. Evans had the figure restored as a boy, but since something very like a tail is waving in the air above him, it is more probably a monkey.

Some idea of the appearance of less palatial houses of the period is provided by a series of plaques in faience (earthenware with an opaque metallic glaze), the "Town Mosaic" (Fig. 1.26). The houses are windowed, two or more stories high, flat-roofed, with an attic or clerestory above. The construction indicated is of stone alternating with squared beams, or round beams with the ends showing. Red-painted window panes imply the use of something like oiled parchment instead of glass.

Middle Minoan II ended in an earthquake, followed by the great period of the palace, to be described in the next chapter.

Archaeological excavation of Neolithic and Early Bronze Age sites in the Aegean basin has made it possible to reconstruct ground plans, analyze pottery, and—sometimes—assess works of art. No archaeologist would deny that this work of reconstruction, analysis, and criticism has a fascination of its own. But such archaeologists as Schliemann, Dörpfeld, Tsountas, Evans, and Blegen are not satisfied with catalogues of mute stones, broken pottery, fragmentary sculpture, and bits of fresco. What they have dug up is history, especially cultural history, and cultural history means—at least to the archaeologist with imagination—not chronological tables, categories of vases, catalogues of works of art—though these are indispensable starting-points—but the inferences from these. And these inferences are about *people*. The development from the primitive ground plan of Troy I to the sophisticated buildings of Troy II implies the material growth of a people from subsistence living to prosperity, and their spiritual growth from savagery to civilization. But the burnt layer between Troy I and Troy II implies further that the growth was not peaceful. Troy I yielded only local pottery; Troy II imported some of its earthenware. The inference is a broadening of cultural as well as commercial horizons: contacts with Hittites, northerners, islanders. This means not only mercantile profit, but

Fig. 1.25 Knossos, Palace of Minos, Saffron-gatherer fresco. Heraklion, Museum. (Pendlebury, 1954, Pl. XI, by permission of Max Parrish, London)

the mental stimulus that comes from seeing the cities of men, and knowing their minds. The fall of Troy I is far from the only evidence of violence: "Priam's treasure" is probably loot, which leads to the melancholy reflection that for 4300 years civilization has meant war. Troy VIIa fell, which leads to the even more melancholy reflection that in 4300 years man has not learned that they that take the sword shall perish by the sword.

The close-packed plans of Thermi V, Poliochni, Sesklo, Dimini, and Phylakopi may have been evolved out of the necessity for protection, but they came to be the way Mediterranean people preferred to live, as in many villages they still do: close together, with common party walls to their houses, but finding their livelihood outside the villages, in the fields or on the sea, and returning after labor to the intimacy of their close-knit neighborhoods, and the friendly gossip of their outdoor living room, the town square. There is a lesson of continuity here, as there is in the controlled excitement of Dimini's geometric pottery, to which the descendants of Dimini's people returned for inspiration after 1600 years. We have seen, too, how the unity of the plans implies a centralized government of kings and subjects, the beginning of the long and not always happy history of monarchy in the Western world.

At Orchomenos, the evidence of the silos with the burnt layer above enables the archaeologist to reconstruct the pathetic picture of a peaceful agricultural people overwhelmed by invaders. We know from Miss Goldman's excavations that the people of Eutresis, though poor, domesticated animals, were not averse to a convivial cup of wine, and were rich enough to import bronze from Asia Minor and obsidian from Melos. The babies' nursing bottles from Tiryns humanize the site; the massive remains of the round tower monumentalize it. Most of us find the former more interesting than the latter. The potter's surplus stock from Zygouries prompts reflection on the pathos of the small proprietor ruined by invasion. The figure trying to get over the wall of the sacred enclosure from Vounous may cause us to ponder on how old and shameful the human tendency to exclusiveness is. Asine's Early Helladic trade with Egypt, Lerna's unique Early Helladic palace give us a new view of the prosperity and sophistication of Greek mainland peoples in the third millennium B.C. The traders from Melos who ran the station at Hagios Kosmas traveled in the sort of boats pictured on Cycladic "frying pans," and helped to provide the wealth to

Fig. 1.26 Knossos, Town Mosaic. Faience plaques, giving details of Minoan houses. Heraklion, Museum. (Matz, KMT, Pl. 45, by permission of the British School in Athens)

support the sculptor of the Cycladic harper, whose work does not suffer from comparison with Henry Moore's.

But the most eloquent archaeological evidence for the way people lived in the Early Bronze Age comes from Knossos. The first impression a visitor to Knossos gains, as I see from my own journal for Easter, 1936, is of the profound difference in tone and atmosphere from the culture of classical Greece. This is not surprising, for the Middle Minoans were probably not Indo-Europeans, as the classical Greeks were. The very name of Knossos is earlier than the arrival of the Indo-Europeans (possibly Anatolian), and so are the names of Corinth, Athens, and Tiryns. Other words in classical Greek that are survivals from the older language give a surprisingly accurate picture of the culture: the word for the sea itself, *thalassa*, which made Minos' commercial fortune; names for trees and plants: cypress, terebinth (turpentine-tree), artichoke; chestnut, absinth, cherry; flowers: narcissus, hyacinth; herbs: mint, oregano; articles of luxury or leisure: purple mussel, bathtub, chessboard, lyre. This gifted people gave to the classical Greeks many of the softer and more attractive aspects of their nature. The later taste for city life is already clear in Troy and Thermi, Poliochni and Sesklo. The talent for sculpture, the joy in color and design, is visible in Cycladic statuettes and Kamares pottery. The exalting of the female principle over the male is suggested by the "idols," which hint in turn at the importance of women. The love of gardens, music, and leisure is implied in the pre-Indo-European vocabulary itself. This civilization came to its flowering at Knossos. It was the civilization that Sir Arthur Evans loved: "set in beautiful Mediterranean country, aristocratic and humane in feeling; creating an art brilliant in color and unusual in form, that drew inspiration from the flowers and birds and creatures that he loved. It provided him with enigmas to solve and riddles to interpret, and opened a new world for eye and mind to dwell in: a world which served to isolate him from a present in which he had found no real place."

The Greek-speaking invaders who upset all this added some stiffening, vigor, directness, and adventurousness to this charming pursuit of pleasure, and Greeks retained to the end some of the superstition, coarseness, passion, and cruelty of their non-Greek Neolithic ancestors as well; but our Greek heritage would seem far less attractive to us without the contribution of the prehistoric people who were not, linguistically speaking, Greeks at all.

2 "Mycenae, Rich in Gold" (Greece in the Late Bronze Age, 1900-1125 B. C.)

In about 1900 B.C. or a little earlier the culture of the pre-historic non-Greek Aegean, as archaeology reveals it, was destroyed. Many settlements were violently overwhelmed by the invasion of a people who, there is some reason to believe, were the first Greeks. About that time Troy emerged from the doldrums of Troy III-V into the prosperity of Troy VI. It was in this period, as study of animal bones from all layers of Troy showed, that the horse began to be used here. Blegen found that this settlement was destroyed by a disastrous earthquake about 1275 B.C. Its circuit walls were patched, the stones of its fallen houses reused for much less pretentious new buildings. Imported pottery is no longer found: the inference is that prosperity has sharply declined. This settlement, Troy VIIa, lasted for about a generation; then it in turn was violently destroyed by fire and looted. Blegen thinks this is Homer's Trojan War; he dates it about two generations earlier than is usual, about 1240 B.C. The survivors tried to pull their town together again (Troy VIIb1), only to have it taken over, without signs of violence, by a people, perhaps from Thrace, whose barbarity is clear from their ugly pottery. By 1100 B.C. this culture fades, and Troy never rises to prominence again.

Fig. 2.1   Troy VII*a*, house walls built against circuit wall of Troy VI (Page, p. 72, by permission of the University of California Press)

From Troy VII*a*, the Troy of Priam and Helen, Hector and Andromache, Blegen's excavation has stripped most of the glamor. Houses, accurately described as "a series of sheepish cubicles," are jammed together, close against the circuit wall (Fig. 2.1). The danger of siege apparently drove many nearby villagers into the citadel, where crowding created slums, and food was stored and dispensed under emergency conditions. Blegen found much evidence of burning and violence: scraps of human bones in the streets, a skull in a doorway, a skeleton of a man, struck down in flight and left without burial. But Priam's Troy, though patched, was still powerful: the beetling walls are still impressive. To breach them took ten years of siege and, according to legend,

one final piece of ingenuity (ruse or siege-engine), the Trojan
Horse.

Troy fell before Agamemnon, King of "Mycenae, rich in
gold." The citadel of Mycenae, under the shadow of crystal-
line mountains, overlooking the rich Argive plain, had early
attracted Schliemann. He went there to dig in the autumn
of 1876. With his usual luck he hit, within the walls, in less
than seven weeks of digging, upon a grave circle. It was
crammed with gold diadems, cups, and masks (Fig. 2.2). It
contained, too, the pathetic bones of royal children, their
hands and feet wrapped in gold leaf. There were inlaid
bronze daggers, portraying lion hunts not native to the
Peloponnese; and bones which his imagination enlarged to

**Fig. 2.2   Mycenae, shaft Grave V, gold death mask.
Schliemann thought it was Agamemnon, but the grave
is much earlier. Athens. National Museum. (Matz, KMT,
Pl. 87, Foto Marburg)**

giant size. On November 28, 1876 he sent his famous tele-
gram to King George of Greece (a Dane), congratulating
him on the discovery of the graves of his ancestors. Soberer
work was done between 1877 and 1902 by Tsountas, the
excavator of Dimini and Sesklo; in 1920-23, 1939, and 1950-
55 by that Nestor among Englishmen, A. J. B. Wace, and
in 1952-54 by the Greek Archaeological Society with the
coöperation of the dynamic Greek-American, George Mylonas. Their excavations made it clear that Mycenae was
destroyed, luckily for us (unluckily for the Mycenaeans) while
it was still fairly prosperous. The thousand yards of its
twenty-foot-thick fortification walls, long concealed under
Schliemann's dump, proved to be as monumental as the walls
of Tiryns. Pausanias, who saw those great stones in Roman
times, said that a pair of mules could not budge the smallest
of them. The existence of Mycenae's walls, palaces, and rich
tombs implies prosperity, derived from territorial expansion,
trade, and dynastic intermarriages like that of Mycenaean
Menelaus to Spartan Helen.

The entrance to the citadel of Mycenae is through the
famous Lion Gate, surmounted by the oldest piece of monumental sculpture in Europe (Fig. 2.3). The noble beasts face
each other heraldically in the relieving triangle over the
lintel. Between them is a tapering column, anticipating Frank
Lloyd Wright. No doubt they symbolize the power of the
lords of the Mycenaean palace. Sherds under the threshold,
each, as always, a page of history, place the gate and the
adjacent curtain wall in the period which Blegen and Wace
named Late Helladic III*b* (about 1250 B.C.). Agamemnon
must have driven through the gate in his chariot on his way
to the ships to embark for Troy. But there is evidence of
earlier occupation of the site, and a place so rich would always have had need of walls. Mylonas found an earlier
phase in the northern circuit (see plan, Fig. 2.4). To yet a
third phase belongs the eastward extension, which nowadays
overlooks a shady grove of wild olives. It is equipped with
an awe-inspiring ninety-three steps, which run underground
to a cistern outside the wall. Outside the walls, the ridges are
covered with thyme and asphodel, and today are loud with
bees. Here, where the nightingale sings in the plane trees, lay
the lower city. There Wace in 1952 excavated the House of
the Oil Merchant, containing thirty-eight clay tablets inscribed in the script called by Sir Arthur Evans Linear B.

The center of the citadel was occupied by the palace,

Fig. 2.3   Mycenae, Lion Gate, with Schliemann and Dörpfeld. (DAI, Athens)

whose excavation is chiefly due to Tsountas. It was approached by a ramp and, in a later phase, by a grand staircase, recently restored (Fig. 2.4, southwest of the middle L). Its most impressive surviving room is a megaron, facing west on a court (Fig. 2.5). The megaron had a raised central hearth, a gaily painted floor, walls covered with frescoes of warriors, horses, chariots, and women, and a roof supported by four tall slender wooden columns. Sherds date the megaron as contemporary with the Lion Gate. North of the megaron is a bath, whose blood-red stuccoed walls have led the modern Mycenaeans to identify it as the very room in which Agamemnon was murdered. Both east of the palace, by the circuit wall, and also westward, within the Lion Gate, near Schliemann's grave circle, are remains of houses grand enough to have belonged to palace officials: the House of the Columns (N on the plan), is one of the most impressive Mycenaean *houses* (as opposed to palaces) yet excavated. The House of the Warrior Vase (F) is named from a famous find of the late thirteenth or early twelfth century (Fig. 2.6) now in the National Museum in Athens, along with the other objects from this area. On the vase six unidealized warriors, all different, with provision bags on their spears, march off leaving a woman grieving behind them. The Ramp House (G), yielded a fresco of bull-leaping. Tsountas' House (K) provided a fresco of masqueraders wearing asses' heads. The Granary (C), so called from the carbonized grain found in jars within it, produced a pottery style that has given its name to a late phase of Mycenaean ceramics. These houses were looted and fired while Late Helladic IIIc pottery was in use, perhaps about 1125 B.C.

Outside the citadel, westward, Wace excavated more private houses: the House of the Wine Merchant, with its store of 500 unused vases, closely packed. Here also is the House of the Oil Merchant, with its huge storage jars, each in its alcove, its inscribed tablets, already mentioned, to which more has been added by more recent excavating of further foundations discovered in widening the modern road for tourist buses. If these are private houses, and not quarters for palace staff, the tablets suggest a wider range of Mycenaean literacy than had hitherto been suspected. Wace found, too, the buildings he christened the House of Shields and the House of Sphinxes. They yielded an unmatched series of exquisite carved ivories, probably all that is left of inlaid wooden furniture. These houses were destroyed in the twelfth

Fig. 2.4 (above) Mycenae, citadel, plan. A, Lion Gate; D, Grave Circle A; L, Palace; S, stair to cistern. (Wace, *Mycenae*,

Pl. 19, by permission of Princeton University Press)   Fig. 2.5
(opposite) Mycenae, court in front of megaron, reconstruction
drawing. For details of construction, compare Knossos Town
Mosaic, Fig. 1.26. (Wace, *op. cit.*, Pl. 30)

century B.C. by the cataclysm called the Dorian invasion,
which destroyed Bronze Age civilization. The Warrior Vase
portrays the kind of men who vainly tried to ward off the
destruction.

Outside the citadel, too, are chamber tombs—Tsountas
published fifty-two of them—where broken pottery found
above suggests a final toast drunk to the dead, and the
goblets smashed afterward. Figurines found in these tombs
may represent either nurses (in children's graves) or goddesses. Limited pottery sequences warrant the inference that
these tombs were violated a century before catastrophe befell
the city proper. More interesting, among the architectural
remains outside the citadel, are the beehive or tholos tombs,
of which nearly eighty are now known on the Greek mainland and adjacent islands. Of the ones near Mycenae only
one, at Dendra some seven miles southeast, was found un-
plundered. From its treasures, as displayed in the National
Museum in Athens, we can get some idea of the richness of
the Mycenaean tholos tombs before the ancient grave-robbers
did their work.

The Dendra tholos tomb was discovered by an American,
Dorothy Burr, now the wife of Homer Thompson, director
of the American excavations in the Athenian agora. Out for
a mule ride one April Sunday in 1926, on a busman's holi-
day from Blegen's dig at Prosymna, she noticed some
farmers trying to remove from a field some large flat
blocks, among which she recognized the lintel of a tholos
tomb. Three pits in the tomb floor yielded treasures as exotic
as they were valuable (Fig. 2.7): a massive gold ring; a
great Mycenaean necklace; an ostrich egg, probably an import
from Egypt, with a silver neck, gold-edged bronze banding,
and glass paste appliqué; a gold cup with an octopus
motif; bronze swords (of a type in use after 1400 B.C.), with
gold-mounted hilts and ivory or agate pommels; and a gold-
and-silver cup decorated with bulls' heads. This cup, filled
with red Nemean wine and passed round the company,
prompted Dimitri, the innkeeper of La Belle Hélène nearby, to exclaim, "Twice God has let me drink from gold cups:
in Vaphió in '89 when I was with Tsountas, and again
today. Now I can die content!" The dig ended on the
fiftieth anniversary of Schliemann's first setting spade into
his grave circle at Mycenae.

Such treasures must once have filled the romantically
named "Treasury of Atreus," the "Tomb of Clytemnestra,"

Fig. 2.6 Mycenae, Warrior Vase. Athens, National Museum. (Schuch-hardt, *Schliemann's Excavations*, Fig. 285)

Fig. 2.7 Dendra, tholos tomb, finds. Note especially the ostrich egg, bottom center. (Persson, 1931, Pl. 8; by permission of C.W.K. Gleerup, Lund)

and the other seven tholos tombs near Mycenae, but nowadays what awes the visitor is their size and the obvious skill of the great architect who built them. The Treasury of Atreus is the largest and the most famous. Today its name seems less fantastic than it used to; for it certainly once contained a treasure, and its date, established by pottery under the entranceway or *dromos,* and by the style of building, is contemporary with the Lion Gate, and therefore with the traditional date (mid-thirteenth century B.C.) of Atreus himself. It is one of the most impressive monuments of the Mycenaean world, nearly fifty feet in diameter, over forty-three feet high to the top of the beehive (Fig. 2.8), and with a lintel block weighing 120 tons. The beehive shape is built up in thirty-three courses of stones. Above the foundation course, each ring of blocks is cantilevered to overlap the one below, until finally the circular top block is set to crown the whole and give the impression of a vault, a false impression, since the top block is nonfunctional as a keystone. On both sides of the lofty entrance were half-columns in a green stone, perhaps from Sparta; they are decorated with chevrons and spirals.

Fig. 2.8   Mycenae, Treasury of Atreus, interior, showing twenty-two of the thirty-three courses. Note enormous lintel block. (Saul Weinberg)

Only slightly smaller and slightly later than the Treasury of Atreus is the "Tomb of Clytemnestra," some 150 yards west of the Lion Gate. Here, in October, 1951, in the course of repairs, workmen stumbled upon some pieces of a grave monument on its original base. Soon after, the Greek archaeologist Dr. John Papadimitriou, and the Greek-American George Mylonas discovered three more worked stones, set on a curve. It looked to them as though they had hit upon another grave circle, like the one Schliemann had discovered within the wall seventy-five years before. Excavation proved them right: there was a circle, and within it twenty-four graves. of which fourteen yielded highly significant finds, dated by pottery to Middle Helladic III, or about 1650 B.C. These included bronze swords with alabaster pommels, ivory-handled bronze daggers, and the remains of a leather scabbard in gold appliqué. There were vases in silver and bronze, a death mask in electrum, and quantities of gold leaf. Jewelry included gold and silver earclips and gold diadems strengthened with bronze wire. Mylonas was particularly touched by the discovery of a child's gold rattle and thin gold curlers. He found, too, boars' tusks which had once covered helmets, and a belt in gold appliqué. The masterpiece of the collection was an exquisite rock crystal bowl in the form of a duck (Fig. 2.9). A fluted silver cup, bags of obsidian arrowheads, and an Egyptian scarab in lapis lazuli complete the selection from the rich roster of finds. They are now in the National Museum in Athens. Skeletons from two of the graves revealed macabre medical details: one had a fractured skull, neatly trepanned, the earliest such operation known in Europe; between the lower right ribs and the iliac crest of the other were two green-brown, faceted and polished stones: they were gallstones, suggesting a rich diet, worthy of a Homeric hero. This unfortunate seems from his gnarled joints to have suffered also from arthritis.

These are fabulous finds. Three quarters of a century earlier, Schliemann, excavating *his* grave circle (Fig. 2.10), had brought mythological Greece within the orbit of early Greek history. Within the circle he found six shaft graves containing nineteen burials; their rich contents made this, until the 1951 finds, the outstanding single discovery in Greek archaeological research. Schliemann, mistaking the disorder of fallen grave roofs for Aegisthus' guilty haste, thought Agamemnon was buried here, but the pottery dates

Fig. 2.9 Mycenae, duck vase in rock crystal from Grave Circle B, now in National Museum, Athens. (Mylonas, 1957, Fig. 61, by permission of Princeton University Press)

the graves far earlier, between 1580 and 1500 B.C. All the Mycenaean burials, shaft graves, chamber tombs, and *tholoi* belong to one unbroken tradition: all are family graves, all are furnished for the journey to Hades (including sometimes the occupant's favorite hound), all are burials, not cremations; all are heaped with earth, all marked with gravestones engraved or plain, all involved a funeral meal and libation or pouring of liquid offerings. Construction techniques show that the beehive shape is only an extension of the grave-circle principle. The exciting discoveries at Mycenae caused many a heightened heartbeat among the excavators, an excitement that seldom shows in their factual reports. But all the excavators of Mycenae, from Schliemann to Mylonas, were humanists, keenly aware that they were digging up not things but men: these weapons, wielded 3500 years ago, brought victory or defeat to real men, the vases once held priceless ointment for real women, the bones are of real people. Not the least reward of archaeology, as Mylonas says, is to infer from withered flowers the hour of their bloom.

Eight miles south-southeast of Mycenae lies the sister citadel of Tiryns, whose pre-Mycenaean history as archaeology reveals it we have already traced. Its remains, dated after 1900 B.C., are even more impressive than the massive

MYCENAE
SKETCH RESTORATION
OF GRAVE CIRCLE
WITH FIRST STAGE OF GRANARY

Fig. 2.10 Mycenae, Grave Circle A, reconstruction drawing. Visible, from the top down, are the triangular back of the Lion Gate relief, the Granary, the *stelai* over the Shaft Graves, the Ramp House, and the House of the Warrior Vase. (Wace, *op. cit*, Pl. 22) round tower described in the last chapter. The pottery reveals, in Late Helladic III, about 1400 B.C., a vigorous and ambitious period of construction, which produced in three phases the most monumental fortification walls known from the Mycenaean age (Fig. 2.11) and the surviving palace. Tiryns in mythology is Heracles' city: do his victories over local beasts symbolize Tirynthian victories over local barons?

Kurt Müller, the excavator of Tiryns, learned his archaeological techniques from Dörpfeld, and his results are a model of interpretation, acute, accurate, scrupulous, and thorough. Since most of but not quite all the pottery was cleared away either when the top of the acropolis was leveled off to build the palace or when Schliemann excavated in 1884, the relative dating had to be done mostly by acute observation of materials, dimensions, and construction styles. Thus the earliest phase, best seen in the citadel wall on the southwest, used sizable but not giant blocks of gray limestone, finished smooth on the outer face. Phase II, which involved northward and southward extensions of this wall and a new eastern approach by ramp, was built with large blocks of red stone. Phase III includes the great false-vaulted "casemates" (galleries) on east and south, and the bowing out of the west wall (undergoing restoration in 1961). This protects a new stair, reminiscent of the approach to the cistern at Mycenae: it has a pitfall thirty feet deep and a gate at the top. To Phase III belong the vast extension to the north, doubling the size of the citadel to provide a place of refuge at need to the population of the probably unwalled lower city; and the frescoed megaron with its throne, painted pavement, hearth, columns, and forecourts. All this gives evidence that this was the height of Tiryns' wealth and power. Phase III is identified by its use of gray and red stones, mixed, some of them gigantic, none as smoothly finished as in Phase I. Just enough pottery survived (including a few sherds painted with signs in Linear B script), to make an absolute dating possible. It shows that Phase I is Late Helladic (Mycenaean) III*a*, early fourteenth century. Phase II begins late in the same century and lasts well down into the thirteenth. The magnificent Phase III is dated a little later than the Lion Gate at Mycenae (i.e., after 1250, on the evidence of a new east gate, like the Lion Gate in material, dimensions, and plans, but showing slight improvement in detail). This is the phase whose Herculean ruins astonish the modern visitor. Its existence implies friendly relations with Mycenae, which must have regarded

I.BURG

II.BURG

III.BUR

Fig. 2.11 Tiryns I, II, III Phases. The walls of Phase I are jogged, as in Troy VI (Fig. 1.4). For Phase III, cf. Fig. 1.15. (Müller, 1930, Pl. 4, by permission of DAI, Athens)

Tiryns' walls not as a menace, but as merely a legitimate defense of Tirynthian treasure.

The approach today is by the same route that would have been taken by a visitor in Mycenaean times: up the ramp, a sharp right turn at the east gate, a sharp left along a narrow passage between massive beetling walls to yet another gate, the twin to the Lion Gate at Mycenae; then on to a forecourt, keeping the casemates on the left. All this time the right or shieldless side of the visitor was exposed to defenders on the walls, but from this point on the architecture changes, from a closed and forbidding to an open and welcoming mood. From the forecourt another right turn takes the visitor through the palace entrance gate or propylon, into a court paved with white stucco; from its northwest corner opens, off-center, the entrance into the main court in front of the megaron. This court was porticoed on three sides, and contains an altar on the axis of the megaron. The contrasting red and gray of the stonework, the brightly painted front of the megaron entrance (Fig. 2.12), the carpet-like painted floor of the inner propylon, its alabaster frieze, with its elongated rosettes, in Cretan style, bordered with spirals picked out with beads of blue glass paste, made the

Fig. 2.12 Tiryns, court and megaron entrance, reconstruction water color. The details (tapering columns, portico, figure-eight shield) show Minoan inspiration. (Müller, 1930, Pl. 42)

whole ensemble strikingly colorful. The megaron itself closely resembles those of Troy VI, the palace at Mycenae, and, as we shall see, the Palace of Nestor at Pylos. It had a painted floor, in which octopus and dolphin motifs alternated with geometric patterns, and a stripe like the border of a carpet marks the location of the throne-dais against the east wall. Frescoes of a boar hunt, a chariot race, a festal procession of women with offerings, and bull-leaping enlivened the palace walls in one phase or another with a range of seven colors: white, black, blue, two tones of red, yellow, and green.

West of the megaron are suites of apartments, one with a red-trimmed bright blue floor enlivened with painted dolphins; and a bathroom floored with one single colossal limestone block. East of the main megaron is a smaller one, perhaps for the Queen Mother, or Crown Prince, since it, too, had a throne; the floor was painted with rosette-embellished stripes. In an adjoining room, north of the stairwell, the dolphin-octopus motif recurs in the painted pavement. Both megara face south, the quarter from which in summer the cooling sea-wind blows across the Argolid from the Gulf of Nauplia. The sleeping rooms have an eastern exposure, for coolness in the evening. Wooden beams built into the stone courses of the walls provided a cushion against earthquakes, but also a hazard of fire. The roofs were flat; their height has been calculated from the diameter of column-bases and the height of stairwells; some inner rooms must have been lit by clerestories, others by light-wells. The whole palace complex gives evidence of great technical competence and architectural skill in the manipulation of space: the appropriate seat of a considerable kingdom, related to or at least on friendly terms with Mycenae, prospering no doubt on the spoils of the destruction of the Palace at Knossos and the fall of the Minoan Empire. But it too fell to violent assault by the Dorians and perished in flames. The blocked drains in the bath give evidence of a lower cultural level in the Sub-Mycenaean age. Tiryns, like Mycenae, never regained its former grandeur.

By 1939 the discovery in the southwest Peloponnese, near classical Pylos, at the north end of the Bay of Navarino in Messenia, of more "royal" tholos tombs than anywhere else except Mycenae led Greek archaeologists to invite Blegen to join them in more extended excavation. On the height of Epanò Englianós, three miles north of the beach of sandy Pylos on a steep plateau crowned by magnificent olives, Blegen found the ruins of an extensive complex of buildings, calcined and fused by an intense conflagration, which sherds established as a palace of late Mycenaean date. It is identified by Blegen as the Palace of Nestor, the aged, garrulous king of Pylos in Homer's *Iliad,* and host in the *Odyssey* to Odysseus' son Telemachus as he searches for his father. The excavation, interrupted by World War II, was reopened in 1952 and has been continued every year since. Successive campaigns have revealed (Fig. 2.13) a central palace block with at least forty-six rooms on each floor, including forecourt, main and subsidiary megara, and storage rooms; an older southwest block, with throne room, hearth, painted pavements, and toilet facilities; and an artisan's quarter with armory, wine-cellars, and storerooms to the south and east. Out of one of these very storerooms Nestor's maid may have broached the eleven-year-old wine in honor

Fig. 2.13 Pylos, palace, plan. The Archives Room, where the Linear B tablets were found, is in the lower left corner of the central block, where megaron with central hearth can also be identified. Artisan's quarter to the right, older palace to the left. Note circuit wall and gate discovered in 1960. (Blegen, 1961, Pl. 53.1)

of Telemachus' visit, as described in the *Odyssey*: "They took
their places on the settles and chairs, and the old man prepared a bowl of mellow wine for his guests, from a jar that
had stood for ten years before the maid undid the cap and
broached it." In 1960 innumerable fragments and chips of
ivory were found in this area, as well as 500 diminutive
bronze arrowheads. The plan closely resembles that of the
palaces at Mycenae and Tiryns. No less than eight pantries
were found, filled to overflowing with orderly nests of unused
pottery. One set of 800, found right beside the front door,
suggests the need for instant hospitality for visitors, attested
by the Homeric poems. Beside the throne room was found
a kind of bar, with provision for setting large wine jars to
cool, for the refreshment of those awaiting audience. Over
8000 whole pots in all were found, of which all but a dozen
are Late Mycenaean III^h and *c*: they date the destruction
about 1200 B.C., a generation after Blegen's date for the destruction of Troy VII*a*. Earlier ware in deeper levels, going
back to Middle Helladic, proves that the site had been occupied since about 1900 B.C. by modest houses, which were
swept away in Late Mycenaean III*b* to make room for the
palace.

The main megaron has a magnificent version of the usual
Mycenaean round central hearth, thirteen feet across, edged
with a flame pattern and with painted spirals running horizontally round the raised rim. The floor has a chessboard
design, as at Tiryns, with abstract and octopus patterns,
and a space marked out for the throne, which was flanked
by a frescoed griffin on one side, a lion on the other. Many
colorful fresco fragments found fallen from above show
that all the important rooms were gaily decorated, with
figures of gods, tanned men in spotted white tunics, women,
panthers, lions, boars, deer, sphinxes, dogs, horses, marine
creatures; processions, duels, sieges, a lyre player perched
on his own colorful private mountain: he may be Apollo, or
Orpheus. A bathroom with a built-in bath and a kylix or
footed shallow drinking cup smashed in the tub may either
imply that Mycenaeans drank wine while bathing, or it may
have contained oil for anointing, as Nestor's daughter
anointed Telemachus on his visit: "She bathed him and
rubbed him with olive oil; she gave him a tunic and arranged
a fine cloak around his shoulders, so that he stepped out of
the bath looking like an immortal god." One pottery kylix,

excavated in 1957 (and now in the National Museum in Athens), is a foot high and a foot wide, the largest ever found: it reminded Blegen of Nestor's gold cup in the *Iliad,* which was the size of a soup tureen. The 1959 campaign revealed at last traces of an early fortification wall with gate and tower, and trial trenches below the citadel uncovered the house walls of a lower town, which supplied the last features necessary to make the palace and its environs perfectly parallel to those of Mycenae and Tiryns, and to clinch it as, like them, the seat of a powerful and wealthy dynasty and, like them, doomed to fall, not long after the siege of Troy, to the merciless and uncivilized Dorian invaders.

All this is important, but another Pylos find, dating from the very first week of the first campaign, made possible the most important breakthrough in the history of early Greek archaeology. In *The New York Times* of April 28, 1939 was announced Blegen's discovery, in an Archives Room in the south corner of the central palace, of over 600 fragments of clay tablets, inscribed in a script identical with the one identified by Evans at Knossos a generation before, and named by him "Minoan Linear B," to distinguish it from an earlier "A" script with some different characters, and from still earlier hieroglyphics. In 1936, when Evans lectured in London on this tantalizing writing, in his audience was a fourteen-year-old English schoolboy, Michael Ventris, who vowed to take up the challenge of this undeciphered script. Sixteen years later, with the aid of the Pylos tablets and techniques of cryptanalysis learned in World War II, he had cracked it.

Both Evans and Blegen had observed, from the pictorial nature of some of the signs of the script, that they were dealing with lists, catalogues, or inventories of persons, domestic animals, cereals, and other commodities, with numbers or quantities recorded in a decimal system. Since the Pylos deposit was the first one found in mainland Greece, Blegen was able to conclude, without being able to read the script, that the Mycenaeans were not illiterate, that they were capable of orderly methods of administration, and that the strikingly similar palaces of Mycenae and Tiryns must also have contained such tablets, and hence their bureaucracy must also have been literate. The failure of the excavators

to find the evidence there must have been due to sheer
chance or to the fact that the conflagrations which destroyed
those palaces did not always bake the clay of the tablets hard
enough to preserve it. (Even the better-baked Pylos tablets
had to be dried for days on specially constructed wire-mesh
frames before they could be handled.) Wace in fact did, as
we have seen, later find Linear B tablets at Mycenae. The
finding of tablets on the mainland in the same script as those
known since 1900 at Knossos created the strong presumption
that all the tablets, Pylian and Cretan alike, were written in
some early form of Greek. This justified the further inference
that the Palace at Knossos in the level at which the tablets
were reportedly found (Late Minoan I-II, fifteenth century
B.C.) was occupied by Greek-speaking invaders. Evans went
to his grave in 1941 denying this, but Ventris proved it true.

Ventris began by distinguishing on the tablets some
eighty-eight signs, uniform on the mainland and on the Cretan tablets. Eighty-eight signs are too many for an alphabet,
too few for such a system of ideographs as Chinese, or
Egyptian hieroglyphics. Therefore the system must have been
a syllabary, in which the signs might stand for *ba, be, ka, ke,*
etc. With some 2500 tablets to deal with, Ventris was able
to find which signs were statistically frequent, average, or in-
frequent; initial, medial, or final; to determine which signs
were regularly paired or linked, and which never associated. On the assumption, rendered safe by the mainland
finds from Pylos, that the language of the syllabary was
Greek, he could guess that the most frequent initial signs were
a and *e*, as they are in classical Greek. Earlier work by an
American, Alice Kober, had established that the word-endings
(ascertained by noticing the upright strokes, or dividers, marked
in the clay) involved vowel variation, and showed that certain
signs shared the same consonant, others the same vowel, and
that there were characteristic inflectional vowels, as in the
Greek or Indo-European inflections for gender, case, and
number. Thus a series (called "Kober's triplets") might
run ⊤�兊⥄⼊⊟, ⊤⼕⥄⼊⼔, ⊤⼕⥄⼔⼔, or ⼔⣕⣴⼊⊟, ⼔⣕⼊⼔,
and ⼔⣕⼲⼔. The way in which certain sign-groups were used
suggested that they referred to certain categories: places,
persons, trades or occupations, and commodities. Ventris
had available nearly 1700 tablets from Knossos; place names
near Knossos survived down into classical times; he could

play some hunches. For example, in the first series above, which comes from Knossos (where Linear B may have been invented by Minoan scribes at the order of Mycenaean masters), the initial sign had already been noted as high-frequency, and therefore a vowel. Now the name of the harbor town of Knossos was known to be Amnisos. These four syllabic signs were therefore guessed to represent *a-mi-ni-so*. Another very frequently occurring Knossian sign-sequence, also cited above, shared one sign with this: - - *so*; why should this not be *ko-no-so* = Knossos? The other final signs would be adjectival case-endings, to be extrapolated from Greek: *ja, jo*. The first syllable of *ko-no-so* occurred often together with one of two signs, either ⟨⟩ or ⟨⟩, together with pictorial ideograms clearly meaning *MEN* and *WOMEN*. The classical Greek for "boy" is *kouros* (involving a lost digamma or *w*-sound; "girl" is *kore*. These two pairs of signs might then be transliterated *ko-wo* and *ko-wa*, and the final signs in each could then be substituted, as a pair of case endings, in another of "Kober's triplets." Another sign, ⊙ , occurred with high frequency in the final position. These are lists: the sign might be an enclitic (tacked-on) *and*, like *-que*, "and," in Latin, *te* in classical Greek; Ventris assigned it the value *-qe*. Already Ventris had possible equivalents for twelve of the eighty-eight signs, and each verified hunch would produce a chain reaction substituting knowns for unknowns in more tablets. It was time to systematize these relationships in the form of a grid.

Ventris' grid (Fig. 2.14) provided space for five vowels across the top and twelve or thirteen consonants down the sides; i.e., equivalents for up to sixty-five out of the eighty-eight signs in the syllabary. It will be noted that there is no *b, c, f, g, h, l, v,* or *x: b* and *f* (=*ph*) are labials, for which *p-* does duty in the syllabary; *c* and *g* are gutturals, for which *k-* does duty; *h* is not an expressed consonant but a rough breathing; *r* and *l* both seem to be represented in the syllabary by *r,* as when a Chinese speaks English; *v* is not a letter in the classical Greek alphabet; and *x* is a double letter (= *ks*). How to find more clues? Among Blegen's tablets found in 1939 at Pylos was one where the signs ⟨⟩ =⟨⟩, ⟨⟩ =⟨⟩ were repeated with the *WOMAN* ideogram. In the Greek dialects the word for "mother" is *mater;* suppose ⟨⟩ =⟨⟩ = *-ma-te;* then ⟨⟩ =⟨⟩ = *pa-te* = *pater* "father," and two more

Fig. 2.14 grid — Basic values and Homophones (Linear B syllabic signs shown graphically; phonetic labels transcribed below):

						Homophones
a	e	i	o	u		a_2 (ha?)
da	de	di	do	du		ai
*a	je	—	jo	ju		ai_2?
ka	ke	ki	ko	ku		ai_3?
ma	me	mi	mo	mu?		*87 (kwe?)
na	ne	ni	no	nu		nwa
pa	pe	pi	po	pu		pa_2
—	qe	qi	qo			pa_3?
ra	re	ri	ro	ru		pte
sa	se	si	so	su		pu_2?
ta	te	ti	to	tu		ra_2 (ri-ja)
wa	we	wi	wo	—		ra_3 (rai)
za	ze	zi	zo	zu?		ro_2 (ri-jo)
*22	*47	*49	*63	*64		*85 (si-ja?)
*65	*71	*82	*83	*86		ta_2 (ti-ja)

Fig. 2.14 Linear B grid. (Ventris-Chadwick, 1956, p. 23, by permission of Cambridge University Press)

syllables are added to the grid. Pairs of words identical except for one sign were helpful, too; the variation would indicate alternative spellings, and a relation could be established between pairs of signs which would differ by only one letter. Thus a Pylos tablet read ♈♈♈♈, a Knossos one ♈♈♈♈. Frequency tables showed that ♈, ♈, ♈ were vowels. Another Knossos tablet contained the sequence ♈♈♈♈♈ along with ♈♈♈♈. The *pater* deduction had established ♈ as *pa*, ♈ as *-te*. The Amnisos-Knossos deduction had established ♈ as *-si*, *Pa- si te-?-?* might be *pasi theois*, classical Greek for "to all the gods." In such a context surely the word "priest" or "priestess" might be expected: the classical Greek is *hiereus*, *hiereia.* Thus it was easy to transliterate the unknowns, with their numerous vowel signs, as *i-e-re-u, i-je-re-u, i-je-re-ja,* and a link between $\mathcal{A}$ = *e* and $\mathcal{X}$ = *je* was established. All these new values could be added to the grid.

A high-frequency pair at Pylos is $\mathcal{A} \vdash$: if this is "Pylos," and in the syllabary *r* = *l*, as seemed likely on other grounds, then the syllables *pu* and *ro* can be added to the grid. It developed that the Linear B syllabary had its own rules for spelling, different from those of classical Greek (naturally, since an alphabet produces one kind of conventional spelling, a syllabary another). In addition to the peculiar behavior of labials, gutturals, etc. already noted, *q* apparently stands for a sound which in classical Greek resolves into *k, p,* or *t; l, m, n, r,* and *s,* final or before another consonant, are omitted; consonant clusters are broken up into two syllables; initial *s* is omitted before a consonant; the semivowels *j-* and *w-* are indicated. Once these peculiarities were understood a consistent vocabulary and grammar began to work itself out. The transliterations that made sense became too frequent to be explained as coincidence, and the language was established as Greek. Chadwick illustrates how the guesses became virtual certainties, by postulating that work on an English cipher might establish the combinations XYZ and ZYX as nouns, XY and ZY as verbs, XYYZ and YZZ as adjectives; *G, O,* and *D* then become the only possible equivalent for *X, Y,* and *Z.* Ventris announced his provisional results in June, 1952. In May, 1953, Blegen found a tablet at Pylos with a picture of a tripod on it, and beside it a sign-series which by Ventris' grid worked out as *ti-ri-po-de* (Fig. 2.15). The decipherment was an accomplished fact, and the Greek language was proved to have a 3300-year history, which only Chinese can rival. Ventris died tragically in a motor accident in September, 1956; his work is being carried on by John Chadwick (Cambridge), and Emmett L. Bennett, Jr. (University of Wisconsin), and many other scholars from many countries.

The decipherment yielded at once a vast number of personal names and names of occupations. Personal names make up 65 per cent of the vocabulary of what we must now call Mycenaean Greek. They include some that recur in classical Greek mythology and history, such as Theseus and possibly Alkmaion; god-names, Athena, Poseidon, and Dionysus:

Fig. 2.15 Pylos, tripod tablet. The four signs to the right of the second tripod in the top line read, according to Bentris' grid, *ti-ri-po-de*, thus clinching the soundness of his decipherment. (Ventris-Chadwick, 1956, fac. p. 111)

enough to suggest strongly the Mycenaean origin of Greek myth. Over 100 names of occupations were deciphered in the first report. They show a sophisticated division of labor and interest in luxury goods, and include goldsmiths, ship-wrights, masons, bakers, cooks, woodcutters, messengers, longshoremen, oarsmen, coppersmiths, fullers (dry cleaners), saddlers, shepherds; as well as the Homeric names for King and Leader of the Host. Later, Ventris and Chadwick were able to add the words for doctor, herald, potter, forester, carpenter, bowmaker, flax-worker, carder, spinner, weaver, bath attendant, and unguent-boiler.

At Pylos the tablets included inventories of inlaid furni-ture and costly objects in ivory, gold, silver, and lapis lazuli. They revealed the workings of an organized bureaucracy, working down from King and court through military leaders, administrative officials, charioteers, mayors of surrounding villages, craftsmen, and landworkers. It was this palace bu-reaucracy that fell when the Dorians invaded; with it Greek literacy disappeared for centuries. The tablets established re-ligion, too, as involving offerings of agricultural produce, precious objects, men, and women, to named gods: Poseidon, Zeus, Hera, Hermes, Dionysus, and perhaps Artemis. They tell us what Greek was like 500 years before Homer; what elements in Homer are Mycenaean and what late; what the origins of classical Greek mythology, religion, and art are. They proved (because Linear B was derived from the still-undeciphered but non-Greek Linear A in Crete) that there was communication, verbal and cultural, between Greeks and Minoans. If Greeks could communicate with Cretans, they could presumably communicate with other cultures; e.g., the Hittites, who used tablets at this time. Thus One World in the Near East in the thirteenth century B.C. becomes an es-tablished fact.

When in the fall of 1953 I excitedly announced the news of Ventris' decipherment to a colleague, he asked drily, "What is the poetry like?" The answer is that so far there is none; nothing but inventories and prosaic documents of that kind. But they are enough to bring the Mycenaean world out of the darkness of prehistory into the light of historic docu-mentation, and there is good reason to believe that the Homeric poems as we have them derive ultimately from Mycenaean oral epic.

Neleus, founder of Nestor's dynasty at Pylos, took to wife a princess from Orchomenos in Boeotia; the tholos tomb there, Schliemann's so-called "Treasury of Minyas" (mentioned above, Chapter 1) is to be dated as contemporary with the Tomb of Clytemnestra at Mycenae. Besides the tholos tomb, bits of fresco showing architectural details and bull-leaping (which involved catching the bull's horns and somersaulting onto his back and off again) hint at the Mycenaean palace, or at any rate an upper-class house, at Orchomenos, which the tomb presupposes, and so does a stirrup-vase (a squat, flat-bottomed container for liquids, named from the shape of its handles) painted with Linear B signs. The wealth, prosperity, and sophistication which these finds imply clearly resulted from the draining of the nearby Lake Copais. When this operation was repeated in the late nineteenth century of our era, the contractors found the dikes that bounded the ancient drainage canals. Since these are built of polygonal blocks in the same technique as the later phases of the circuit walls of Mycenae and Tiryns, a late Mycenaean date is established for them. On the tiny rocky island of Gla near the lake's east shore, French and German excavators discovered a citadel larger than Mycenae and Tiryns together, walled in salients like the southwest side of the acropolis of Tiryns, with a main gate that probably boasted a relieving triangle in the Mycenaean manner, though nothing above the lintel is preserved. Against the inner north face of the circuit wall at its highest point, with a fine view over the lake or the rich fields, was built an L-shaped palace or villa whose plan (Fig. 2.16) strongly resembles, as we shall see (Fig. 2.26), the villa excavated by the Italians at Hagia Triada in southern Crete. Like Mycenae, Tiryns, and Pylos, Gla has megara (plan C, P), and traces of drainage conduits, painted pavement, and frescoes. Unique finds include clamps of lead for joining the wooden door jambs to the walls, and pilasters and half-round columns in stucco, apparently used as moldings to frame frescoes or relieve the monotony of solid-painted walls. Like Mycenae, Tiryns, and Pylos, Gla came to a violent end by fire, probably in the twelfth century B.C.

Detailed accounts of other Mycenaean sites on the mainland would unnecessarily complicate the story. It must be noted in anticipation, however, that Athens and Demeter's holy city of Eleusis also flourished in Mycenaean times, apparently without falling before the Dorian invaders who de-

Fig. 2.16 Gla, palace, plan. Recent excavation has revealed an entrenched camp with long walls south of the palace. (BCH, 1894, Pl. VI)

stroyed many Mycenaean sites. But their story can be told more intelligibly as a unit later on. Meanwhile, the Cyclades give evidence for the state of culture at Phylakopi and elsewhere in the islands in Mycenaean times.

Phylakopi I, a phase of the city described in the last chapter, appears from its pottery to have come to a violent end, at about the same time as many mainland cities, about 1900 B.C. or a little earlier. This, then, is the point of transition between Middle and Late Cycladic. Phylakopi II is a Late Cycladic city, walled, with frescoed houses, streets crossing at right angles, and evidence of close connections in trade and culture with Crete; perhaps it was even a Minoan colony. The best evidence for this Minoan influence is the flying fish fresco (Fig. 2.17), found in association with Cretan Kamares ware, and therefore to be dated about 1600 B.C.

It is a gay freehand piece, in marine blue, yellow, red, and black; in it the fish dart now up, now down, with wings now closed, now outspread, against a background of rocks, sponges, and fish eggs. Phylakopi III centers around a new palace (no trace of earlier phases below) with a megaron in the mainland style and a central hearth. With the palace goes mainland, not Cretan pottery. The style is Late Mycenaean III, and the finest piece is the Fisherman Vase, on which four men with Picasso-like eyes walk on a pebbly beach carrying miniature dolphins by the tail in each hand. The style is close to that of the Warrior Vase from Mycenae. One sherd, otherwise undated, bears syllabic signs which, interpreted as Linear B, apparently comes from Lyktos in Crete; if the language is Greek, the pottery was imported after mainland invaders had taken Crete over. Phylakopi III declined with its mainland neighbors, and about the same time, under the stress of the Dorian invasion of about 1125. Other islands, Naxos, Kea, Delos, Kythnos, Seriphos, Amorgos, Paros, Siphnos, Tenos, Kimolos, yield late Mycenaean wares, which cease after the mainland palaces were sacked, but there has been little or no systematic excavation and cultural details are lacking. The important conclusion is that Cretan influence ceases after the mainland folk sacked

Fig. 2.17 Phylakopi, flying fish fresco. Athens, National Museum. (Émile Séraf)

Knossos, and mainland influence ceases after the Dorians sacked the Mycenaean palaces. Thereafter the Cyclades, like the rest of the Aegean world, lapse into the poverty-stricken "Dark Ages" that yield little to the excavator.

Crete remains. We left it, at the end of the last chapter, in the midst of the Middle Minoan period, before the prime of the palaces at Knossos, Mallia, Gourniá, and Phaistos. The culture to be described is as on the mainland of vast extent in time, nearly 800 years. An earthquake at the end of Middle Minoan II*b*, about 1800 B.C., gave the architects of the New Palace at Knossos a free hand for expansive plans. Prosperity resulting from sea trade, piracy, and tribute provided the means. Knossos, archaeology tells us, was for about a century (1580-1480 B.C.) the center of an international power, the first in European history.

The wealth, enthusiasm, and imagination of Sir Arthur Evans reconstructed chiefly this phase of the palace (Fig. 2.18), not always, it is to be feared, with complete fidelity to the archaeological data, but the result is vivid, picturesque, and colorful enough to satisfy the most jaded tourist: the bright frescoes; the famous downward-tapering painted cypress-wood columns; the huge storage jars, taller than a man, have been restored or left *in situ* to lend the Palace of Minos more human interest that any other prehistoric Greek site. The palace as reconstructed is a great six-acre square, 400 feet on a side, built around a central court, and dominating a flourishing city (almost entirely unexcavated) with a population estimated by Evans at 82,000 (100,000 if the port town of Amnisos, three miles away, is included). Its state entrances and public rooms were on the south and west. In the rich storerooms beneath them Evans found the lead linings of chests that had once contained objects of value. From the west porch a dog-leg corridor, frescoed with a processional scene, led first south, then east. Out of the middle of its eastern leg opened northward a propylon, not unlike the one at Tiryns, decorated with a fresco of cupbearers. From this, one ascended a broad staircase to an audience hall on the upper story. Opening out of the northwest corner of the central court is a suite of rooms belonging to a late phase of the palace, including one with a ceremonial seat in gypsum flanked by frescoed griffins. Evans called this the "Throne Room," but the lustral area and kitchens adjoining make it more likely that it was used for

Fig. 2.18 Knossos, Palace of Minos, air view. 1, grand staircase to audience chamber; 2, Throne Room; 3, Theatral Area; 4, Central Court; 5, magazines of great *pithoi*; 6, 15, horns of consecration; 8, Hall of the Double Axes; 9, Northeast Magazines; 10, Pillar Hall; 11, Propylon. (Scullard, *Atlas*, Pl. 14, by permission of Elsevier, Amsterdam)

some cult ceremony requiring a high priest (perhaps the King) to live here for several days running. This "Throne Room" may have been the seat of the power of the Mycenaean invader who took over the palace late in Late Minoan I, a greater feat than the taking of Troy. There is certainly a close resemblance to the throne rooms of Mycenae, Tiryns, and Pylos. When the room was excavated, vases for anointing oils were found on the floor as they had fallen. Perhaps— it is all conjecture—the final catastrophe (about 1400 B.C., wrought by Mycenaean overlords impatient of Minoan recalcitrance, who pillaged, massacred, burned, and withdrew) overwhelmed the palace at the very moment when an anointing ceremony was going on. The southeast block, Evans found, belonged almost entirely to the New Palace (Middle Minoan IIIb). It contained the Domestic Quarter, the private residence of the king and queen, approached by the Grand Staircase, whose five flights, embellished with a fresco of shields, open out of the eastern side of the central court. Evans' reconstruction of the Grand Staircase is one of the major feats of modern archaeological rebuilding. It gave access to the airy Hall of the Double Axes (so called from the masons' marks cut in the building blocks). That in turn opened, through seven of its eleven doorways, on an L-shaped portico and terrace with a view over the valley below, where, Evans believed, was the bull ring where Theseus and his Athenians performed before King Minos and his daughter Ariadne. (It is equally possible that the bull-leaping was done in the central court.) South of this Hall, and isolated from it by a dog-leg corridor, are the charming apartments centering on what Evans called the Queen's Megaron, with its vivacious fresco of blue dolphins (cousins to the flying fish of Phylakopi), with bubbles flying off their fins, set in a border of coral and sponges. Although this megaron has five doors and seven windows, it does not open on the eastern terrace: its blank eastern wall was painted, in compensation, with a landscape. Adjoining it on the west was a bath and (a comfort to those who equate civilization with plumbing) a flush toilet. A room to the south has been called the "Nursery" because its entrance has a low gypsum barrier which might have been a gate across the door of a baby's room.

The northeast wing was the artisans' quarter, where Evans identified the palace laundry and small cells with grooves for sliding doors, which he thought were kennels. In the long north-south corridor of this wing he found an elegant gaming board in rock crystal, blue glass paste, silver, ivory, and gold. To the northwest is the impressive stepped "Theatral Area," overlooked, Evans thought, by a "Royal Box." It could hardly have been used for bull-leaping, since it offered spectators no protection; perhaps it was used for ceremonial dances. From the "Armoury," which faces the road leading west from the Theatral Area, comes a tablet recording in Linear B numerals 8640 arrows. Sealings with the Linear B ARROW ideogram were found here attached to the charred remains of two wooden boxes containing arrowheads and their carbonized shafts.

Middle Minoan is the period of the undeciphered Linear A script, many of whose signs anticipate Linear B, but the Linear B tablets belong to a later and prosperous period when Mycenaean invaders occupied the palace. Another earthquake, about 1580 B.C., destroyed the magnificence, but the restored palace and its dependent houses show frescoes of very high standard, depicting scenes from nature and wild life; blue monkeys, partridges, hoopoes. There are also proud human figures: the Priest-King (found near the entrance from the Processional Corridor into the central court) with his swelling chest, powerful muscles, and lean thighs, wears a coronet of lilies and peacock plumes. The cup-bearers, lining the south propylon walls, wear silver earrings, necklaces, bracelets, and anklets; silver belts inset with gold pinch in their waists. The masterpiece of this period is the "Parisienne" (Fig. 2.19), the very type of elegant, slightly decadent young Cretan womanhood, with her ivory-white skin, big, bold dark eyes, dark curly hair falling in unrestrained ringlets over a low forehead, retroussé nose, full-coral-red lips, and delicate chin. In the Harvester Vase of the same period from Hagia Triada (Fig. 2.20), a spirit of riotous drunkenness pervades the scene: a band of peasants with winnowing fans over their shoulders are bawling a song at the top of their lungs, while a man, blind drunk, trips and falls over another who turns to roar a jest at him. They are roistering while Knossos burns, for just about this time (ca. 1450 B.C.) the Linear B tablets begin, the palace adds its throne room of the mainland type, and tombs and pottery in the Knossos area become strongly Helladic; i.e., Mycenaean. Pretty clearly the Minoan kingdom and palace were now taken over by a mainland prince. Perhaps mythology reflects this in the story of the slaying of the Mino-

Fig. 2.19 Knossos, La Parisienne, fresco fragment. Heraklion, Museum. (Evans, 1921-36, IV. 2, Pl. XXXIE, by permission of Messrs. Macmillan and the Trustees of the Sir Arthur Evans Estate)

taur in the Labyrinth by the Athenian prince Theseus.

Evans spent a fortune restoring the Palace of Minos, not always—to repeat—with complete accuracy. But the vivid reds and blues of the columns, the fresh colors and lively motifs of the frescoes, the giant vats in the storerooms make it one of the most rewarding sites to visit in the entire ancient world. It is all too easy to forget that there are other sites in Crete, not as accessible, not as well publicized, not as boldly restored, but vitally important for an understanding of Minoan culture as a whole. Of these the most important are the palace of Mallia (a French dig, since 1922); the town of Gournia (American, 1901), both east of Knossos; and the palace of Phaistos and the villa of Hagia Triada (Italian, since 1901), near the south coast.

Mallia, eighteen miles east of Knossos, proved, since its walls were stuccoed but not frescoed, to be a provincial

Fig. 2.20   Hagia Triada, Harvester Vase. Heraklion, Museum.

palace, smaller and less elegant than Knossos, but very like it in general plan, with its complex of *insulae* grouped about a central court (Fig. 2.21). The French excavators found numbers of Minoan sherds at the first stroke of the pick: the site had not been inhabited since the catastrophe, perhaps the result of local rivalries, which overwhelmed it earlier than the other Cretan palaces, early in Late Minoan I, about 1600 B.C. As at Knossos and, as we shall see, at Phaistos, the main entrance is on the west. Here it is in a recess protected by bastions. It opens into a narrow corridor, narrowed still further by a door at its east end, which connects with a wider north-south corridor with storerooms opening off it, as at Knossos. The thick buttressed walls of some of these were planned to bear the heavy weight of a story or more above. Bits of gold leaf were found in the storerooms, but clandestine diggers had long ago carried off nearly everything of intrinsic value. Potsherds remained, in which, as always, the history of the site could be read; and in the Domestic Quarter opening off the northwest side of the central court was found a stone votive ax splendidly worked into the shape of a leopard, the hide rendered with running spirals; and a bronze sword a yard long with a gold-plated hilt and rock crystal pommel. Since the site had no natural source of water, a series of eight circular reservoirs for catching rain was built in the southwest corner. In the northwest quarter the rooms, grouped around their own stucco-paved court, included a sunken lustral area like the one adjoining the throne room at Knossos. In a room just south of the court a number of clay tablets were found, inscribed in early Cretan hieroglyphic. Its signs recur at Knossos, and in the same grouping, which warrants the inference that the language used was the same in both places. The *insula* west and southwest of the stuccoed court was for artisans: one room had so many fragments of ivory in it that it must have been a workshop. The block south of this contained a potter's shop under the monumental stair. South of the stair the open, naturally well-lit vestibule facing on the central court is the largest room in the palace: it was perhaps the entrance to the rooms of state.

The central court had porticoes on its north and east sides, and possibly all the way round. Since dowel holes in the blocks between the columns show that this space was barricaded part way up, it may be that the court (and by inference those in other Cretan palaces) was used for the

Fig. 2.21 Mallia, palace, plan. Note resemblances to Knossos: magazines, central court, pillar hall. The reservoirs mentioned in the text belong in the lower left corner. (Chapouthier, 1942, p. 78)

dangerous sport of bull-leaping, in which as we saw, acrobatic athletes vaulted between the horns of the bull, turned a somersault, and vaulted off over his tail, a feat that Spanish bull-fighters have declared impossible, but which is portrayed on Minoan frescoes and in ivory statuettes.

East of the central court are more storerooms, with low platforms in which oil-jars are set; channels led the overflow to collecting jars (*pithoi*) sunk in the floors. Measures and weights were found here, and traces of carbonized wheat and lentils. The pillared hall north of the central court was full of incense-burners: it was the crypt of an important room above. The block north of this contained more storerooms, one of them a pantry, crammed with broken pottery, which could be pieced together. (It is a useful archaeological principle that where masses of sherds can be pieced together, they represent a deposit; where they cannot, they represent a dump.) The rooms in this block, too, are grouped around their own court. One of them contained two-part molds of imported stone, for bronze-casting. A paved causeway led up to another entrance, on the northwest.

The French have also dug trenches in the area round the palace, Mallia town, which, they calculate, would hold a population of 12,000. In the rich necropolis 500 yards north of the palace, where the pottery shows the burials to be of the inhabitants of an earlier phase of the palace than the one described above, the chief find was a gold pendant (Middle Minoan I) whose motif (Fig. 2.22) is a pair of bees arched round a honey-cake, with a gold bead in a gold cage above. The jewel is soldered, and the granulated work is very fine. One of the villas has been restored as a small museum of Minoan daily life.

Another series of villas, excavated by the Greeks, published by the French, at Tylissos, eight miles west of Knossos, ranges in date from Early Minoan to Late Minoan III. All the villas showed similar ground plans. Among the finds were a bronze talent, vases containing pigments (red and yellow ocher, copper oxide), Linear A tablets, tables of offering made of steatite, fine-toothed saws for work with ivory, and a cylinder seal, an import from Hittite Anatolia. The Tylissos villas were more elegant than those of Mallia town: some rooms were frescoed, with crocus and lily motifs. The Tylissos houses, together with Mallia palace and town, are of particular interest as showing that neither the palace nor the domestic architecture of Knossos is unique; it is all part

Fig. 2.22 Mallia, necropolis, gold bee pendant. Heraklion, Museum.

of a common Minoan architectural language, of which Mallia represents a provincial phase.

The best excavated and most interesting Minoan *town* is Gournia, near the coast, twenty-five miles southeast of Mallia. It was dug in 1901-03 under the direction of an American woman, Harriet Boyd Hawes, who compared its steep, stepped streets and crowded multistoried house blocks (Fig. 2.23) with Naples; it also presents analogies with Phylakopi III and with Dorion IV (Malthi). The palace (plan, G) does not enclose a central court, as elsewhere; the court (H) is rather the agora or market place of the whole town. This petty king kept his vassals at no greater distance than would a medieval lord. A vast quantity of weapons, tools, and utensils in bronze, stone, and clay gives a full and lively picture of the life of a minor Cretan city of the second half of the sixteenth century B.C. (Late

Minoan I*b*); there is some reason to believe that toward the end Gournia was an important center for the production of an elegant pottery that rivaled the late "Palace Style" at Knossos.

The other major Cretan palace site is Phaistos, near the south coast, thirty-six difficult miles by road southwest of Knossos. The Italians under Luigi Pernier began to excavate it in May, 1900, as Evans was ending his first campaign at Knossos, but the final publication did not appear until 1951, and digging, under Doro Levi, is still going on, as it is at Knossos under Sinclair Hood of the British School at Athens. The excavators of Phaistos claim it gives, because here restorations have not exceeded the evidence, a better and clearer idea than Knossos of a palace dating from the height of Minoan civilization. Reconstruction at Phaistos has been limited to rebuilding a few vertical walls to no great height, leaving a groove between the genuine Minoan stonework and the modern reconstruction; and roofing over a few rooms to preserve stratification, pavements, or artifacts left *in situ*. Clarity at Phaistos results from a fixed line of stratification between an earlier and a later palace, provided by a concrete-hard second-palace pavement laid down over the leveled remains of the first palace, whose foundations had inadequate footings, so that an earthquake toppled it in Middle Minoan III, about 1650 B.C., to judge by the pottery. This pavement (which incidentally suggested to Pernier that the palace-dwellers went barefoot indoors, oriental fashion) provides as clear a baseline as the marks of the Persian fire of 480 B.C. on the Acropolis at Athens, or the layer of Vesuvian ash over the Pompeii of A.D. 79. Beneath this pavement the first palace stratum averages about five feet thick; below that again, trial pits have yielded over nine feet of sub-Neolithic and Neolithic deposits with traces of huts, bones of boar, hare, and wild goat, obsidian flakes, stone weapons and tools. The absolute dating of Palace I depends indirectly on Egyptian artifacts. None was found in the first palace level, but first-palace pottery presents exact analogies with sherds found at nearby sites in association with Egyptian scarabs and amulets of the XIIth Dynasty (after 2000 B.C.). The synchronism is clinched by imported pottery of the Phaistos first-palace type found in a XIIth Dynasty stratum at Kahun in Egypt. In both places archaeology has revealed this to be a period of great prosperity and ambitious building.

Fig. 2.23 Gournia, town plan. (Hawes, 1908, plan at back)

Fig. 2.24 Phaistos disk. Heraklion, Museum.
(Evans, *Scripta Minoa*, I, Pl. XII, by permission
of Clarendon Press, Oxford)

Parts of the first palace were reused in the second. In
the first palace the excavators distinguished forty rooms, including a shrine and sacrificial trench in the west court. The
façade projected farther west into the west court than did the
façade of the second palace, and the entrances were less
monumental, but otherwise the plans of the two were much
the same: the central court was common to both. The most
famous find from the first palace is the Phaistos Disk, discovered in 1908 together with a number of Linear A tablets,
in a Middle Minoan III*b* context in the basement of an
archives room at the west end of the northeast block. It contains (Fig. 2.24) forty-five different hieroglyphic symbols, im-
pressed on both faces with separate stamps like movable type,
in a spiral running from the outside in, with vertical word-
dividers. The Disk has never been deciphered. Any decipher-

ment without more evidence is intrinsically improbable, but a recent (1959) attempt uses initial, medial, and final frequencies, which allegedly match those established for Linear B, to argue that the language is a Cretan dialect of Greek, listing, for pilgrims, a set of sacred precincts lucky and unlucky, pure and polluted. Since the Disk was found in association with tablets in Linear A (twenty-four more, allegedly of Middle Minoan I*a*, were found in 1953 and 1955), and Linear A is definitely not Greek, the 1959 effort needs and fails to explain an unlikely double shift of language, between the date of the Disk and the intrusion of Mycenaean Linear B. A 1962 attempt starts the decipherment from the center and works out, counter-clockwise. Assuming that the signs on the Disk are the ancestors of the signs on a tablet from Énkomi in Cyprus (see below, p. 132), it emerges with on one face a list of sacrifices, on the other a poem about the "yielding" of the mortal Ion of Sardis to the goddess Tharso-Athena. Until more examples of the Phaistos signary are found, this attempt, too, must be labeled "not proven."

The plan of the second palace (Fig. 2.25) presents many analogies with Knossos, whose power may have reduced the lords of Phaistos to peaceful coexistence. It nearly equals in size the Palace of Minos; like it, it includes a "theatral area" (the steps in the northwest); west and central courts; *insulae,* functioning either as storerooms, or as living quarters, or as rooms of state. The west court is dominated on the north by a magnificent flight of steps with a wall at the back. If the area was used for bull-leaping, these steps were unsafe for spectators, and in any case would not hold many: in a posed excavation picture, fifty-three persons overcrowd them. We may suppose the spectators used the north terrace (94 in the plan) above, or the windows of the palace façade on the east of the court. The main entrance to the palace was by a splendid fifty-foot-wide flight of steps, built convex, to shed water; its blocks are up to nine feet long. It leads east, out of the northeast corner of the west court; the excavators describe it with pardonable pride as the most monumental thing in Minoan architecture. Across a broad landing at the top is a double propylon (monumental entrance), its outer portion supported by a single column, as at Pylos later. But the whole ambitious plan leads not to a great audience hall, as at Knossos (the Italians doubt Evans' reconstruction) but to a light well and a blank wall. (Beneath the light well is a labyrinthine storeroom of Palace I.) Entrance to

Fig. 2.25 Phaistos, palace, plan. The resemblance to Knossos and Mallia is striking. (Pernier - Banti, 1947, Fig. 53)

the rooms of state was not straightforward, as in later classical architecture, but by a devious, pure Minoan dog-leg corridor leading to the left out of the inner propylon and into a peristyle (74) with traces of an Early Minoan house in the middle, and lower levels going back to Neolithic times. The whole palace is built on terraces, and this is the highest of them all, with a breath-taking view across the Geropotamos Valley to snowcapped Mt. Ida, the throne of Zeus, beyond. The peristyle has an entrance, again divided by a single central column, from the south as well, whence a vestibule and a choice of stairs lead to the central court (40) below. North of the peristyle, six double-leaf doors opened into a lozengepaved reception hall. North of this again, and not opening directly upon it, is a suite of isolated small rooms, with stuccoed walls painted with marine plants. The suite includes a sunken bath and latrine, reminiscent of the Queen's Megaron at Knossos. East of the peristyle, and deviously connected with it by a dog-leg stair, is another luxurious suite (50) with double porticoes and stuccoed walls painted with four-petal red rosettes within white disks. Particularly elegant pottery was found here. It is unlike the contemporary Palace Style at Knossos, and Luisa Banti, Pernier's immediate successor at Phaistos, thinks it may come from a center at Gournia. South of this suite is a small open court (48), out of which opens a corridor (41) open to the sky (it has an open gutter down its middle), which leads to the central court. Looked at from the court, it is monumentally framed by half-columns (like the Treasury of Atreus at Mycenae), and frescoed niches. In the northwest corner of the central court is a platform that may have had something to do with bull-leaping. The porticoes on each of the long sides of the central court were supported by an alternation of pilasters and columns as at Mallia and, as there, may have been barricaded part way up to protect spectators of the dangerous sport. The southern end of the central court together with the whole southeastern corner of the palace have slipped into the ravine, but ruts in the surviving open space suggest that the court had a south entrance for wheeled traffic.

Near the northwest corner of the central court a vestibule (25) leads into a series of storerooms symmetrically opening on a central corridor. Their thick walls suggest a story above, with a room of state like the one over the crypt at Mallia. One of the storerooms (33) contains storage jars so tall a terracotta stool was needed for peering into them. They once contained the tribute, in oil, wine, or grain, of the vassals of the prince of Phaistos. The southwest block must have contained living quarters: it has at least two sunken baths (19, 21). A later building in the extreme southwest, differently oriented, is an archaic Greek temple, dedicated, as we know from an inscription, to Rhea, a fertility goddess lineally descended from the Cretan Mother Goddess herself, a nature goddess, Mistress of Animals, fostering fertility. Her statuettes, sometimes in ivory and gold, represent her in a high tiara, a bodice revealing her breasts, and a flounced skirt, with snakes coiled around her.

The palace area east of the central court contained more living quarters, intermediate in elegance between the crowded rooms on the southwest and the sumptuous suites on the north. There is a sunken "lustral area" (63*d*) in which the excavators found nine bronze double axes, handsome vases, and "horns of consecration"; a latrine adjoins. This suite opens eastward onto an L-shaped portico strongly reminiscent of the portico on the east of the Domestic Quarter at Knossos. It, too, enjoys an extensive view, across the rich

Fig. 2.26 Hagia Triada, villa, plan. (Pernier-Banti, 1935, Pl. 17.8)

plain of the Mesará. North of this is an industrial quarter, centering on a trapezoidal court (90) with a smelting furnace in the middle: slag was found in it. A gatehouse, differently oriented, marks a northeast entrance. From it a flight of steps led down to the dependent houses in one of which (101) the Disk was found. Like the other Cretan palaces, the second palace at Phaistos was destroyed all at once in Late Minoan I*b* by a surprise raid, as vases found on floors all over the palace and lamps *in situ* show.

What was destroyed embraced altogether 104 rooms, grouped into *insulae* differentiated in function. The architectonic aim is not grandiosity, as in Egypt, or subordination to a central megaron, as at Mycenae or Tiryns, but variety of line and color, achieved by façades with setbacks, terraces and flat roofs of various heights, the play of light and shadow on white gypsum stucco, blue-gray local stone, red cypress beams and columns; the alternation of light and darkness in propylons, light wells, peristyles, porticoes, and open courts of various shapes and sizes. If color is the key at Knossos, line is the key at Phaistos. To many modern tastes its cool restraint will seem preferable to the baroque extravagance of Evans' restorations.

Two miles west of Phaistos, reached by fording the Geropotamos, is the sumptuous and elegant villa of Hagia Triada. Pottery dates it contemporary with or slightly later than the second palace, and it was destroyed at the same time, though megaron-shaped rooms (lettered on the plan, Fig. 2.26) show that it was reoccupied by the Mycenaean invaders. In post-Mycenaean times it was not in use (whereas the archaic temple shows the Phaistos palace was), and therefore it is richer in frescoes, tablets (150 in Linear A were published in 1945),* seals, gems, bronze (including nineteen

---

* Since Hagia Triada has supplied the largest number of Linear A tablets yet found, the Swede Arne Furumark has been emboldened to try to decipher them (in an unpublished Berlin lecture of 1956). The tablets, like Linear B, are inventories, under headings, by categories, totaled. Though the ideograms are often different from those of Linear B, those for men, looms, textiles, vases, tripods, axes, grain, figs, honey, wine, fish, and miscellaneous tools and equipment are clear. The signs for whole numbers closely resemble Linear B; those for fractions are different, but their interpretation is still in doubt. The categories of words dealt with are place names, personal names (individuals and groups), commodities, and vocabulary words. Furumark distinguished categories by a method of exclusion; e.g., headings with

hide-shaped copper ingots from Cyprus, each weighing a talent: were they innovations of the Mycenaean invaders?), and such rarities as the famous painted sarcophagus. Though it was excavated in 1903-05 and 1910-14, the final publication has not yet appeared. Its L-shape anticipates the fortified palace or villa at Gla. Its northwest corner presents the same combination of propylon, airy main room, and L-shaped portico that we have seen in the Domestic Quarter at Knossos and in the eastern *insula* at Phaistos; this time the view is of the sea. East of the propylon, behind a room lined (as sometimes at Phaistos) with benches whose risers bear a triple groove like the triglyphs of classical Greek temples, is a small room with a raised slab which, spread with animal skins, would make a bed. North of the propylon is an elegant room frescoed with a cat stalking a pheasant. South of this block, and in the north wing, are pantries and storerooms; beyond them on the east another small but elegant signorial suite. To the south is a paved courtyard. Opening on it at the northeast, and independently oriented, is a Mycenaean shrine paved with stucco painted with marine scenes like those at Pylos and Tiryns. To the north is a Minoan village, rebuilt in Mycenaean times with a porticoed market anticipating Hellenistic plans, and Trajan's market of a millennium and a half later in Rome. About 150 yards north of the village is a necropolis, where in a stone-lined trench was found the famous painted limestone sarcophagus, in a context with Late Minoan III sherds, and perhaps dating from the Mycenaean occupation. It portrays (Fig. 2.27) a cult of the dead, in which the double axes are Minoan,

subheadings in fractions cannot refer to persons. Like Miss Kober, he used spelling variants to detect what signs are closely related. He claims to have distinguished gender, vowels, and syllables, and, without using Linear B, to have established that the nineteen signs in Linear A identical in form with Linear B are identical also in sound. On this basis he sets up a grid, and offers decipherments of place names corresponding to known sites; e.g., Alasija (Cyprus), Samos, and Kydonia, Dikte, and Sitia in Crete: commodities (coriander, sesame, figs), and words corresponding to those used in Linear B for deficit, total, grand total, and "warehoused." The place names and an alleged third person singular verb ending in -ti point, he claims, to an Anatolian origin for the language: he apparently thinks, though he does not say, that Linear A's affinities are with the language of an Indo-European people of Anatolia called the Luvians. A rival attempt at decipherment, by the American Cyrus Gordon, concludes that Linear A is a Semitic language. Both cannot be right, so the question remains open, but another large find of Linear A tablets would probably settle the matter.

Fig. 2.27 Hagia Triada, sarcophagus. Heraklion, Museum. (Pernier, *Monumenti Antichi* 19, Pl. I) the offering of a curve-prowed boat Egyptian, and the deified deceased rising from the tomb at the right, Mycenaean. A lyre-player like one on the sarcophagus has now been found on a Pylos fresco; it appears on the dust jacket of this book. This pomp and circumstance, this heroizing of the great dead, has more in common with the implications of a Mycenaean beehive tomb than with the comparative simplicity of a Minoan burial; the inference is that we are faced with a Minoan artist's attempt to cope with portraying the strange funeral cult practices of his new Mycenaean masters.

The archaeological sites and finds described in this chapter, at Troy and on the mainland, in the Cyclades and on Crete, are our main historical documents for a span of time as long as from the coronation of Charlemagne in 800 to Shakespeare's birth in 1564, or from Magna Carta (1215) to our own day. It all adds up to a coherent picture of the material, social, religious, artistic, and intellectual life of the Aegean peoples of 1900-1125 B.C., upon whose cultural heritage the classical Greeks drew. Knossian frescoes reveal the small, wiry, brunette Minoan physical type; Mycenaean gold masks show the broad-faced, mustachioed men whose descendants fought at Troy. Tombs, frescoes, and tablets make clear the richly colored dress and costly gold adornment of the ruling classes. Storerooms, shaft graves, and again the invaluable tablets make real for us the inlaid bronze swords and daggers, the boars' tusk helmets, the scabbards in gold-appliqué of these ancient warriors. Patient, intelligent excavation has fixed the ground plans of palace, villa, citadel wall, and town. For social life our most valuable evidence comes from the tablets and the pottery, though the tombs, too, betray the wide cleavage between classes. The tablets show that the government was monarchical, with a literate bureaucracy; that the division of labor was sophisticated, with many luxury trades; imported pottery shows the extent of international trade relations, between mainland and Cyclades, between both and Crete, Egypt, and Anatolia. As to religious life, the frescoes supply evidence of anthropomorphism; games such as bull-leaping are connected with cult, and double axes and horns of consecration found in Cretan palaces suggest fetishism, being inanimate objects obviously regarded with awe as containing a potent spirit or magical powers. The Hagia Triada sarcophagus and the tholos tombs suggest among the Mycenaeans if not a cult of the hero dead, at least a solicitude for his welfare on his journey to the other world. Names of gods and goddesses on the tablets show that classical Greek religion and mythology had Mycenaean origins. A highly developed artistic sense is amply revealed by the frescoes, statuettes, goldwork, gems, seals, and painted pottery; Minoan art and architecture is clearly the work of a "wild, irregular, venturesome, colorful" people. The decipherment of Linear B has revealed literacy. Only poetry is lacking; it must have been oral or recorded on perishable materials. Archaeology and the tablets make clear that the first great Greek poet, Homer, when he began to compose in the ninth or early eighth century B.C., drew upon Mycenaean memories; but between him and the great towns and palaces of the Mycenaean-Minoan world stretches the great blank—blank partly because they yield little to the excavator—of the Greek Dark Ages. The Dorian invasion brought that darkness; from that invasion the only major city that escaped was Athens.

3 Mycenaean Athens, the Dorian Invasion, Protogeometric, Geometric

(1250-700 B. C.)

The story of prehistoric Athens, as archaeology reveals it, has been postponed to this point in order to treat it as a unit. Italian excavations on the south slope of the Acropolis and American on the northwest slope have revealed Neolithic pottery and a Neolithic house, and there is evidence that Athens has been continuously inhabited since the fourth millennium B.C. Unfortunately, investigation of the Acropolis itself was undertaken before the era of scientific archaeology, so that basketfuls of precious prehistoric sherds were thrown away; and classical buildings effaced earlier ones, but enough remained to make certain that Athens, like Mycenae, Tiryns, and Pylos, was a fortified citadel in Mycenaean times. Of the palace, two column-bases survived (Fig. 3.1), perhaps not enough to establish which way it faced, but their location south of the classical Erechtheum established the general area of the palace, and a ground plan with megaron and forecourt, as at Mycenae, Tiryns, and Pylos, is most likely.

The first clear light thrown upon Mycenaean Athens resulted from the Swedish-American Oscar Broneer's excavations in the thirties on the north slope of the Acropolis. His

Fig. 3.1 Athens, Acropolis, Mycenaean palace, tentative plan. The only certain elements are the two column-bases marked in black. These are used as a basis for restoring a typical Mycenaean megaron (cf. Fig. 2.13). The dotted lines represent the archaic temple of Athena, above the megaron. The Erechtheum is to the north. (Holland, 1924, p. 166)

intent at the start was to illuminate the classical cult of
Eros and Aphrodite, a spring fertility festival in which the
goddess' statue was ritually washed and her sacred bird, the
dove, sacrificed. Broneer located the cult sanctuary by
spotting two hitherto unnoticed inscriptions carved in the
rock, but when he had removed the dump, sometimes
more than three meters deep, from nineteenth-century excavations of the Acropolis, he found, nearby, traces of a
stair leading down from a postern gate defended by towers
(Fig. 3.2). This discovery was interesting in itself, but Broneer
was able to fit it fascinatingly into prehistory because he
could identify and date the potsherds he found in association
with it. They were of a pattern well known in Mycenae,
called Mycenaean III*b*, and datable 1300-1225 B.C. From
the postern a stair (wrongly shown in Fig. 3.2 as a path) led
down; it was abandoned before the end of the Mycenaean
period (potsherds again), and houses built over it. These in
turn were abandoned, and in a hurry, for Broneer found
coarse household pottery scattered over the floors. But there
was no burnt layer, and the pottery goes on without a
break. What historical inferences are warranted? Surely that
within the seventy-five years covered by the pottery the

Fig. 3.2 Athens, A-
cropolis, Mycenaean
postern and tower,
restoration drawing.
(Holland, 1924, p.
147)

postern was abandoned (for a reason which will emerge in the sequel) and covered over by squatters' houses ("squatters," because their pottery is so poor), which in turn were hastily deserted, surely in the face of a threat of invasion, presumably of the Dorians. Athenian history proudly recorded that the Athenians successfully stood the Dorians off, and Broneer's excavations have proved the truth of the boast. They could thank good planning more than luck: the "Pelasgic" wall of the Acropolis yielded sherds that matched Broneer's, and when the little Nike temple that flanks the Propylaea (the present west approach to the Acropolis) was dismantled for rebuilding in 1936, the bastion on which it stands was found to have, beneath a fifth-century facing, a "Pelasgian" core, again dated by potsherds to the same period as the rest of the wall and Broneer's postern. So the whole of the Acropolis defenses were strengthened at the same time and against the threat of the Dorian invasion. (The date matches that assigned in the traditional Athenian genealogies to Theseus, the Attic Heracles, whose heroic exploits included the voyage to Crete and the slaying of the Minotaur.)

But the tale of Broneer's exciting discoveries is not yet all told. Once some modern squatters' houses were demolished in 1937-38, he was able to return to work on the

Fig. 3.3 Athens, Acropolis, north slope, stair to Mycenaean fountain, restoration drawing of flights III-V. (Broneer, 1939, p. 338)

Fig. 3.4 Athens, plan of prehistoric finds. The chamber-tomb under the temple of Ares is between the 50- and 55-meter contours; the oval between contours 65 and 70 is the Geometric House; the Princess Tomb is the largest south of the 80-meter contour. The Acropolis (lower right) shows in black the palace and the Mycenaean bastion under the Nike temple. Broneer's stair led to the spring marked by arrow in the middle of the Acropolis north slope; the right-hand arrow marks the squatters' houses over the postern stair. (after Travlos, 1960, p. 23)

north slope. Re-exploring an underground passage west of the Erechtheum, which had been known since 1897, he discovered a stairway (Fig. 3.3) leading down, seven flights through a cleft in the rock, to a fountain 130 feet below. He was at once struck by the parallel with the underground stair that gave access to a water supply at Mycenae, and to the stairs protected by the west bastion at Tiryns. And, sure enough the sherds, this time Mycenaean IIIc (about 1225 B.C.), proved the staircase to be of Mycenaean date; presumably it was after this staircase was constructed that the earlier postern was abandoned. That it was an emergency measure is proved by the fact that it was built partly of wood, which in the damp cleft in the rock would hardly last more than twenty-five years unmended, and when this portion collapsed it was left where it fell. When the Dorian menace was past, the Athenians could get their water more simply and openly. The pottery is all of one style: the period of the stair's construction and abandonment was so short that the pottery style did not have time to change.

The American excavations in and around the Athenian Agora or market place have hit upon enough burials (Fig. 3.4) to prove that the area was a cemetery in Mycenaean and Sub-Mycenaean times. One of the richest of these is a chamber tomb discovered under the Temple of Ares in 1951. It contained fourteen to sixteen interments, and the accompanying pottery shows that the tomb was in use from 1450 to after 1200; the later burials, here and elsewhere in the Agora, containing the uninspired plain-banded Sub-Mycenaean and Protogeometric pottery, tell the same story as Broneer's staircase: Athens survived the Dorian invasion without a cultural break. A rich chamber tomb on the north slope of the Areopagus contained an ivory box carved with deer and griffins; at least 100 gold ornaments; fine Mycenaean IIIb pottery; and a bronze ladle, mirror, and hairpins. Clearly its occupant was a woman, perhaps royal, to judge by the gold; perhaps she had lived in the palace on the Acropolis in the generation before the Dorians came: the excavators call her final resting place the Princess Tomb.

For twelfth-century Athens the archaeological evidence is slight indeed: only enough to prove that the Athenians hung on through troubled times. The date when the evidence begins to be copious again, about 1100, is the date ascribed by Greek historical tradition to the Dorian invasion. How can this date be reconciled with Broneer's archaeological evidence, which dates the passage of the Dorians a century earlier? The answer may be that the Dorians came not in a single assault but in a series of waves. Herodotus supplies a clue with his story of Hyllos son of Heracles (another name for the Dorian invasion is the Return of the Sons of Heracles) who fell in a duel at the Isthmus of Corinth, after which his men promised not to return for three generations.

This story shows that the ancient Greeks were at least as aware as any modern archaeologist that the Dorian invasion took time. Their invention to fill the gap masks a historical fact: the unrest caused by these migrations of Greek-speaking clansmen from the northwest lasted a hundred years. The traditional date of the invasion marks the end of that time of trouble. And Broneer in 1957 found a towered fortification wall at the Isthmus with Mycenaean pottery dated 1250-1200 in the fill, which proves that it was not the Athenians alone who put up a fight against the invader. But Athens was bypassed; the Peloponnese beyond the Isthmus bore in the end the full brunt. Tiryns, Pylos, and finally Mycenae fell. The invaders swept on, into the south Aegean islands, southwest Asia Minor, and Crete. Wherever they established themselves, the language in historical times was Doric— Greek with a broad *a*. Meanwhile, Athens survived to become a haven, according to tradition, for refugees, especially from Pylos.

The archaeological evidence for this was provided by German excavations (1927-1938) in the cemetery in the Ceramicus, the ancient Potters' Quarter of Athens, where three roads diverged: one to the port of the Piraeus; a second, the Sacred Way westward to Demeter's holy city of Eleusis; and a third, the road to the grove of Akademe, which Plato was to make famous. This cemetery yielded an uninterrupted 500-year sequence of pottery. The graves that concern us were found in clearing between and under the foundations of the Pompeion, a building in which gear used in processions and festivals was stored between times. Under and around this building the Germans excavated 108 graves, laid out in eleven uneven rows, and cut as deep as a man can shovel. They judged by the homogeneous pottery that these particular graves all belonged to one epoch, but the diverse groupings of the graves suggest that they span at least fifty years. They were poorly furnished, usually with nothing but an oil flask, a pitcher, and a cup. But the interesting thing is the style of the pottery and what can be deduced from it. One group resembles the Close Style at Mycenae, so called because of its close-packed, complicated patterns. In the Ceramicus ware (Fig. 3.5) this is reduced to freehand concentric semicircles on the shoulder, and broad and narrow bands, or wavy lines between bands, on the belly of the jar. The Germans named this pottery Sub-Mycenaean. With it were found long bronze shoulder pins, and *fibulae* (safety

Fig. 3.5 Athens, Ceramicus, Sub-Mycenaean pottery. Note crude freehand design. Ceramicus, Museum. (Karo, *An Attic Cemetery*, Pl. 5)

pins) used to fasten a kind of dress new to the Greek world, the Doric peplos, a square of woollen cloth folded around the body and pinned at the shoulder. There were also a few rings of iron, which in this use and at this date (*ca.* 1125- 1075 B.C.) must still be a precious metal. No weapons at all were found in association with this pottery, but in three cases the pottery was found not in inhumation graves but in cremation burials. Other such mixed burials, found on Salamis with Sub-Mycenaean pottery, and in a cemetery at Perati in Attica in association with Egyptian scarabs of the XIXth Dynasty, prove that cremation was beginning to be introduced into Attica, and carry it back perhaps as early as 1214 B.C. The inference is that the Ceramicus graves belonged to a people with unbroken Mycenaean connections (on the evidence of the pottery), under some Dorian influence (on the evidence of the pins), in an age of transition (on the evidence of the new fashion of cremating the dead). The excavators see in the pottery the last echo of courtly Mycenaean art; in the potters, refugees from the Dorian terror that ran rampant in the Peloponnese after the middle of the twelfth century B.C. Surely not the potters alone came; there must have been some survivors among farmers, ex-landed proprietors, and leading members of noble clans; perhaps it is their graves that turn up in the Attic countryside, where many Mycenaean and Sub-Mycenaean sites are known (Fig. 3.6). Cremation does not necessarily indicate an intrusive race of invaders: the Achaeans, who buried their dead at home, cremated them before the walls of Troy; cremation is a logical way to dispose of the bodies of persons dying in far places.

But Sub-Mycenaean is not the only new style of pottery the Germans discovered in the Ceramicus. Seven of the graves contained a severe abstract ware (Fig. 3.7), decorated with compass-drawn circles and semicircles, cross-hatching, and lozenges between bands—a throwback to the old-fashioned designs, Middle Helladic and earlier, which we saw at Orchomenos, Eutresis, and Dimini. All these pots— the Germans named them Protogeometric—came from cremation burials, all were associated with iron *fibulae* and iron weapons, the latter perhaps an index not so much to change of race as to troubled times. Protogeometric ware ushers in the Iron Age in Athens, the age when, as the old Boeotian poet Hesiod was to write 200 years later, "never will men cease from toil and misery by day and night as they

Fig. 3.6 Attica, prehistoric sites. Over 100 are known. (Travlos, 1960, p. 17)

pins) used to fasten a kind of dress new to the Greek world, the Doric peplos, a square of woollen cloth folded around the body and pinned at the shoulder. There were also a few rings of iron, which in this use and at this date (*ca.* 1125-1075 B.C.) must still be a precious metal. No weapons at all were found in association with this pottery, but in three cases the pottery was found not in inhumation graves but in cremation burials. Other such mixed burials, found on Salamis with Sub-Mycenaean pottery, and in a cemetery at Perati in Attica in association with Egyptian scarabs of the XIXth Dynasty, prove that cremation was beginning to be introduced into Attica, and carry it back perhaps as early as 1214 B.C. The inference is that the Ceramicus graves belonged to a people with unbroken Mycenaean connections (on the evidence of the pottery), under some Dorian influence (on the evidence of the pins), in an age of transition (on the evidence of the new fashion of cremating the dead). The excavators see in the pottery the last echo of courtly Mycenaean art; in the potters, refugees from the Dorian terror that ran rampant in the Peloponnese after the middle of the twelfth century B.C. Surely not the potters alone came; there must have been some survivors among farmers, ex-landed proprietors, and leading members of noble clans; perhaps it is their graves that turn up in the Attic countryside, where many Mycenaean and Sub-Mycenaean sites are known (Fig. 3.6). Cremation does not necessarily indicate an intrusive race of invaders: the Achaeans, who buried their dead at home, cremated them before the walls of Troy; cremation is a logical way to dispose of the bodies of persons dying in far places.

But Sub-Mycenaean is not the only new style of pottery the Germans discovered in the Ceramicus. Seven of the graves contained a severe abstract ware (Fig. 3.7), decorated with compass-drawn circles and semicircles, cross-hatching, and lozenges between bands—a throwback to the old-fashioned designs, Middle Helladic and earlier, which we saw at Orchomenos, Eutresis, and Dimini. All these pots— the Germans named them Protogeometric—came from cremation burials, all were associated with iron *fibulae* and iron weapons, the latter perhaps an index not so much to change of race as to troubled times. Protogeometric ware ushers in the Iron Age in Athens, the age when, as the old Boeotian poet Hesiod was to write 200 years later, "never will men cease from toil and misery by day and night as they

ΠΡΟΪΣΤΟΡΙΚΗ ΑΤΤΙΚΗ

ΘΗΒΑΙ

Ἀσωπός π.

Ὠρωπός

Μαλθυάσα

Λιθαιρών

Ἐλευθεραί

Πάρνης

Δεκελεια

Μαραθών
ΚΑ.

Μπρτατι

Διόνυσος

Πεντελή

Νέα Μάκ.

Φυλή   Ἀχαρναι

Κηφισιά

Χαλάνδρι

ΜΕΓΑΡΑ

Ἐλευσίς

Αἰγάλεως

ΑΘΗΝΑΙ

Ὑμηττός

Σπάτα

Λιόπεσι

Λουτ

ΣΑΛΑΜΙΣ

Πειραιάς

Φάληρον

Κορωπι

Βραώνα

Μαρκόπουλο

Τι.

Ἀμ.Κοσμάς

Γλυφάδα

Πάνειον

Κερατέα

Βουλιαγμένη

ΑΙΓΙΝΑ

Ἀνάβυσσος

0   10   20   30   Χιλιόμετρα

Fig. 3.6   Attica, prehistoric sites. Over 100 are known. (Travlos, 1960, p. 17)

Fig. 3.7 Athens, Cera-
micus, Protogeometric
vases. Note characteristic compass-drawn circles.
Ceramicus, Museum. (Karo, *op. cit.*, Pl. 6)

plunge to their ruin. . . . No reverence for the man who
keeps his oath. . . . Right shall rest in the power of the
hand; there will be no sense of honor." Grim enough the
beginning of the Iron Age was in the rest of Greece: almost
no buildings survive from the period, and the gifts in the
tombs are pathetically poor. But Athens, bypassed by the

Dorians, did not suffer complete Iron Age depression: the pottery actually shows a technique improved over Sub-Mycenaean. And there was no violent transition from bronze to iron: Sub-Mycenaean and Protogeometric pottery are occasionally found in the same Ceramicus grave.

The distinguishing mark of Protogeometric pottery is the compass-drawn circle. Freehand skill was a Cretan talent, imitated in Mycenae; with the fall of Mycenae, invention faltered, and mainland potters went back to the age-old geometric tradition, which had been kept alive by farm families in home weaving, leatherwork, wood carving, and basketry. It is this old tradition that came to the fore, we may suppose, when the centers of courtly life and art were destroyed. With the battles, raids, and displacement of persons that followed their fall, pottery sank to its lowest level. But the improved techniques of Protogeometric ware, early in the eleventh century B.C., mark the gradual return of peace and prosperity. This is especially marked in a strong, fortified, urban community such as Athens, where the genealogies of the kings are unbroken. But the new pottery probably symbolizes some profound inner change in Athens. The traditional date of the shift from kings to aristocratic archons matches the date—early eleventh century—of the shift from Sub-Mycenaean to Protogeometric pottery in the Ceramicus cemetery. According to tradition, the father of Codrus, the last king of Athens, came from Pylos. The father's name, Neleus, appears in the genealogy of Nestor of Pylos. Blegen's date for the sack of the Pylos palace makes the synchronism possible, but does not quite prove the connection. Codrus was said to have sacrificed himself to save Athens from the Dorian invasion. His younger sons allegedly led a migration to Ionian Asia Minor, of which more will be said later. Ionian Protogeometric pottery is enough like Athenian to prove a cultural connection, but scholars disagree as to which way it ran. From King Codrus' eldest son, Medon, some famous Athenian philosopher-statesmen traced their descent: Solon, the tyrant Pisistratus —whose name also occurs in the genealogy of Pylos—and Plato.

The earliest wells in the Athenian Agora yielded an amount of Protogeometric pottery so large that it may be used as evidence for a marked increase in population. But this population was not predominantly of a new race. The Germans measured the skulls from the Ceramicus, and, though they would perhaps have been glad, in 1939, to report evidence of Nordic supremacy, like honest scientists they reported their findings objectively. The skulls of Mediterranean type outnumbered the Nordic in a proportion of three to two. A 1945 American study of over 100 skulls, from the Ceramicus, the Athenian Agora, and elsewhere in Attica concludes that it is a process of biological blending, rather than dominance by any single racial type, which produced the greatness of Athenian civilization. Athens, like America, was a melting pot, and this may have been one of the sources of her strength, as it is of ours.

When the Dorians finally overthrew Mycenae, they destroyed, if not a great empire, at least prosperous commercial connections with the Near East. Late Mycenaean pottery has been found at over fifty sites on the Asia Minor coast; on the island of Kea, fifteen miles off the east coast of Attica; on Rhodes and Cyprus, in Syria and Egypt, and in a dozen more sites in South Italy and Sicily. On the island of Kea, in August, 1961, the first life-size Mycenaean (twelfth-century B.C.) terracotta statuary was found. It probably represents the Mother Goddess. The latest phase of Phylakopi on Melos is entirely Mycenaean, and at Miletus, on the Asia Minor coast, evidence for Mycenaean settlement goes back to 1500 B.C.: there are three settlement strata, separated by destruction layers; the fourteenth-century settlement had a circuit wall with gates and tower. At Ialysos on Rhodes the Italians excavated a settlement whose lowest levels (sixteenth century B.C.) show exclusively Minoan pottery. With the fall of Knossos Minoan pottery at Ialysos ceases, to be superseded by Mycenaean, but the site was suddenly and inexplicably deserted before the end of the fifteenth century, leaving pottery scattered on the floors. Another example is Énkomi on Cyprus, an island whose copper made it a center of trade and an object of cupidity throughout the Aegean world. At the earliest settlement level (ca. 1600 B.C.) the pottery, unearthed by French excavations, is entirely Cypriote; at about 1450 (while the Mycenaeans were ruling in Knossos) Mycenaean pottery begins; this is the date of the House of Bronzes, so richly furnished that it must have belonged to a ruler, perhaps the Mycenaean governor; its riches were protected by a massive towered circuit wall. This phase was destroyed by an earthquake (1365 B.C.), then rebuilt, to prosper to the end of the Mycenaean period. The evidence of prosperity comes from rich tombs, one of which contained gold-leaf diadems, toe-rings, and forty-five large gold Mycenaean necklaces. Another yielded two gold pectorals (like the one illustrated in *The Mute Stones Speak*, Fig. 2.20) and a gold cup decorated with bulls—like the one from Dendra, p. 78, in the technique called niello, which involves engraving, lining with black, and granulating with gold. Then, in the late thirteenth century, Enkomi was again destroyed, perhaps by the "Peoples of the Sea" who are a part of the same phenomenon as the Dorian invasion; but it rose again. In this phase its weapons are iron and its pottery is Sub-Mycenaean. This might suggest that the invaders passed on, and that its new settlers were Mycenaean refugees from the mainland, but the contents of Mycenaean tombs were impiously tossed out when the tombs were reused, and the pottery is clumsy imitation. The excavator sees here an example of the contamination of a Bronze Age culture by a foreign element, or, to put it another way, an early example of captive Greece taking captive her fierce conqueror, but the evidence is equivocal, and, on balance, the hypothesis of a Mycenaean refugee settlement has a slight edge, especially if we take into account legends that Cypriote Salamis, Paphos, and Lapithos were founded by heroes returning from the Trojan War. In the tomb under the Temple of Ares at Athens, later burials treat earlier ones cavalierly without any change of race, while poor pottery is just as likely to imply poor Mycenaean potters as imitative foreign ones. The best argument for the Mycenaean refugee hypothesis is that here, as perhaps nowhere else in the Aegean, literacy survived: two clay tablets in a Cypro-Minoan syllabary have been found here, in a disturbed level that is dated *ca.* 1225, but the tablets might be later. One of them has allegedly been deciphered as Cypriote Greek, referring to a boundary dispute, but since another attempt makes it into poetry about Jason and Medea, we may safely say that the Cypro-Mycenaean script is still a mystery. The conservative Cypriotes, always mercifully spared any catastrophic change, continued to use a Bronze Age syllabary until after the rest of the Greek world had adopted the Phoenician alphabet. The Cypriote dialect is related to Arcadian; mountainous, landlocked Arcadia in the central Peloponnesus must have been one of the places where the Mycenaeans took refuge from the Dorians, and some Mycenaeans almost certainly migrated to Cyprus.

Greek historical tradition recorded that refugees from Pylos became kings of Athens, and that in the sixth generation after the fall of Troy one of the princes of the royal house led a band of settlers to Asia Minor, the so-called "Ionian migration." Taking Blegen's date for the fall of Troy VIIa, and figuring three generations to a century, we may place the date of the migration somewhat before 1000 B.C. What can archaeology do to confirm or deny the tradition? Very little deep-level excavation has been done along the Asia Minor coast, but excavations on the island of Kos in 1940-41 revealed Protogeometric tombs in unbroken association with a Mycenaean settlement; tombs at Assarlik in Caria as long ago as 1887 yielded pottery with the telltale compass-drawn semicircle of Attic Protogeometric, in association with iron weapons. That more excavation would yield more evidence of this kind is indicated by a joint British-Turkish dig (1948-51) at Old Smyrna, northeast of the modern city. The excavators found that some of the pottery in deep levels on the site resembled that of Troy I-II, and thus showed that habitation there went back a very long way. But, at a level dated by them about 1000 B.C., a pottery begins to appear that is in décor very like the Protogeometric found by the Germans in the Ceramicus in Athens, though the shapes are local. This is the kind of evidence that may be used to justify the hypothesis of *émigrés* from Athens teaching local potters to make the ware they had been used to at home. If the hypothesis is sound, archaeology has at last confirmed the historical tradition of the Ionian migration.

The excavators were extraordinarily lucky. In the midst of the time of trouble following the Dorian invasion, its victims were too impoverished to build buildings that would last, and very little of the architecture of this dark age survives, not even ground plans. But in Old Smyrna the archaeologists found, under the platform of a seventh-century B.C. temple, the remains of apsidal buildings. An oval, one-roomed mud-brick house contained Protogeometric pottery, which the excavators date about 900 B.C. Architecturally it is unimpressive, but as illustrating from what humble beginnings the brilliant culture of later Ionia arose, the house is of the highest importance, not least because one of the inhabitants of Old Smyrna may have been Homer himself. We have seen such ground plans before, at Orchomenos and elsewhere; apparently the Dorian invasion forced its survivors back to the past for the inspiration, such as it was, of their architecture as well as their pottery.

The new settlement developed. By 850 Old Smyrna had a circuit wall of mud brick, with bottom courses of stone to prevent enemy undermining (Fig. 3.8). The wall enclosed a densely populated town, which by now had houses rectangular in plan, some of them resembling mainland megara; their north-south orientation suggests an axial town plan. By the late eighth century the wall had been strengthened until it was over fifty feet thick. In the late seventh century Old Smyrna fell before King Alyattes of Lydia, at a date well beyond the lower limit of this chapter. Just before its fall it may have looked like the imaginary reconstruction shown here (Fig. 3.9) to illustrate what developed out of the humble beginnings of the Ionian migration.

Fig. 3.8 Old Smyrna, earliest wall, reconstruction sketch. (Cook, 1958, p. 51, by permission of British School, Athens)

Did Crete, too, feel the impact of the Dorian invasion? Two sites, Karphí and Vrókastro, supply the clearest answer. Karphi, over 4000 feet above the sea in the mountain range of Dikte, but only twenty miles east-southeast of Knossos, was identified as a prehistoric site by Evans as long ago as 1896, but was not excavated until 1938-39. The workmen included two Albanian murderers, a lame sheepstealer, and a (possible) leper from Cyprus. Donkeys, and girls to wash sherds, were hired at the same rate: thirty-five drachmas (then about thirty cents) a day. The dig aroused great local interest: schoolmasters brought small boys up 1200 feet from the plateau to be shown the finds. What was unearthed was a city and a cemetery. It must have been a city of refuge, for its most inaccessible part was settled first.

Fig. 3.9 Old Smyrna in the late seventh century B.C., reconstruction drawing. (Cook, 1958, p. 15)

There was (Fig. 3.10) a Great House, large, sheltered, elaborate, with a megaron in the mainland style; a temple, with an altar, and a ledge for cult statues (one, put together out of 500 pieces, derives from Minoan prototypes); a Priest's House (nearly as large as the Great House), so named because it had direct access to the temple; a bazaar quarter; opening on the main square a room found full of pottery, which may have been a tavern, like the *kaphenion* of a Greek village today; paved streets, *terrazza* courtyards, limestone walls, wooden columns, flat roofs. The tombs are the beehive type, showing, like the megaron of the Great House, mainland influence. Safety pins show that the inhabitants dressed in Doric fashion; the pins occur in iron as well as in bronze, and therefore belong to a period of transition. There were

Fig. 3.10 Karphi, plan. 1, temple; 8, 9, 11-18, Great House; 58-61, 80, Priest's House; 49, tavern. (Pendlebury, 1937, Pl. IX, by permission of British School, Athens)

no cremation burials, and no gold: nothing of intrinsic value was found either in the town or in the tombs; but no trace of conflagration either: the inference is that the site was peacefully abandoned; the inhabitants took all their valuables with them. The pottery is either the debased and spiritless imitation of Late Minoan III called Sub-Minoan, or the designs show the compass-drawn circles of Protogeometric. Such pottery, in Crete as on the mainland, is usually dated 1100-900 B.C. How may we read these stones and sherds? Their date is that of the Dorian invasion; the city is inaccessibly perched: the citizens must have been refugees. The megaron is Mycenaean, the cult-statue is Minoan. This suggests a Mycenaean minority ruling over a native Cretan population, both alike the victims of a scourge that had overwhelmed Knossos. In the 300 years since the late fifteenth-century sack of the palace, a good deal of race mixture must have taken place; lords and vassals alike, like true Cretans, armed themselves and took to the hills. Since Karphi is the largest and richest of the cities of refuge, it was probably the seat of the old regime. Intensely conservative, and probably poor, it imported nothing for 200 years. The pottery, in which Minoan motifs persist beside the Protogeometric; and *fibulae* and iron, which are rare, suggest knowledge but distrust of Dorian fashions. For 200 years the rulers of Karphi must have lived in their eyrie like robber barons; then, the invaders having been at last absorbed, they deserted their mountain fastness and moved down into the plain.

Vrokastro ("Jew's Castle"; its ancient name is unknown) lies three miles east of Gournia, on a steep limestone spur 1000 feet above the sea. It was excavated by an American woman, E. H. Hall, in 1910 and 1912. The likeness of its situation and its finds to those of Karphi is striking. Here too is a settlement and a cemetery, on an inaccessible crag sheer on two faces, affording a good seaward lookout. Its houses are humbler, but its abundant pottery (the site yielded thirty baskets of sherds a day) is better stratified than Karphi. The top layer was a mixture of Late Minoan III ware (showing a strong Mycenaean influence in its slip [clay coating], polishing, and lustrous paint) with compass-drawn Protogeometric. Miss Hall compared it with the Mycenaean pottery from Phylakopi III. In one house hundreds of scraps of bronze indicated a smithy. The tombs were of two kinds: chamber tombs, rubble-lined and pebble-floored, containing inhumation burials in which Protogeometric pottery was

Fig. 3.11 Athens, Ceramicus, Geometric vases. Note typical hatched meanders, upper right. Ceramicus, Museum. (Karo, *op. cit.*, Pl. 10)

found in association with bronze *fibulae* and iron blades. One spearhead of cast bronze was found fastened to a shaft made of iron, than which nothing could be more transitional. Matching finds (iron blades, seals of glass paste, peplos pins) from Salamis, Mycenae, Enkomi, Assarlik, and the Argive Heraion place the chamber tombs in a familiar context. The most significant find was a bronze tripod with volute-topped legs; one like it from Enkomi is dated about 1000. Some of the seals can be matched in Egypt from the XX-

XXIst Dynasties (1075-850 B.C.). The other type of burial consisted of cremations in bone-enclosures or ossuaries. Among the finds iron preponderates, and the pottery is Geometric, identified especially by hatched meander patterns (cf. Fig. 3.11). Similar examples come from Dodona in west Greece, one of the points of departure for the Dorian invasion; the island of Thera, seventy miles north of Crete, according to tradition invaded by Dorians in the late twelfth century; and the later Ceramicus tombs in Athens. At Vrokastro the top level of the town is Sub-Minoan, ending about 1050 B.C.; the chamber tombs range in date between 1000 and 850; the ossuaries, 850-700. The town and the chamber tombs reflect the same history of invasion and resistance as Karphi; but Vrokastro was not abandoned; it endured, and its last phase, reflected in the ossuaries, tells us a little about how Crete at long last made its peace with the Dorians.

Before we leave Crete let us descend still further in time to describe one of the few examples of architecture from the dark age. In 1935 a farmer leveling his land at Dreros, a dozen miles northwest of Vrokastro, came upon a stone foundation forming a twenty- by thirty-foot rectangle; subsequent excavation, sponsored by the local tourist club, revealed early Geometric pottery, an altar filled with the horns of sacrificed animals, a bench supporting bronze statuettes and a bronze Gorgon's head, a table of offerings, and iron sacrificial knives: enough to prove that the building was a temple, the only one of its period found up to then in Crete where the cult objects were still in place. In the center of the rectangular floor plan were traces of a hearth, with column bases north and south of it (Fig. 3.12) which might have supported a pitched roof with open gable ends to let the smoke escape. The published restoration, with its combination of pitched and flat roof, is bizarre; more probably the pitched roof covered the whole temple, as in the clay model from the mainland (Fig. 3.13). The importance of the Dreros temple is not in this detail, but in the fact that it is dated by its associated pottery—Geometric but not yet orientalizing*—to the early eighth century B.C., and is thus one of the four earliest known temples in Greek lands.

* The term refers to motifs or materials originating in Syria (floral or animal motifs), Phoenicia and Palestine (ivories, faïence), or Egypt (lotus-flower handles on vases).

Fig. 3.12 Dreros, temple, side elevation, front elevation, and plan (showing votive offerings on bench, right rear). The pitched roof probably continued the whole length of the temple. (Marinatos, 1936, Pl. XXXI, by permission of Ecole Francoise, Athens)

Another early temple was excavated by the British (1930-33) on the still, deserted promontory of Perachóra, north across the bay from Corinth, where the blue-gray of the limestone blends with the soft-shaded foliage of the pines and the incredible deep aquamarine of the sea, and the view embraces the heights of Acrocorinth, Helicon, and Parnassus. Here, some twenty yards north of the minuscule harbor, the British unearthed the ground plan, inspired by Middle Helladic buildings, of an apsidal structure that must have looked very like one of the clay models (Fig. 3.13) found on the site. It must have had rubble walls (brick makes poor apses), smeared over with clay and painted; a thatched roof, an open gable, and a porch. Egyptian scarabs and early Geometric pottery date the temple in the early ninth century, earlier than Dreros, and earlier than any temple plan thus far discovered in Greece, unless the possibly apsidal plan of the unpublished temple of Apollo Ismenius at Thebes be of the same date. Under the Perachora temple was a thick stratum of votive offerings; the whole site is richer in these than any other in Greece except Olympia, Delphi, and the Athenian acropolis itself. A similar temple model from Argos and bronzes from Corinth very like the Perachora votives may serve to symbolize the sites with

Fig. 3.13 Perachora, temple model (right). Note Apsidal end, thatched roof, and painted wattle-and-daub walls. The rectangular model (left) was found in excavating the Argive Heraion. (After Payne, 1940, Pl. 9b, by permission of Clarendon Press, Oxford)

which Perachora shows closest connections. Very early inscriptions with dedications to "white-armed Hera," the marriage-goddess, consort of Zeus, with the cult titles Akraia (of the Promontory) and Limenia (of the Harbor) tell us to whom the sanctuary was dedicated. One inscription dedicates a fistful (*drachma*) of iron spits (*obeloi*) to the goddess, and dates from a time of transition (about 650 B.C.) from this primitive currency to coined money; this, and a still later temple on the site, take us down into the archaic period. Close relations to finds from the temples of Hera at Argos, Samos, and the mouth of the Sele near Paestum in south Italy suggest intimate connections in the early Greek world between one Hera cult and another.

A hundred yards east of the apsidal temple the British found the footings of the temple of Hera Limenia (identified by a votive inscription), with a hearth in the center, and a votive deposit of thousands of small objects, including hundreds of scarabs, pottery dating the temple about 750 B.C., nearly 1500 terracotta figurines, fragments of amber and ivory, over 5000 complete rings; mirrors, strigils (for scraping after exercise), sickles, a mask, diadems, mint-fresh bronze nails (which the excavator suggests may have been dedicated by carpenters), a lovely bronze dove which from the curve of its feet may have been held in the hand of the cult statue of Hera; arrowheads, horse trappings, 200 bronze saucers (many found in a sacred pool between the two temples). All in all the deposits totaled between ten and twenty tons. Clearly by 750 B.C. Greece had emerged from her time of troubles.

When the British discovered the apsidal temple plan at Perachora, they were at once reminded of a parallel from Thermon, in Aetolia, above the Corinthian Gulf between sixty and seventy airline miles northwest of Perachora (overland it is much further). Here the Greeks had excavated (1911-14) a complex of buildings ranging in date over nearly 2000 years, from Helladic to late Hellenistic times. The one that interests us lies under the long, narrow archaic temple (Fig. 3.14), and is called Megaron B. Its north wall has a slight curve, and around three sides of it lie eighteen thin slabs of an elliptical portico, the ancestor of the colonnade surrounding a classical Greek temple. Megaron B was excavated before prehistoric Greek pottery had been scientifically classified, and the excavator

Fig. 3.14 Thermon, site plan. Megaron B is under the long, narrow archaic temple. Note the slight bowing of the north wall, and the eighteen column-bases (black dots) in an ellipse around it. (Rhomaios, 1915, p. 231, by permission of Archaiologikë Hetaireia, Athens)

called what he found "Cretan-Mycenaean" and "Geometric"; we would call it now Sub-Mycenaean and Protogeometric, and date the latter in the ninth century B.C. The earlier ware belonged to the village of thatched-roofed apsidal and rectangular wattle-and-daub huts that surrounded the temple; there were enough sherds to reconstruct fifty whole pots. The excavator ascribed the ashes he found in Megaron B to a hearth, not an altar. For this reason, and because he also found storage jars within the walls, he argued that Megaron B was a house, not a temple, and that here we can see the gradual transition from King's House to temple. Nowadays, since temples with hearths have been found at Perachora and Dreros, we are not so sure, and are readier to call Megaron B one of the earliest temples on the Greek mainland.

Of the storied cities of Greece, only Sparta remains to be mentioned. Archaeologists never expected its ruins to be spectacular, for they knew Thucydides had said that if it suddenly became an archaeological site instead of a living city, no one could gauge its actual power by the remains of its temples and public buildings, for it remained a collection of villages, "giving an impression of inadequacy." And indeed British excavations there (1906-1910) found nothing as spectacular as Athens and Mycenae: no Mycenaean remains at all on the site of classical Sparta; the city of Menelaus and Helen lay several miles south; its pottery shows a change of style and a break in continuity, owing no doubt to the Dorian invasion. Digging in 1906 on the classical site north of the modern city in the reed-bed by the Eurotas River, the British hit within the first three weeks upon a temple identified by inscriptions built into neighboring Roman walls as that of Artemis Orthia, the huntress goddess of the mountain. The accompanying pottery at the lowest levels was Protogeometric; the metal finds were iron; there was Baltic amber; the excavators concluded that they had found a village of the Dorian invaders, and they dated their finds in the tenth century. The scanty remains of the earliest temple proved that it was long and narrow, built of adobe brick with a timber frame, divided by a single row of wooden columns into two naves. An altar in front was dated by pottery to the mid-ninth century, the temple proper about a generation later. Later phases do not concern us here, and are of little intrinsic interest. On the acropolis to the

Fig. 3.15 Sparta, site plan. O 15, temple of Artemis Orthia, under Roman theater; K 12, temple of Athena of the Brazen House, on the Acropolis. (Dawkins, 1906, Pl. I, by permission of Society for the Promotion of Hellenic Studies)

northwest (Fig. 3.15) the scanty remains, identified by a
stamped roof tile, of the temple of Athena of the Brazen
House were dated by pottery somewhat earlier, going back
into the tenth century. Four of the five villages of which
classical Sparta was made up were located by means of
stamped roof tiles; evidence was found, in the artistic decline of votive offerings, of the metamorphosis of Sparta
into a military state, with stifled aesthetic interests, in the
sixth century; the Roman theater beside the Orthia temple
was used as the scene of the public ritual flogging of Spartan
boys—a sadistic tradition that lived long. To a period below
the limits of this chapter belongs a series of grotesque terracotta masks (Fig. 3.16), models of those used in ritual
dances; and over 100,000 cheap lead figurines. Sparta in
archaeology looks like Sparta in literature: regimented and
dull. The delicacy of some of the early pottery (700-550
B.C.; cf. Fig. 4.18) alone remains to tell us what fine
aesthetic sense the Spartans stifled to become a militaristic
state.

A final example of a Dark Age temple, the predecessor of a
glorious one of the mid-sixth century, was excavated by
the Germans in 1911 on the island of Samos. Dedicated to
Hera, it was 100 feet long, had a double row of interior
columns, was built of coarse limestone, and is dated in the
eighth century B.C.

This somewhat thankless survey of the age of the nadir
of Greek fortunes can end, at least, on an optimistic note,
with a return to Athens, where the seeds of the vitality of
the subsequent Archaic Age were quickening to a new birth.
There, in 1933, Dorothy Burr (whom we have met as the
discoverer of the rich tholos tomb at Dendra) discovered
evidence for a remote age of Athens in an area ten
yards square on the north slope of the Areopagus. What
she found were the traces of a sixteen- by thirty-six-foot
elliptical house (which she compared with the village houses
at Thermon) with a hard red floor covered in places with
sea sand. There was a central hearth, and platforms for
beds. Under the house was the pathetic grave of a child four
to six years old (archaeologists determine age by the teeth).
It had been buried with two small seashells, a clay piglet,
and a few miniature vases to friend it on its lonely journey
to the house of Hades. The grave was earlier than the house:

Fig. 3.16 Sparta, grotesque terracotta mask from temple of Artemis Orthia, now in Sparta Museum. (Émile Séraf)

the miniature vases were Protogeometric of the ninth century. The house itself was in use, to judge by the pottery, from the late eighth century to about 640 B.C. The sherds ranged from late Geometric through orientalizing to a new exuberant style called Proto-Attic. Geometric pottery is Pan-Hellenic, but Proto-Attic is unique to Athens; it is the first city-state ware; it symbolizes a new era, and its emergence marks the end of the Greek Dark Ages and the beginning of the Archaic Age, when Greece comes forward into the full light of history and the more familiar treasures of early

Greek art and architecture begin to reward the archaeologist's spade.

The archaeological discoveries recorded in this chapter cover over 500 years. On the face of it they are depressing, until one stops to reflect on the heartening evidence they provide for the indestructibility of the Greek spirit in the face of invasion, poverty, oppression, and hard times. The efforts expended by the defenders of the acropolis of Mycenaean Athens were crowned with success. The walls and bastions held, the emergency stairs to the water supply could safely be left to rot, for the attackers failed. Life could go on, more austerely, but undaunted, as Protogeometric pottery shows, with its spirited revival of a sense of design. There was peace at last: there are no weapons in the Ceramicus graves. And Athens could be proud to receive the refugees from less fortunate cities, who, encouraged by their welcome into Athenian civic life, contributed their share to the revival. They helped eventually to develop the new exuberant Proto-Attic pottery. If they died in their new homes, they were buried side by side with the Athenians in the city cemetery, in the fairest quarter of the city. But some of the refugees energetically carried the new amalgamated culture overseas. Some new settlers came direct to Miletus, Rhodes, or Enkomi in Cyprus from their devastated Peloponnesian homes. They did not always prosper, but at Enkomi at least they survived. And the rise of Smyrna, which was to become Homer's city, can pretty safely be attributed to émigrés from Pylos whose stay in Athens gave them encouragement and new energy for the enterprise that lay ahead.

In Crete, Karphi, the city of refuge, shows how age-old is the indomitable Cretan valiance in the face of the foreign invader. Cretans showed it again in World War II, to the unbounded admiration of the whole free world. The men of the resistance endured, too, at Vrokastro; and the remarkable temple at Dreros, together with the ambitious one on another island, Samos, show how spiritual life survived, and even had the vigor to innovate, through troubled times.

Out of the ruins wrought by the Dorian invasion a new spirit, which we can identify as related to that of classical Greece, was beginning to arise, and even to prosper. The evidence for it is the succession of temples at Perachora, with their rich votive offerings. The temple and village at Thermon show that West Greece, too, had the vitality to rise from the blow of the invader, and nourish the outer and the inner man.

Mycenaean Sparta fell, but the temple of Artemis Orthia and the splendid Laconian pottery show to what heights the new Sparta proved capable of rising, even in this Dark Age, before militarism stifled her sense of beauty forever.

Over the "Dark Ages," then, like the light of the strong Greek sun, plays the heartening warmth of the eternally gallant Greek spirit. Thanks to it, by the end of the eighth century Greece is back on her feet again, and the wonders of the Lyric Age are about to begin.

4 The Lyric Age: Greece and the West (700-480 B. C.)

Within the 220 years of the Lyric Age, history comes firmly to archaeology's aid: Olympic victor lists go back to 776 B.C.; Athenian archon lists begin in 683. It is an age of poets, lyric and elegiac: Sappho of Lesbos, Solon of Athens, Theognis of Megara, Pindar of Thebes; and lyric grace and elegiac solemnity are to be seen in its architecture and its art. It is an age that sees the beginnings—on the barren island of Delos, at Olympia in its sandy river valley, at Delphi, on its lovely mountainside—of the great international festivals that were to be the glory of the succeeding classical age. We shall begin with some of the archaic monuments from these places. It is an age of tyrants, strong-minded men who left great public works behind them: Pheidon in Argos, Polycrates in Samos, Periander in Corinth * and her colonies, and especially Pisistratus in Athens.

* An interesting work of engineering, possibly from Periander's reign (627-585), came to light in 1956 near the Corinth Canal. It is the *diolkos,* or road by which galleys were hauled across the Isthmus. Paved with limestone, it averages fourteen feet in width, and has two parallel ruts, five feet apart, in which the wagons ran. On curves, a pair of low walls, to keep the wagons from slipping, replaces the tracks (Fig. 4.1).

It is an age when colonies flourished: it is no accident that its most impressive buildings are in the golden West * or on the way to it: on Corcyra off the Greek west coast, at Selinus in southwest Sicily, at and near Paestum south of Naples (see map, Fig. 4.3). The age ends with the Persian Wars: the great conflict between East and West, which left its mark in many places, even, perhaps, upon those masterpieces, the pediments from the Temple of Aphaia on the island of Aegina, six miles across the Saronic Gulf from the Piraeus, the port of Athens. It is an archaic, an old-fashioned age, with strict conventions of its own, and its own kind of liveliness. To the nineteenth century it seemed primitive, naïve, childlike, a preface, to be dismissed with impatience, to the ripe perfection of the classical fifth century; to our taste there is something tremendously attractive about the strength, the simplicity, the straightforwardness, the discipline, the purity of line of the buildings and the works of art that are our heritage from this age when the world was young.

To follow a straight chronological line (for which see Addendum at the end of the chapter) would involve us in leaping back and forth from one end of the Greek world to the other. More coherence will result from beginning with some account of the buildings and artifacts, from the archaic age, which have been excavated at three of the great international shrines: Delos, Olympia, and Delphi. There follows an assessment of archaic Athens, as seen through her pottery, her buildings, her technology and coinage, and her sculpture. Thirdly, we shall describe the little archaic island town of Thera, and her rich daughter, Cyrene. Fourthly, the burgeoning of architecture and architectural sculpture in the West will occupy us, and we shall end, upon the threshold of early classicism, with Aphaia's temple on Aegina, within eyeshot of Athens.

Since 1879 the French have been digging on the naked waterless rock of Delos, the holy island in the center of the Cyclades where Leto brought Artemis and Apollo to birth be-

---

* Except the archaic temple at Ephesus, for which see page 318 and the archaic Acropolis of Larisa-by-Hermos, between Smyrna and Pergamum. The latter proved especially rich in pottery and in architectural terracottas, and boasted a fine archaic palace (Fig. 4.2).

Fig. 4.1   Corinth, *diolkos*, for hauling ships across the isthmus. (after AJA 61 [1957], Pl. 83.3)

Fig. 4.2 Larisa-by-Hermos, archaic palace, reconstruction drawing. (Boehlau, *Larisa I*, Fig. 29)

Within the map:

0 100 200 300 400
SCALE OF MILES

ETRURIA

CHIUSI

Sele R.

PAESTUM METAPONTUM

SIRIS

SYBARIS

CROTON

PALERMO HIMERA

SICILY MAGNA GRAECIA

SELINUS

CARTHAGE

THE LYRIC AGE:
GREECE and the WEST,
700 – 480 B.C.

Fig. 4.3 Map to illustrate the Lyric Age, Greece and the West, 700-480 B.C.

DELPHI
•THEBES •MARATHON
MEGARA •ELEUSIS •SALAMIS
CORINTH •ATHENS •BRAURON
•ARGOS Saronic •PIRAEUS
gulf •AEGINA LAURIUM
SUNIUM Cyclades
RHENEIA DELOS
PAROS NAXOS

0   20   40   60
SCALE OF MILES
SIPHNOS

SAMOS

CORCYRA
TROY
LESBOS
OLYMPIA
IONIA

CRETE

neath the sacred palm tree. One of the earliest finds there, in the fill between the temples of Apollo and Artemis, was a female figure in Naxian marble, not very far in technique from primitive statues in wood, yet the first large-size marble statue known to us from the Greek world.* An inscription on it reveals that it is a dedication (mid-seventh century) to Artemis by one Nicandre of Naxos. Of Naxian marble too is a row of splendid colossal seventh-century lions (Fig. 4.4), first scientifically described in 1907, which bordered as majestically as a file of Egyptian statues the approach to the sacred palm tree where every spring all Greece celebrated in festival the birth of the heavenly twins. Since the lions are of various sizes, the inference is that they were dedicated in rivalry by various Naxian "tribes" (political subdivisions) or noble families. Their lean bodies, after 2500 years of weathering, still make their effect upon the visitor, the effect of majesty that was intended by the Naxians when they were lords of Delos. To house their Delian offerings they built a treasury (identified by an inscription), and a portico beside it to shelter pilgrims from the hot Aegean sun. Beside the treasury the French found a colossal statue of Apollo, and nearby, again used as fill, numerous statues of Naxian youths and maidens, dedications to the god or goddess for victory won or for marriage expected.

On the island of Naxos itself, only twenty-five sea miles away, another colossal Apollo, thirty-four feet long, lies flat on its back in a quarry. It was intended for Delos but never sent, because the marble turned out to be of poor grade and the face developed cracks. The statue lies in its bed with the rock gouged out around it wide enough for a man to work. The intent was to pry it loose underneath with wooden wedges, which, wetted in the night, would swell and split the statue loose by morning. It would then have been taken on rollers down to the shore of Apollonas Bay and rafted to Delos.

All this ingenuity cost money (derived from the quarries and from mines of emery, an abrasive used for polishing statues, of which Naxos is still the chief source of the world's supply). That the Naxians were willing to be lavish is an index of the value to them of controlling the tiny island where religion and trade, reviving after the Dark Ages, went so profitably, as so often, hand in hand.

---

* For earlier life-size terracottas, see p. 132.

Fig. 4.4   D los, Lion Terrace, leading to temple of Leto, *ca.* 625-600 (Author)

The colossal Apollo symbolizes how the god took over the primacy from his sister. But the earliest temple on Delos was dedicated to Artemis, herself no doubt the descendant of the fertility goddess who in prehistoric times held sway over the minds of men in all the Cyclades and in Crete. In the fall of 1946 a trial trench was dug beneath the floor of the previously identified Hellenistic Artemision. The first stroke of the pick revealed fragments of gold, ivory, bronze, and pottery. The latter, both Mycenaean and Geometric, dated the deposit. It must have been put there deliberately, as we would place objects in a cornerstone. The earliest artifacts prove that Artemis had a cult on Delos from Mycenaean times; the latest date the archaic temple. The finds included an ivory plaque of a proud Mycenaean warrior with a magnificent Cyrano de Bergerac nose, a boar's-tusk helmet, and a figure-eight shield; another with a frieze of animals fighting; fragments of two gold diadems; ducks and bees in gold *repoussé;* statuettes and a miniature double ax and arrowheads in bronze.

The identified buildings of archaic Delos are not many; even the site of the famous altar made of horns is uncertain. More important than buildings was the open meadow south of the Sacred Lake (now dry), the goal of the processions of pilgrims that passed along the Lion Terrace. Here, on this meadow, there was room for sacrifice, cult banquets, choral dance and song, and competitions in athletics and music; here selections from Homer were recited for a prize; here Homer himself was said to have competed. Pindar, too, is associated with the island: he composed a processional ode for the Delian festival.

The archaeologists excavated, on the edge of the festival meadow, a small temple whose foundations are in local granite, its walls of *poros* (limestone) from Attica. This temple symbolizes the decline of the Naxians (who, the archaeologists think, built the foundations) and the rise on Delos of Athenian influence. Athens dominated Delos in the last half of the sixth century under the tyrant Pisistratus, who no doubt favored Apollo of Delos because his enemies, the noble clan of Alcmaeonidae, were enjoying in exile the hospitality of Apollo of Delphi. Pisistratus' estates in Attica were at Brauron: from a port near here, and not from the Piraeus, the Athenians regularly sent their sacred galley to the Delian festival. From Pisistratus' time too, probably, date various secular buildings, a senate-house southeast of the temple, a meeting place for the assembly to the northwest. Pottery dates some houses, in the district round the later theater, to Pisistratus' age. He was famous for his public works and for his patronage of the arts, in Athens as well as on Delos. He "purified" the island (as the Athenians were to do again in 426) by removing all the dead, with the contents of their tombs, to the neighboring island of Rheneia: the pits where the bodies and the pottery were deposited have been excavated, and give mute if grisly evidence of centuries of Delian cultural and trade relations. Pisistratus' connections with Delos provided a precedent and a pretext for Athens' making the island the ostensible center of her maritime league in the next century.

Olympia, in the northwest Peloponnese, was an even more famous international shrine than Delos; its archives went back, as we saw, to 776 B.C., the first fixed date in Greek history. Here, in this beautiful and historic spot, made still more beautiful by the pines they planted long ago, the Germans have been digging since 1875; here, we remember, Dörpfeld learned his trade. He returned to the site in old age to work on the sanctuary of Hera, and published his results over fifty years after his first excavations there. In 1880 a foundation deposit had been found under Hera's temple, and Dörpfeld tried to prove how early it was. He dated its oldest phase in the early eleventh century, directly after the Dorian invasion. Most archaeologists, with a careful eye on the pottery whose importance they learned from Dörpfeld, would now date the earliest Heraion in the eighth century. The building was divided by cross-walls into side chapels which in later ages were filled with offerings of *objets d'art*: it was in one of these that in the spring of 1877 was discovered the Hermes of Praxiteles (Fig. 6.4), perhaps one of the few originals of Greek sculpture independent of architecture that we possess, and now the pride of the museum next to the site. Here too was found the limestone head, double life size, of the cult statue of Hera herself: its almond eyes and fixed smile date it in the archaic period, perhaps mid-seventh century. Dörpfeld noticed that the columns of the temple (Fig. 4.5) were of various dimensions, with different numbers of flutings and different capitals, showing progressive changes. He deduced that the original columns had been of wood, replaced with stone one by one as they rotted.

When the Olympics were held in Berlin in 1936, Hitler, to propagandize the event, gave a large sum of money to reopen excavation at the site of the first Olympics. The results of this excavation were remarkable. One project was to excavate the whole stadium (a job just completed in 1960). In a trench fifty yards north of the stadium starting-blocks,

Fig. 4.5   Olympia, Heraion, *ca.* 645-640. (Émile Séraf)

the excavators hit upon a spot under the stadium wall where in the sixth century B.C., to judge by the pottery, there had been bronze-casters' workshops. The level had been artificially raised in the fifth century: the fill yielded an almost inexhaustible series of finds of the archaic period (mostly sixth century), including twenty-two bronze helmets, greaves (leg-protectors), bronze shield-straps in relief, unique bronze protectors for the upper arm, shield devices in thin bronze plate for nailing on wood, tripods, architectural moldings, victors' dedications, unique local pottery—all of which had been thrown away in antiquity as old-fashioned. The thin bronze plates had to be heated with blowtorches and strengthened with beeswax, gauze, and wooden slats before they could be removed for study. The devices included a winged Gorgon, centaurs, a cock, a bronze she-griffin suckling her young, a goat bitten by a huge snake, and the goddess called the Mistress of Animals, flanked by heraldic beasts. A foot in thin bronze plate came from a statue with a bronze-plated wooden core, like those already known from Dreros, but here life size. One of the dedications was of a jumping weight (used to add momentum, and therefore distance, to the jump) by a Spartan who won "without dust"; i.e., by default: the Spartan record, in athletics as in war (though no longer in the arts) inspired a healthy respect.

Adjoining the spot where these finds were made, and running westward, is a series of eleven "treasuries," where, as at Delos, Delphi, and elsewhere the archives and dedications of wealthy cities were kept. Of the eleven treasuries, six belong to cities of the West or en route to it—an index of the prosperity of these colonies in Magna Graecia (Great Greece, as the Greeks called south Italy and Sicily)—which had been founded from the motherland since the eighth century.

Olympia had not reached its full blossoming in the archaic age, and would not until the great temple of Zeus was dedicated in 457, with its rich cult-statue by Phidias in ivory and gold (the Germans have found the terracotta molds for the gold plating). Here the center of cult interest shifted from the goddess Hera to the god Zeus, as at Delos it had shifted from Artemis to Apollo, but it was for victories at the archaic site that the famous *Olympian Odes* of Pindar were written, and the archaic Heraion is still Olympia's most impressive building, for some of its columns are standing, or have been re-erected, while the gigantic column-drums of

the temple of Zeus have been left where an earthquake toppled them, centuries ago.

Of natural beauty rocky Delos has none; sandy Olympia
is redeemed by its pine trees; but Delphi in its natural amphitheater under the rosy outcrop of Mt. Parnassus, above the
gray-green olive-clad Pleistos Valley, is one of the most
beautiful spots in Greece, if not in the world. The French
have been digging here off and on since 1892; they won the
excavation rights from the Americans by removing their import duty on Greek currants. They found the villagers of
Delphi less complaisant than the government. The modern
village lay directly on top of the sanctuary, and the Del-
phians of the '90's bitterly and even violently opposed being
moved to a new site farther west, even though the reconstruction, which cost $150,000, was entirely at the French
government's expense. Nowadays, reconciled, they proudly
and with some justice regard the unearthing of the sacred
precinct as the work of their own hands.

Delphi is one of the most complicated sites known to
archaeology. An incomplete (German) description of the
buildings and monuments lists 235 items, and the museum
inventory, which does not list all the finds, catalogues over
7,000 objects, some of them, like the bronze Charioteer,
world famous. Inscriptions were so numerous that the excavation director sometimes found himself obliged to transcribe
100 a day.

Before the work began, or the village was moved, ancient
landmarks—the dip in the ground that marked the stadium,
the Castalian spring, the retaining wall of the Gymnasium,
the lower sanctuary, long used as a stone quarry—could be
recognized, with the aid of the ancient Baedeker, Pausanias,
whose meticulous guidebook, written about A.D. 174, with
a contagious affection for religion, history, and art, is often
the Greek archaeologist's best friend. But for detailed study,
tons of stone, earth, and silt had to be removed, over more
than a mile of light railway.

One of the earliest finds connected archaeology with history. Herodotus tells how Cleobis and Biton, two young men,
sons of a priestess of Argos, finding that the draft animals
to draw their mother's car had not arrived on time, themselves drew it the five miles and more to the temple, and in
response to their proud mother's prayer to Hera to grant
them the greatest possible blessing, were vouchsafed, as they
slept in the temple, the gift of death. Their fellow citizens

Fig. 4.6 Delphi, the discovery of the archaic (615-590 B.C.) statue of Cleobis, now in the Delphia Museum, 1893. (de La Coste-Messeliére & de Miré, 1943, Fig. 36)

dedicated statues of them at Delphi. When in May of 1893 the excavators found, propped against an ancient retaining-wall, an archaic statue of a muscular young man, perhaps represented in the very act of drawing a car (Fig. 4.6; the twin turned up the next spring), they hardly needed the inscription on the base to connect the find with Herodotus' story. These, dated on stylistic grounds 615-590, are the oldest large works in Parian marble yet found on the Greek mainland. The low brow, strong chin, square shoulders, and powerful chest at first suggest mere brawn, but the slim waist, slightly bent-forward stance, and straight look give a subtler impression, of eager, dedicated tension. Three generations after these statues were carved, Pindar would sing, in lyric as stylized and as tense as this sculpture, the victories of athletes like these at the Pythian Games at Delphi.

Since 1903 work at Delphi has involved mostly preparing excavation notes for publication, which involves rechecking, which involves new discoveries. The original dig (1892-1903) aimed to get down only to the classical level, and in many places reached only the phase that Pausanias saw; new trenches occasionally reach archaic levels, as when a deposit of archaic carved ivory plaques and gold ornaments was found in 1939 under the Byzantine paving of the Sacred Way. No attempt has been made to reconstruct Delphi for tourists, as Evans reconstructed Knossos, but some walls and columns have been re-erected to give scale, and steps have been restored on the steep Sacred Way (1959). Using as clues the order of over 150 inscriptions (including two hymns to Apollo with the ancient musical notation intact) on the outer faces of the wall-blocks, the gradual taper of the courses from top to bottom, and in some cases the keying letters placed on the blocks by the original masons, and knowing that in a good Greek building there are no inter-changeable parts, J. Replat, with the financial help of the city of Athens, rebuilt the Treasury of the Athenians (1903-06), and it has been given a new column, fluted since World War II. In 1938 three columns of the tholos in the lower sanctuary were reset, and in 1939-41 eight columns of the major Temple of Apollo were re-erected. During the war the museum's major treasures were hidden (the Charioteer in Athens), and in the civil strife of 1945-46 the authorities refused to allow the museum to be reopened or work to be done on the site, on plea of danger from internal disorder,

Fig. 4.7 Delphi, Siphnian Treasury; north frieze, battle of gods and giants (ca. 530 B.C.). L. to r., two giants, Dionysus in panther-skin; Cybele in her chariot drawn by lions, who are attacking a giant; Apollo and Artemis, as archers; a giant, labeled Kantharos, with a *kantharos* (drinking-cup) in his helmet-crest; a fallen warrior; and three more giants, with inscribed shields. (Delphi; Museum)

so that work on Delphi, always slow, became even slower, but over twenty volumes of the final publication are out, and more are expected.

From the archaic period the most important Delphic finds are the fragments, totaling more than half, of the frieze from the Siphnian Treasury. Siphnos had been rich in gold and silver until its mines were flooded (served them right, said the Delphic oracle sagely, for cheating Apollo of his tithe), and it fell before the Samians in 525. Its treasury reflects its ripe prosperity, and, with its lovely maidens (Caryatids) holding up its porch, is a jewel box of Ionian art, the earliest marble building on the Greek mainland. Its site can be identified from Pausanias, and its footings are to be seen on the Sacred Way just before it curves up to pass the Athenian Treasury (see model, Fig. 6.6). The order of the frieze has been reconstructed from careful notes taken in 1894 of the findspots of the various frieze blocks as they lay where they had fallen on the four sides of the footings mentioned above. Careful study reveals that the friezes were originally richly painted, and are by two different hands, so different that when they meet at a corner it is a shock. One, whose interest, like a lyric poet's, is in décor, did the Judgment of Paris on the west (front) face, and Castor and Pollux' rape of the daughters of Leucippus on the south (the side farthest from the Sacred Way). His Aphrodite, adjusting her necklace as she leaves her chariot, might serve to illustrate an ode of Sappho. The other, whose interest like an epic poet's is in narrative, carved the scenes from the Trojan War, and the battle of the gods and giants, labeled with their names, on the north (Fig. 4.7). The latter subject, symbolizing as it does the victory of intelligence over brute force, of order over disorder, of reason over emotion, was a favorite with Greek sculptors. Its treatment here is the major success of the archaic school in the narrative as opposed to the more typical lyric style; the sculptor has reduced to order the violent movement of over fifty figures. The giants outnumber the gods, but they fight with crude weapons, and they lose.

Just above the Siphnian Treasury, round a bend in the Sacred Way, is the sanctuary's most perfect surviving monument, the Athenian Treasury (Fig. 6.6). The metopes (Doric frieze-panels, separated by triple grooves called triglyphs) feature the exploits of the Athenian hero Theseus. The Treasury's date is disputed, but some architectural detail seems to be matched in vase painting of the late sixth century, so that the building may have commemorated Athens' liberation from the Pisistratid tyranny and the founding of democracy by Cleisthenes in 509.

Fifty yards farther up the Sacred Way is another Athenian building, a Stoa or portico set against the great polygonal wall that supports the terrace of the Temple of Apollo. Along the face of the upper step of this portico is an inscription, in letters about a foot high, which reads, "The Athenians dedicated the portico and the arms and the figureheads which they took from their enemies." Who were these enemies, what were the trophies displayed, and what was the occasion commemorated? Learned speculation ranged from the Athenian victory over the Boeotians and Chalcidians in 506 B.C. to Phormio's victory over the Peloponnesian fleet in 429 B.C. Pierre Amandry of the French School found the right answer in 1948. By an analysis of the style of the architecture and the forms of the letters of the inscription he narrowed the date down to the time of the Persian Wars, the years around 480 B.C. He then noticed that the word *hopla,* which ordinarily means arms, was used by Herodotus for the cables of the bridge of boats built by Xerxes across the Hellespont at the time of his invasion of Greece in 480 B.C. After Xerxes' defeat at Salamis, the Athenians sailed to the Hellespont. When they returned, "they brought with them the cables of the bridge to be dedicated in the sanctuaries." Here then at Delphi, festooned against the great polygonal wall and protected by a narrow portico, the Athenians displayed the captured cables of Xerxes' bridge, a proud and distinctive trophy.

This brilliant interpretation by Amandry, so clear, so simple, so surely right once it has been proposed, shows that progress is to be made not only by excavation but by a correct understanding of ancient texts.

If we consider that the Siphnian and the Athenian Treasuries were but two of twenty-three such buildings known to have graced the precinct in its prime, we can get some idea of the dazzling effect of the total display. The treasuries were thank-offerings, and they were designed to dazzle— this too is the Greek way—to affirm success, to display wealth, to defy rivals, and to insult the vanquished. When, as often, the victors of one monument were the vanquished of another, the moral could not have escaped so quickwitted a people as the Greeks: perhaps it is in this context that we should interpret the famous mottoes, "Know thyself" and "Nothing in excess," allegedly inscribed on the Delphic Temple of Apollo. Perhaps it would break our stereotype of Greek restraint—which was really controlled excitement— if we could see one Athenian monument at Delphi of which we are told: a bronze palm tree with gold dates, surmounted by a golden statue of Athena.

The old Temple of Apollo (seat of the famous Delphic oracle and of the stone *omphalos* [belly-button], the navelstone of the world), which crowned the site, was traditionally the fourth on the same spot. It was accidentally burned in 548, and the rebuilding was undertaken (513-505) by that great Athenian noble clan, traditional enemies of the Pisistratid tyranny, the clan to which both Cleisthenes and Pericles belonged, the Alcmaeonidae. The contract, Herodotus says, called for limestone construction, but the Alcmaeonids gained great fame by finishing off the front in Parian marble, as Pindar also mentions in his *Seventh Pythian Ode*, written in 486 to celebrate the victory of one of the clan, Megacles, in a Delphic chariot race. The French excavations have confirmed the accuracy of Herodotus' account of the Alcmaeonids' noble gesture: the steps, orthostates (lowest wall slabs), ornaments of the main door, inner pavement, inner columns, cornice, and roof tiles proved to be indeed of marble. The new temple, much larger than the old, required a longer and wider terrace, which ruthlessly wiped out a number of old shrines. Four generations later an earthquake destroyed the Alcmaeonid temple; the ruins the visitor sees today are of the fourth century. The motifs in the pediments glorified Apollo not as purifier, singer, or prophet, but as warrior. The subject of one was his epiphany, of the other (as on the Siphnian Treasury) the victory of the gods over the giants. In the nearby precinct of the goddess Earth, Apollo was portrayed again as a warrior, but this time as a baby vanquishing the serpent—the Python— to found his shrine.

The Alcmaeonids building their great temple, like the Siphnians building their treasury, felt their prestige at stake, as dedicators always did in the palmy days of this great international shrine. And so the offerings of the archaic period are always of high quality, using the purest of the styles and materials peculiar to each city, the finest of its craftsmen, or, failing them, the finest that could be hired elsewhere. Doric force, Ionic grace, Attic measure, all are here. They are the three legs of the Delphic tripod; lacking any one, it would fall. Delphi was a microcosm which, with the oracle's advice about the planting of colonies, influenced the whole Greek world. Here met east and west, mother cities and colonies, mainlander and islander. Here great events were commemorated in a living museum of history and of art. The treasures of the Delphi Museum do not represent a hundredth part of the sanctuary's ancient wealth: barbarians and emperors, villagers and connoisseurs have seen to that. We do not possess a single *objet d'art* of the many praised by Pausanias, with the exception of a bronze snake base of a golden tripod in Istanbul. What we have is but the small change from a great fortune, the pale reflection of a radiance that once illumined the whole ancient world.

No small part of Delphi's glory was due to Athens. Archaic Athens could make dedications because she was prosperous. The cause of her prosperity was her increased commerce, and part of the evidence for it is her splendid pottery, the study and sensitive classification of which is one of the great triumphs of Greek archaeology in the last fifty years.

The ware that succeeded Geometric in Athens is called Proto-Attic. It goes back to the very beginning of the seventh century or even a little earlier, and shows a delight in curves, a vitality, a robust individuality, massive, powerful, sometimes crude, in revolt against the discipline of the Geometric. The style develops into one of broad contrasts, turbulent and impatient. One of the finest examples, (Fig. 4.8) an amphora fifty-six inches high, containing a child burial, was discovered by George Mylonas in 1954 in his excavations of the cemetery at Eleusis, and is now in the Eleusis Museum. He dates it about 675. On the neck is the earliest known illustration of the famous scene from the *Odyssey,* of Odysseus blinding the drunken Cyclops (note the wine cup) by boring into his eye with a huge sharpened stake. On the shoulder a lion enthusiastically attacks a slinking boar; on the body a pair of Gorgons in split skirts flee in dismay from Perseus (his winged boots just visible at the right) who has just beheaded their sister Medusa. Perseus is under the protection of Athena, resplendent in a long white robe. This is the earliest known rendition of Gorgons, and the painter is clearly experimenting, not without humor: the Gorgons are

Fig. 4.8 Eleusis, Proto-Attic amphora, over four feet high (ca. 675). Subjects: Odysseus blinding Polyphemus, Gorgons (with meshed teeth) fleeing. (Eleusis, Museum)

more bewildered than fearsome. For a Gorgon to make the flesh creep, Greek art has to wait nearly 100 years (see Fig. 4.19).

This riotous indiscipline reduces itself in a couple of generations to the order and delicacy of Attic black-figure, so called because the design was painted in black silhouette against the handsome light red background of the clay. The most famous and elaborate example of black-figure ware has been known since 1844. It comes, like much of the best Attic pottery, from Etruria, near Chiusi, and is called from its discoverer the François Vase. The style dates it about 570. It is now in the Archaeological Museum in Florence. Its six bands with their over 200 figures, labeled as on the Siphnian Treasury, make up a meticulously detailed anthology of archaic myth, relieved by touches of humor, as when objects as well as figures are labeled: "Water-pot," "Stool," "Fountain." In Fig. 4.9, for example, the top band shows Theseus and the young Athenian hostages, disembarking, probably on Delos, where they will dance their crane-dance, after their escape from the Cretan Minotaur. One young man (*under* the ship) is so eager that he swims ashore. In the upper left corner is something new in Greek art: individual pride in artistic creation, symbolized by the signatures of the potter, Ergotimos, and the painter, Kleitias. Next below, Lapiths, led by Theseus, fight centaurs. In the central band, gods and goddesses magnificently mounted in chariots and richly dressed take the curse off the nymph Thetis' marriage to the mortal Peleus by bringing gifts to the wedding. Their son was Achilles, doomed to die at Troy. On the handle adjoining, Ajax carries Achilles' limp, dead body from the field. Kleitias' mood could change from rollicking humor to deeply tragic irony. Next below, burlesque again: Hephaestus, drunk, mounted on a jackass and escorted by Silens, returns triumphantly to Olympus to release Hera from the diabolical chair he invented as revenge on her for ejecting him from heaven. Kleitias has drawn Zeus's fearsome consort stuck fast in a chair she cannot get out of. Below, stylized animals; on the foot, pygmies and cranes fight it out in a burlesque battle, which would remind the spectator of Theseus' crane-dance on Delos, thus harking back to the scene on the top band and binding the whole composition subtly together. For elegance of drawing and coherence of plan this vase has no equal in archaic painting. And the artist's chaffing, intimate treatment of his myths should teach us not to be too stuffy about our Greeks, while the stark pathos of the Ajax-

Achilles scene should remind us that for them, sophistication was neither shallow, brittle, nor unfeeling.

About 530, Attic red-figure was invented to give the artist a freer medium for line drawing, making it possible for him to exalt the human figure and pay closer attention to anatomy, and set the figures in much more complicated positions. Recent experiments have so convincingly reproduced the ancient techniques that their publication will be very useful to forgers. The artist made a preliminary sketch with a

Fig. 4.9   The Francois Vase, a masterpiece of Attic black-figure (*ca.* 570). Florence, Museo archeologico.

pointed charcoal stick, then outlined his figure with a broad band of heavy glaze. Next, he filled in the background with a dark brown, glistening, heavy, creamy slip, made by mixing clay with water in the presence of a colloidal agent such as wood ash, whose function was to remove the heavier particles from the clay. After the slip was applied, the pot was placed in the kiln and heated to 800° centigrade. (A skilled potter can judge the temperature in the kiln by observing the incandescent color, and ancient potters experimented with temperature on test pieces.) This first stage of firing took place under oxidizing conditions; i.e., by admitting air through vents. At 800° C. the potter cut down the oxygen by closing the air vents and throwing in green wood. He now raised the temperature to 945° C., then lowered it to 875° C., by which time the green wood was all consumed. Then he opened the air vents, and oxidizing conditions again prevailed. The reducing process had changed the red ferric oxide in the clay to ferrous oxide: at this stage the whole vase was black. The reoxidizing affected only the unslipped, porous parts of the vase, the parts that contained the drawing. These turned back to red, while the background, covered with slip, was nonporous and remained black. Some black lines in finished red-figure ware stand out in relief. The recent experiments prove that this effect was produced with a still heavier slip, thickened with honey, which the potter or painter applied with a syringe like a pastry tube. Egg white brushed on to the relief line could be used as an adhesive for applying gold leaf if desired; the gold would not melt in the kiln because the melting point of gold is higher than the highest kiln temperature the potter wanted to achieve. Burnishing with a polishing stone and polishing further with a soft cloth helped to bring out the metallic luster of the slip when it was fired.

The handsome pots, in varied and graceful shapes, that resulted from this ingenious and practical technique took over the whole Greek market. Since many of the pots are signed, many artists' techniques have long been recognizable. The discriminating eye and retentive memory of J. D. (now Sir John) Beazley, at work on these pots over the last fifty years, have associated hundreds of unsigned pots and fragments with known painters, and reduced the history of the red-figure style to an admirably convincing classical order.

One distinguishing mark of the new style is the frequent abandonment of myth in favor of scenes of everyday life.

a

Fig. 4.10 Wurzburg, cup by the Brygos painter (*ca.* 490):
revelry and aftermath. (Saltman, *Attic Vase-Painting*, Pl. 26,
by permission of the Harvard University Press)

An example is the shallow drinking cup in Würzburg (Fig. 4.10) by the Brygos Painter (at work about 500-470; this cup perhaps of 490). On the outside a bearded man, somewhat the worse for drink, in a cloak and slippers, mishandles a girl and tries to snatch from her the drinking cup she is balancing in her left hand. The delicate finality of the gesture by which she brushes him off has been described as "one of the finest impressions ever achieved by an artist." Our cup was no doubt designed to hold transparent white wine, which would have left visible the delightfully Attic cautionary tale painted on the inside, wherein a young man is being sick, his head tenderly held by a flute-girl, perhaps the same girl who repulsed the advances of the older man on the cup's exterior. One is reminded of Aristotle's notion of temperance, which, he says, lies in a mean between drunkenness and total abstention. The object-lesson, plus the perfect composition, combine to make a work of art that is Greek in the best sense, in which perfection of form is wedded, with sophisticated humor, to subtlety of content.

Typically Greek, too, is the conservatism with which redfigure was adopted. At the beginning, artists produce transitional pots, black-figure on one side, red-figure on the other. Another example of conservatism: in 566 the Panathenaic festival was introduced, with prizes of amphorae filled with olive oil. At the time the competition was founded, blackfigure was the conventional style: Panathenaic prize amphorae continued to be painted in black-figure for centuries, even after red-figure had become the vogue on all other pottery; and the latest examples belong to a time when even redfigure had died out. After 480, red-figure painters began to split into more or less manneristic schools; by 450, vasepainting had sunk to a minor art; by 320, the *genre* was finished. But in its prime it supplied to Greek commerce the handsomest containers the world has ever known.

Sixth-century Athens, in which the black-figure and redfigure vases were painted, was dominated by two strongminded figures, Solon (archon 594/3: the split date means that the Attic civil year began in July) and Pisistratus (tyrant probably 560-556 and 546-527). They brought prosperity, reflected in an ambitious building program, a new coinage, and a flowering of the arts. One pious duty was to build on the Acropolis, in thanksgiving, a worthy temple to Athena, the city's patron saint.

In modern times, hardly had Greece been freed from the

Turks when, in 1833, Greek archaeologists set to work to clear the Acropolis of all vestiges of the hated Ottoman domination, and to uncover the remains of the glorious past. Four slabs of the Parthenon frieze were found in the 1833 campaign, the first guards of the Acropolis antiquities were posted, and in September of 1834, in the presence of the new King, a column of the Parthenon was re-erected, and the temple decked with myrtle and olive boughs. The great classical monuments were uncovered in rapid succession: the Nike Temple and the Propylaea steps in 1835, the Erechtheum in 1837. In that same year the Greek Archaeological Society was founded: it held its first meeting in the Parthenon, then still disfigured with a Turkish minaret that survived till 1905. The building of the Acropolis Museum began in 1864; in 1875, with funds supplied by Schliemann, the Frankish tower at the Acropolis entrance was taken down. But not till 1885-90 was excavation in depth attempted.

Among the incalculably rich finds, of which more will be said later, the area south and southeast of the Parthenon yielded in 1888 a remarkable three-bodied monster in *poros* (limestone) now in the Acropolis Museum. It tapered away

Fig. 4.11 Athens, triple-headed sea monster from pediment of a poros temple (*ca.* 570). (Acropolis Museum)

in a coiling mass of tails in a way which revealed clearly that it had been carved to fit into the acute angle of a pediment. Most archaeologists assign the sculpture to the early archaic predecessor of the Periclean Parthenon, the Hekatompedon ("Hundred-Footer"), whose foundations now lie concealed under the surviving building. The limestone had been brilliantly painted, and the colors were still vivid when the piece was found, though they have faded since. The right-hand head (Fig. 4.11) had a blue moustache and beard, and hence, inevitably, was nicknamed "Bluebeard." The eyes had a blue iris with a deeply incised pupil, the eyelids were dark, the lips red. The flesh was rose-colored, the tails blue and red. The hair is white, and crimped in front into a high fringe. From the opposite angle of the pediment comes another snaky-tailed group of Heracles wrestling with Triton, "the Old Man of the Sea." In the center was a pair of lions. Other similar fragments belong to the opposite pediment.

Pisistratus built another temple, whose plan has been unearthed. It is visible in the frontispiece, between the Parthenon and the Erechtheum. It lay over the site of the old Mycenaean palace. It had marble figures in the pediments, of Athena battling the giants. After the battle of Marathon (490 B.C.) the Athenians demolished the "Hundred Footer" to make way for a new temple, the "Older Parthenon," built of marble from the newly opened Pentelic quarries. This temple remained unfinished when the Persians sacked Athens in 480. Some of its column drums, showing damage by fire, are still visible, built into the Acropolis wall.

Besides his temple on the Acropolis, Pisistratus planned a temple to Olympian Zeus. It was abandoned at his death, taken up again in Hellenistic times, and not destined to be finished until the Roman Emperor Hadrian's time (A.D. 135). It thus has one of the longest building records in the history of architecture. But not all Pisistratus' public works projects were doomed to frustration. To him or his sons are to be ascribed an ambitious drainage system; a shrine of Eleusinian Demeter under the north slope of the Acropolis; a new market place with temples and secular buildings, including housing for law court and council, with a room for the deposit of official weights and measures.

American excavations in the Athenian agora, to be described in detail in the final chapter, have added much to our knowledge of the city's appearance in Pisistratean and earlier times. The excavators found that early Athens clus-

Fig. 4.12 Athens, Agora about 500 B.C., plan. (Agora Excavations)

tered close round the Areopagus and Acropolis; down to
the early sixth century the Agora, like the Roman Forum,
was a cemetery. It was taken over for public purposes because it was the most open and level area of any extent
under the shelter of the Acropolis, and because it was on the
direct route from the Acropolis to the Dipylon Gate. The
earliest civic building, two rooms under the Metroon, on the
west side of the Agora (see plan, Fig. 4.12), probably dates
from the time of Solon (594/3). In 1931 a flood revealed
the Pisistratean Great Drain down the west side of the Agora,
which fixed the line of later buildings west of it. Tiles in it
stamped "Mother of the Gods" came from the nearby
Metroon, in which the excavators distinguished sixteen complex levels. It began as a small archaic temple, was expanded
to house the city's archives and after 150 B.C. was remodeled
into four rooms of various sizes sharing a 129-foot portico
that faced the morning light; the slope of Kolonos Agoraios
sheltered the buildings on this side of the Agora from the
scorching afternoon sun. (Not everyone sought shade:
Diogenes the Cynic philosopher, whose only request from
Alexander was that he get out of his sun, set up his tub
[a *pithos*] in a sunny spot on this side of the Agora, perhaps not in Athens but in Corinth.)

Also Pisistratean proved (1935) to be the Southeast Fountain House, a lobby with side compartments for water basins;
its building produced a remarkable outburst of representations of fountain houses on black-figure vases. Pisistratean
too is the Panathenaic Way, where passed the procession instituted by the tyrant and immortalized on the Parthenon
frieze. On the flat, this road was metaled with layer after
layer of firmly packed gravel; on the slopes, at least in Roman times, it was paved with large slabs. Rectangular sockets
at the curb may have had something to do with snubbing
or braking the ship-float that carried Athena's peplos (the
ceremonial embroidered garment offered to the goddess at
the Panathenaic festival), or with some means of spectator
control. Pisistratus built the earliest (apsidal) temple of
Apollo Patroos, where citizens were registered and the city
fathers took their oaths of office. The mold for its bronze cult
statue was found in a pit nearby. Like most of the Agora's
Pisistratean buildings, it was destroyed in the Persian sack
of 480/79, and not restored until the fourth century.

From Pisistratus' tyranny dates the predecessor of the
Tholos, in this phase an irregular court surrounded by

rooms. It was the headquarters of Athenian government, where the Committee of the Council in charge of Athens for the day took their meals, and where a number of them slept at night, so that responsible persons might be always on call. This practice continued long after Athens ceased to be politically important: a Hellenistic decree, found in 1938, authorizes the purchase for the Tholos of furniture, mattresses, and crockery.

Pisistratus' son, Thucydides tells us, built an Altar to the Twelve Gods. The excavators in 1934 found between the rails of the Athens-Piraeus electric railway the footings for the altar fence, and the pits for the plantings of olive and laurel that surrounded it. It became the zero milestone, the place from which distances from Athens were reckoned, like the Miliarium Aureum in the Forum at Rome.

The Pisistratids left the Agora a loose series of small buildings in an arc along the west side of a graveled area crossed by the Panathenaic Way but eroded by freshets. The south edge is typical of how the Agora developed: at first a Bronze Age track serving a hamlet, then a cemetery path, finally (toward the end of the sixth century) a formal boundary. Cleisthenes, the founder of democracy, began in 509 to monumentalize the Agora and straighten its boundaries; some of his stone markers were discovered, one of them *in situ*. His chief building was the Old Bouleuterion (Council House) built to accommodate his new Council of 500. At this time the Assembly moved to the Pnyx, and dramatic contests were transferred to the south slope of the Acropolis. However, the Orchestra in the middle of the Agora, where they had been held, continued in use as the place where lots were drawn for jury duty and other public functions (for Athens carried the premise of democracy to its logical conclusion, and assumed that any citizen was capable of discharging any civic responsibility except the conduct of war). Near the site of the Orchestra a number of interesting machines for drawing and recording the lots was found; though Hellenistic, they almost certainly reflect earlier practice. The ingenious interpretation of these enigmatic objects is due to Professor Sterling Dow of Harvard. A hole is drilled vertically through the left side of the stele (Fig. 4.13), widening to a funnel at the top, opening on the face of the stele at the bottom. The slots at the right are for the tickets of those wanting jury duty. An official dropped into the fun-

Fig. 4.13 Athens, Agora, allotment machine, reconstruction drawing. (S. Dow)

nel a number of white balls for jurors to be empaneled and black balls for jurors to be dismissed. Each ball, emerging at the bottom of the tube, determined the use or rejection of a whole horizontal row of would-be jurors. Once the chosen jurors were empaneled, they were assigned by lot to the court where they would sit. The last-minute allotment was obviously designed to prevent corruption of a jury sitting on a given case, and a check of the dicast tickets would prevent a juror's collecting for duty he had not performed. The assumption throughout is the realistic one that human nature is not proof against temptation.

The democratic Athens established by Cleisthenes had soon to face the Persian menace. Herodotus tells how the 192 Athenian heroes who fell at Marathon in 490 were buried on the battlefield under a mound. Greek archaeologists excavated the mound in 1890 and, nine feet below the level of the plain, hit upon an artificial floor of sea sand and marble chips, with one to four inches of ash, charcoal, human bones, and black-figure *lekythoi*. The next year they found a sacrificial trench lined with fired brick and containing the bones of animals, pottery used in the funeral banquet, and quantities of arrowheads in flint (from Ethiopia) and bronze. One set of bones in a special pot might, they conjectured, be the remains of the Polemarch or Minister of War, who gave up to Miltiades his turn to command and fell fighting.

The funds to execute all these ambitious schemes came in part from the exploitation of newly discovered veins of silver in the Laurium district of Attica, in the mountains near Sunium, not far from Pisistratus' estates at Brauron. In 1860, examination of the slag from the ancient workings proved that it was worth reprocessing for silver, lead, manganese, and zinc. The engineers coöperated with archaeologists of the French School in Athens, and made possible a fruitful study of the mining processes of Pisistratus' day and after.

Laurium's geological strata are limestone and schist. The Greeks early discovered, perhaps as early as Mycenaean times, that the ore lay between these strata, and their tunnels for it, reused by the modern engineers, are like wormholes in wood. Red iron oxide on the surface, which usually accompanies lead crystals, supplied the clues for digging. The tunnels are seldom more than a meter high, so that the workmen—usually slaves and criminals—had to work on their knees or their bellies, but this, with the tools at their disposal, was probably preferable to enlarging the tunnels to man's height. Since the ore was carried out in sacks, not cars, there was no need for the tunnels to run level. Archaeologists have found rings for chaining the slaves, driven into the tunnel walls, and lamps with a ten-hour capacity, but the shifts were probably only two hours long. Where the tunnels went deep into the mountainside horizontally, they were also connected with the surface by vertical shafts from

200 to 350 feet deep, up which the baskets of ore were run on pulleys. Parallel or inclined shafts with dampers supplied ventilation. The mines were underground cities, with streets, wells, squares, crossroads, and workshops. They were state property, but let to entrepreneurs on seven- to ten-year leases, at ridiculously low rates (twenty to 150 drachmae a year.) Since 1949 over seventy-five inscriptions (of the fourth century) recording such leases have been excavated in the Athenian Agora.

The ore was pulverized with mortar and pestle, then washed so that the heavy lead would settle. Numbers of ancient washing basins survive. Methods of extraction were efficient: the surviving slag heaps never showed more than 12 per cent mineral deposit. The lead was extracted by melting it with iron, in the presence of a catalyst such as calcium carbonate; this yields ferrous sulphide and pure lead. The lead flowed out of the high-chimneyed furnaces down channels into forms for ingots. The Athenians extracted silver by filtering the lead ore through a porous material, bone ash or certain clays, and superheating the silver-bearing lead with an excess of oxygen. Archaeologists have identified the treasury where the precious metal was kept: a tower at Sunium where they found a bronze pinion wheel designed to engage a ratchet for lifting such heavy objects as bar silver, and also a weight (1,000 tetradrachms) inscribed with a mint magistrate's name. The silver kept there was .978 fine. The total production has been calculated at over 2,000,000 tons of silver-bearing lead. The richest veins were not exploited early; it was hardly worth while to work the Laurium mines intensively until rivals were eliminated, as after the Siphnian mines were flooded in 525, and after the mineral-rich island of Thasos in the north Aegean fell to Athens (463). In the years after Marathon the surplus silver from the Laurium mines was struck into handsome ten-drachma coins (Fig. 4.14) for distribution to the citizens as a bonus. But in 484 they voluntarily surrendered the bonus: Themistocles used it to build the triremes that beat the Persians at Salamis.

One of the finds from the Acropolis excavations of 1886 was a small hoard of silver coins hidden before the Persian sack and never recovered. Some of the coins bear the familiar Athenian device of the owl and Athena; others are stamped on the obverse with a four-spoke chariot wheel; the reverse is deeply cut with what numismatists call an "incuse square," intended to prove that the coin is silver all the way through, and not just base metal plated. Ancient coins were struck from blanks placed between two dies. The lower, let into an anvil, produced the obverse; the upper, let into the end of a punch, produced the reverse. When the silversmith struck the punch with a hammer, the blank received simultaneously the impression of both dies. Since punch-dies wore out faster than anvil dies, sequences of coins can be arranged by careful attention to the degree of wear on their anvil-dies.

Other obverse devices besides the wheel occur on early Athenian coins found elsewhere than in the Acropolis hoard. The devices include, among others, the triskeles (three bent legs radiating from a center), the forepart of a horse, the hindquarters of a horse, a bull's head, and a horseman. These same symbols occur as shield devices on vase paintings, and are therefore intended to identify persons, like the shield devices of King Arthur's knights. Greek literature makes clear that they were the badges of various noble clans. The triskeles and the chariot wheel are associated with the Alcmaeonidae (Pindar wrote an ode on the chariot victory of the Alcmaeonid Megacles at Delphi); the bull's head with a priestly clan called the Eteobutadae, etc. The choice of the hindquarters of a horse must be ironic, mocking: this device shares the same anvil die with the Alcmaeonid chariot wheel: the most likely mocker of this clan would be its enemy, Pisistratus. The chariot-wheel types in the Acropolis hoard have been approximately dated, from the die sequences and from similar devices on datable vases, 589-561: * they fit the period between Solon's archonship and Pisistratus' first tyranny, when the nobility was in the ascendant. The owl-Athena series from the same hoard is dated on the same sort of evidence 555-527; it therefore falls within Pisistratus' period of exile and his second tyranny. We may suppose that while he was jockeying for power he used his personal, mocking, horse's hindquarters type; when he had won control he chose a device that would symbolize all Athens, and not just narrow clan interest. He chose the owl and Athena, which remained Athens' symbol right down through

---

* Some scholars (not all) think this dating (C. T. Seltman's) is too high. Even so, Seltman's ingenuity is worth recording, and the numismatic evidence that the Pisistratids broke the power of the nobility and prepared the way for democracy is not in doubt. The owl-Athena series is unquestionably Pisistratid, and the owl and Athena continued to symbolize Athenian democracy as long as it lasted.

Fig. 4.14 Athens, silver dekadrachm, Athena and owl, *ca.* 486. (Seltman, A Book of Greek Coins, Pl. 47, a & b)

Roman times. Some of the earlier owl-Athena types in the Acropolis hoard bear an unusual lettering, found also on Attic coins from Paeonia, far to the north, where Pisistratus was in exile (probably 555-546). This series used up no less than twenty-six anvil dies, an index to great mint activity. Pisistratus was amassing a war-chest to pay the troops who were to secure his return. Some of the later Pisistratid coins are as handsome as medals: they may have been struck to commemorate Panathenaic festivals. After 546 the Attic mint produced no more individual badges, though the Alcmaeonids still used them on coins they struck in exile at Delphi.

The coin propaganda, therefore, marks Pisistratus as the precursor of Athenian democracy, since his choice of the owl-Athena type remained the democracy's symbol to the end. However little the propaganda may have fitted the facts, the change from aristocratic badges to the owl-Athena type is concrete evidence for what the historians tell us: that he broke the political power of the Athenian aristocracy.

Though Pisistratus might break the aristocrats' political power, he could not so easily undermine their social position. The outward and visible sign of their prestige was the dedication of statues of their sons (*kouroi*) and daughters (*korai*) on the Acropolis. When the Athenians returned to their blackened shrines after the Persian sack in 480 B.C., they determined to waste no time on repairs or patching, much less on antiquarian respect for archaic art (the Greeks were so modern!), but to make a clean sweep of the debris and start the beautification of the Acropolis afresh. During the 1885-90 Acropolis excavations, on two fruitful days in February, 1886, fourteen of the finest sixth-century statues of maidens (now in the Acropolis Museum) were found packed together in a hole northwest of the Erechtheum. These serene, festal types of aristocratic Athenian young womanhood are known, rather unfeelingly, by their inventory numbers. One of the loveliest, No. 679 (Fig. 4.15), the small-scale Peplos Korê (only four feet high, in Parian marble), explains why one Greek word for "statue" is also the word for "delight." It is in as nearly perfect condition as an ancient statue can be (the lower left arm is missing; the dowel hole for it is visible in the photograph). It must have stood under cover from the time of its dedication, about 530, until the Persians overthrew it: it shows no signs of weathering, and its ancient painting is well preserved. The

Fig. 4.15 Athens, Acropolis Museum, Peplos Koré, *ca.* 530, detail. (Lullies, *Greek Sculpture*, Pl. 43, by permission of Hirmer Verlag, Munich)

maiden wears a green necklace, her robe is green-bordered at the throat, her sleeve bears a pattern of green running spirals. Her hair, lips, and iris are dark red; pupils, brows, and lashes black. Her ears are pierced for earrings, and she originally wore a bronze coronet, of which the insertion holes and some of the nails survive. The sculptor has rendered to perfection her taut vitality, the independence of her body beneath her dress. This is archaic art at its lyric best. It successfully reproduces the forms observed in nature, and yet conforms to the language of a convention (the archaic smile, the hair style) as precise and exacting as the rhythm of the most strictly metrical verse. The Peplos Korê, then, is a true product of the lyric age of Greece. It achieves the universal

Fig. 4.16   Thera, site plan. 5, temple of Apollo Karneios; 7, votive inscriptions; 13, theater; 17, Agora; 20, stoa; 24, palace; 26, gymnasium; 27, commandant's headquarters (RE, 1934, Sp. 2285-6)

Stadt Thera

1 : 3130

0   50   100   150

without falsifying the unique. One feels that it was from the loins of girls like these that sprang the heroes who commanded at Marathon and Salamis.

The search for inscriptions for the massive Berlin *Corpus*, in which all Greek inscriptions were to be collected, led to the excavation (1896-1902) by Baron Hiller von Gaertringen of a charmingly sited little archaic Greek mountain town, Thera, on the picturesque volcanic island of Santorin, in the Aegean some twelve hours' steaming southeast of Piraeus; some think it is Plato's lost Atlantis. Hiller first went there to study some very old (seventh century) rock-cut inscriptions, recording boy-love of the Spartan sort. He soon decided that their meaning would not be clear without the excavation of the buildings adjoining (see plan, Fig. 4.16).

Hiller dug and published the site at his own expense: his four volumes on Thera are charmingly discursive, more a personal journal than a formal excavation report. He was on the friendliest terms with his forty-five workmen: they made him an honorary citizen of their village, and, led by their bearded Arcadian foreman, danced their age-old dances in front of the Thera museum at its dedication. At the start of the 1900 season the island band, the Phira Philharmonic, resplendent in uniform, played in the recently discovered Hellenistic theater. They were very proud: "we have a theater just like the Athenians." It had been covered by the excavation dump, and was accidentally discovered by the foreman working on his own in Hiller's absence, an incident typical of the informality of the whole dig. The workmen camped during the excavation season in neat stone huts like igloos, built from such nonsignificant ancient stones as the dig turned up. The site was virtually inaccessible; Hiller nearly killed his mules getting his gear up the mountain. He and his galaxy of volunteer assistants—a roster of the best-known archaeologists of the day—lived and worked in tents, and, with the full consent of the local abbot, in a chapel convenient to the site. Wind was a constant difficulty; the digging had to be shifted from one side of Thera hill to the other, depending on the quarter from which it blew. It ripped the excavation tent, and whisked a mule loaded with ancient pottery off the mountain path to his death. The finds had to be brought down on sledges 1140 feet over slithering volcanic pebbles, and then transported in home-made wagons over roads whose ruts and potholes only the seasoned traveler in out-of-the-way Greek places can visualize.

Within ninety minutes of the start of the first day's dig, Hiller had found seven new rock-cut inscriptions, and a cloudburst washed away the earth from the rock face and revealed many more. He transcribed them by painting the rough letters with water color for legibility and then taking their imprints on oiled paper. The site proved rich, too, in inscriptions conventionally cut in *stelae*: Hiller's eventual grand total was 1070. One of them identified the temple of Apollo Karneios (the Ram Apollo), protector of flocks. At his festival at vintage time, handsome nude youths danced in his honor; it is they who occasioned the rock-cut inscriptions.

The temple itself is set in bedrock, and in the rock of its threshold pious pilgrims scratched the outline of their feet. From its cella two entrances, one with a double set of doors for greater security, led to treasuries cut in the cliff face. Thera was at the height of its prosperity between 631, when it was founded, and 571, when it replenished a colony at Cyrene in North Africa. The building of the temple probably belongs to the years of its prime. South of the temple Hiller discovered a very ancient structure built over a very archaic rock-cut inscription: this was the Heroon or shrine of Theras, the city's founder. Hiller could gauge the level of the ancient mountain road to the site by noticing how high up the rock the inscriptions were cut. Some of them could be reached only by three ladders lashed together. Generations of traffic and erosion had worn the road down to its present level.

Thera proved rich in pottery as well as inscriptions, some of it as early as the ninth century. The necropolis from which most of it came was so prolific that the catalogue could not keep up with the finds. The unique, fully developed Geometric style that the Dorian settlers brought with them to Thera never underwent the rich orientalizing influence that, as Hiller picturesquely puts it, makes Attic ware look beside Theran like a finely educated cosmopolitan beside a bureaucrat of the better class.

Besides inscriptions and vases, Thera yielded a large coin hoard, 760 pieces, of the seventh and sixth centuries. Thera's trade relations with Aegina must have been close, for over 70 per cent of the coins found were minted on that island.

Thera's daughter-city, Cyrene, is an Italian excavation (1914-23; 1956 to date). Interest in it was first aroused when a cloudburst late in 1913 flooded the temple area and uncovered the voluptuous Aphrodite now in the Terme Museum in Rome, perhaps a copy, made for a bath, of a bronze original by Polyclitus. As in the mother city, the most important temple was Apollo's (see plan, Fig. 4.17), dated in the early sixth century, and Cyrene, like Thera, has a huge necropolis; its burials range over the thousand years from the sixth century B.C. to the fourth century A.D. Beside Apollo's temple was one to his sister Artemis. The Italians hit upon a foundation deposit in it, containing objects of gold, silver, bronze, hematite, ivory, and amber; ostrich eggs, Corinthian and Attic vases, and lamps, ranging in date from the seventh

Fig. 4.17   Cyrene, plan. Temple area in upper left quadrant, necropolis at top, Agora near center, temple of Zeus 800 yards northeast. (TCI Guide, *Colonie*, fac. p. 489)

Fig. 4.18 Arkesilas cup, Laconian ware from Vulci, in Etruria (about 550). The king of Cyrene, under canvas on the deck of a ship, supervises the loading of silphium. (Paris, Bibl. Nat., Cabinet des medailles)

to the fifth century. Its prosperity was founded on the export of silphium (asafoetida), which enjoyed wide currency in the ancient world, apparently as an aphrodisiac. The plant appears on Cyrene's coins and on a famous archaic Laconian cup of about 560, now in the Louvre. Arkesilas, King of Cyrene, is portrayed (Fig. 4.18) supervising the loading of bags of silphium onto a ship. Some of the profits were used to support the arts: Cyrene has yielded three fine archaic

kouroi and two *korai,* of the mid-sixth century B.C.; and
Pindar was subsidized to write his longest and most splendid
ode, the *Fourth Pythian,* for a king of Cyrene, "the city of
noble horses . . . at the shining breast of the sea." Her
prosperity lasted down to the end of the archaic period and
beyond: the evidence is the temple of Zeus (480-450). It
is a giant (104 × 225 feet); only the temple of Zeus at
Agrigentum and Temple G at Selinus, both to be described
later, exceed it in size. It is larger than either the Parthenon
or the temple of Zeus at Olympia, which was one of the
Seven Wonders of the World. Cyrene's Agora is mainly Roman, and will be described in the last chapter, but a copy
of the original foundation decree from Thera was set up in
it, and one of its porticoes was discovered in 1956 to be of
the sixth century.

Tradition had it that on the very day on which the Greeks
beat the barbarians at Salamis, the Sicilians in the West beat
their barbarian foe, the Carthaginians, in a sea battle off
Himera. Thus did the colonies pay their debt to the mother
cities. The archaic age was, as we saw, an age of coloniza-
tion, and some of the colonies rivaled or outstripped the
homeland in wealth and in artistic sophistication. For example, Corcyra, modern Corfu, off the Greek west coast,
early achieved prosperity as Corinth's staging point for voy-
ages to Italy and Sicily: from Corcyra's highest mountain top
the Italian coast is visible on a clear day. In the fields south
of the modern town farmers kept turning up ancient architectural blocks, and in December, 1910, they found, upside
down where it had fallen, an extraordinary series of pieces
of early archaic limestone sculpture, of which the most striking was a fearsome Gorgon (Fig. 4.19), obviously, from the
shape of the block, belonging to a pediment. During further
excavations the following spring, Kaiser Wilhelm II happened to be vacationing on the island. He took a personal
interest, summoned Dörpfeld to the spot from Olympia,
and won from the Greeks a concession for the Germans to
dig. It was Dörpfeld's pupils who published the Gorgon
pediment from a building which inscriptions proved to be
the Temple of Artemis. It is illuminating to note the mathe-
matical precision of which Greek architects and sculptors were
capable in the early sixth century. The excavators found
that the pediment fell into five groups, rendered on three
panels each, symmetrically related in width (the outer two
not shown in the photograph): the measurements in meters

Fig. 4.19 Corcyra, pediment of temple of Artemis, *ca.* 580, with Medusa, her sons Pegasus and Chrysaor, and lion-panthers. (Lullies, *op. cit.*, Pl. 15)

are 3.02, 3.10, 3.35, 3.10, 3.02. Enough remained of the
temple cella ground plan to prove that it was exactly as long
as the pediment, and exactly a third as wide. Some of the
original cornice was found. It is of terracotta, an old-
fashioned material that went out of use by 580 B.C.: therefore the sculptured pediment is usually dated 590-580. It
was carved probably by a Corinthian sculptor, during the
last years of Periander's tyranny in the mother city. The balance in the pediment is not lifeless. It shows double movement, toward the middle, and toward the corners. It fore-
shadows the ripe archaism of Aphaia's Temple on Aegina,
and the classicism of Olympia and the Parthenon.

The central Gorgon figure is stupendous—over nine feet
high—and terrible, with her frightful grin, bared teeth,
protruding tongue, and scaly snakes for hair and belt. Her
face is frontal, but her bent knees are in profile: the archaic
convention for rapid running. Her chiton (shirt reaching to
the knees) was originally painted red, her snakes blue, the
feathers on her boots alternately red and blue. She was
flanked heraldically by her sons; on her right was a
rampant Pegasus (the symbol of Corinth). All that remains
are his forefoot resting on her arm, his hindquarters, and
part of his wings, which are feathered exactly like his
mother's. On her left is Chrysaor of the golden sword (this
to be restored under his mother's left arm); he has blue
hair bound with a red fillet, and a rather bestial grin, obviously inherited. The gigantic felines, a cross-breed of lion
and panther, are orientalizing in style, and subtly varied:
the left one is angry, the right one placid. But all, Gorgon,
brood, and beasts, are apotropaic; i.e., they are where they
are to ward off wicked powers from Artemis' temple and
its contents. With the myths of Artemis they have, of
course, nothing to do: archaic architectural sculpture never
bears any relation to the divinity of the temple to which
it is attached. In the corners of the pediment (not shown)
were unrelated mythological figures. Myth is just beginning
to conquer the apotropaic. When it conquers, something
solemn, awesome, and hieratic is lost from Greek religious
art. But the tension between the apotropaic and the mythological led in the end to the classical pediment. The discovery of this sculpture opened a whole new chapter in
Greek art history, a chapter concerned with one of the many
early sculptural schools, a selection from which was to
make the classical style.

Selinus in southwest Sicily had, like Corcyra, close trade relations with Corinth, as has been proved by Protocorinthian pottery that had long gathered dust in the storerooms of the Palermo Museum, until it was examined scientifically in 1958. Selinus, however, was ultimately a colony not of Corinth but of neighboring Megara, home of the bitter Tory poet Theognis (flourished 548-40). On the acropolis of fever-ridden Selinus, two young English architects named Angell and Harris excavated at their own expense in 1822-23, and were rewarded by the discovery of some of the finest archaic metopes ever unearthed. (Metopes are squarish sculptured slabs that run above the columns of a temple.) The Bourbon government of the Kingdom of Naples interrupted the work, and Harris died at twenty-three of fever in Palermo in 1823, but Angell lived to publish his finds. One of the finest (Fig. 4.20), now in the Palermo Museum, from the temple called C, portrays Heracles carrying on his shoulders, trussed like game to a pole, two Cercopes, imps who had annoyed him by changing themselves into blue-bottle flies and troubling his sleep. This, unlike the Corcyra pediment, is real provincial work, with a charming primitive quality of robust realism, and a good instinctive feeling for geometric composition. Because of the time lag involved between art in the metropolis and art on the periphery, provincial work is always difficult to date, especially when, as here, there is nothing but style to go by. Estimates of the date of this metope therefore vary from 570 to 530; the lower date is the more likely.

The treasures of Selinus have neither been completely excavated nor definitively published. On the acropolis are at least three other temples, and blocks of houses; there are silted-up ports on either side; metopes from a very early temple were found built into the acropolis north wall; the city proper to the north has never been excavated. Local clandestine diggers consistently rob the sanctuary to the west of its rich crop of very early votive figurines. Only in the east, where there are three more temples, is work going on, and this is limited to re-erecting columns to attract tourists. Of the eastern temples (called, with customary archaeological caution, E, F, and G), E too has yielded metopes, also in the Palermo Museum, but, lovely as they are, they are fifth-century, and fall below the lower limits of this chapter (see Fig. 5.21). G, dedicated to Apollo, is colossal, begun as early as 540, and still unfinished when

Fig. 4.20 Selinus, temple C (570-530), metope of Heracles and Cercopes. Palermo, Museum. (Villard, 1955, Pl. 96)

the Carthaginians sacked Selinus in 409. Selinus, inadequately excavated and published, may stand as the type of provinical city of the archaic age, rich, but remote from the creative centers of art, which it imitates energetically but without understanding.

Paestum, Greek Posidonia, in south Italy below Salerno, is a different case. There in 1934, at the mouth of the river Sele, two devoted archaeologists, Paola Zanconi-Montuoro and U. Zanotti-Bianco, working with private funds, and following clues in ancient literary sources, discovered to their intense joy the largest archaic find in the history of Greek archaeology: an almost complete series of sandstone metopes from a small building (at Olympia or Delphi it would be called a "treasury") in a sanctuary of Hera. Corinthian pottery in the fill dated the building after 575. The work was long drawn out. The excavators had no derricks, no roads, no vehicles but ox-carts. Malaria and pneumonia laid them low, and 1940 found them in a race against war, which finally claimed all their best workmen. Fortunately the finds, stored in a hut on the site, were ignored by both sides in the war, and between 1948 and 1952 it was found possible to toughen the friable metopes by sponging them with sodium silicate, to repair them with brass pegs, and to install them in a specially built museum near the more famous temples of Paestum proper.

The metopes survive because they were carved in sandstone. If they had been in limestone or marble, they would long ago have been reduced to useful whitewash in local kilns. Even so, many of the metope blocks were found in reuse in ancient buildings more or less remote from where they belonged. Of the thirty-two more or less complete metopes, eleven are unfinished. In them, the relief is blocked out in angular fashion, but not rounded. Only a sudden catastrophe could have halted the work thus in mid-course. Since the frieze blocks had to be put in place before the building could be roofed, and the sculptors naturally worked more slowly than the carpenters, the metope blocks were mounted anyhow, finished or no. The excavators believe the emergency was the threat to the sponsoring city, Siris, from the coalition against her, sometime between 570 and 560, of the neighboring cities of Sybaris, Metapontum, and Croton.

The excavators have been able to assign almost every metope to its place on the treasury, by careful observation

Fig. 4.21 Heraion at mouth of Sele, metope of Heracles and Cercopes, 570-560. Paestum, Museum. (Fototeca)

of the subject of the relief, the cuttings on the back for the ends of roof beams, masons' marks, or, where the metope was not reused, the spot where it fell. Seventeen metopes related to Heracles, ten to the Trojan War; the rest portray miscellaneous myths. For the sake of comparison and contrast with Selinus, I have chosen (Fig. 4.21) the rendition of Heracles and the Cercopes, where the treatment is much crisper, more mature and detailed; e.g., one of the Cercopes is bearded, one is not. Here the stiffness is not primitive but deliberate, to enhance the humor of the situation: one may imagine that the culprits are stiff with fear of the muscle-bound hero and his mighty club. On the other metopes, archaic humor abounds, as on the François Vase: Heracles tries to stuff the boar in on top of Eurystheus, who set him his labors, and is hiding in a large jar; Odysseus rides a tortoise; centaurs have human or horse feet according as they are considered more human or more beastly. The total effect is one of freshness, intelligence, refinement, boldness, and skill, by more than one sculptor. One feels this work was done by pioneers. The excavators claim that the treatment of the myths was influenced by a pioneer lyric poet of the Far West, Stesichorus ("the Choirmaster") of Himera, but their argument is more ingenious than cogent, since of Stesichorus' poems hardly more than titles survive.

There was a temple to Hera also on the site; some of its metopes, of graceful dancing maidens, survive. Their technique is riper, and they are dated 510-500. It is possible to argue, from religious buildings in Magna Graecia dated 575-475, of which Selinus and the sanctuary at the mouth of the Sele are only two of many examples, that the fervor, skill, and detail of their architectural sculpture was not matched again in Europe until the Middle Ages.

Five miles southeast of the mouth of the Sele lie the three handsome temples of Paestum proper, so rightly beloved of travelers—though in antiquity no one saw the golden-brown patina: the limestone was stuccoed over. Of the three temples the middle and most perfect is classical (Fig. 5.20) and does not concern us here. The other two are archaic. Excavations since World War II, which have yielded over 1,000,-000 small finds, have produced *graffiti*, inscriptions, and foundation deposits like the one under the archaic Artemision on Delos. These have proved that the three-mile circuit of the city wall is of sixth-century date, that the

Fig. 4.22   Paestum, Basilica, *ca.* 550 (Author)

southern temple, called since the eighteenth century the "Basilica," was dedicated to Hera; the northern ("Ceres") to Athena. Paestum was little visited till the nineteenth century. The railroad did not come till 1884, and the area was infested with malaria and brigands.

The "Basilica," unusually wide in proportion to its length, was built about 550 of limestone with some sandstone details, visible in the photograph (Fig. 4.22) between the two courses of the architrave. The sandstone was used where it was desired to have a soft stone on which to carve moldings. The upper course reveals U-shaped lifting grooves, through which ropes were passed to raise the blocks. These were never intended to be seen; this course was originally two blocks thick; the front blocks, together with the pediment and the cella walls, were long ago carried away. Some of the blocks are built into the eleventh-century churches of nearby Salerno and Amalfi. Different columns show different details under the sturdy, spreading Doric capitals; these may have been artisans' signatures. The details were picked out in color, always the same color for the same element. This is part of the formal lyricism of archaic architecture: red for the rings under the capital and the projecting band at the top of the architrave; blue or black for triglyphs, and red and blue for leaf ornaments.

The Temple "of Ceres" (Fig. 4.23) is of a greater delicacy, and a more comfortable size: like the temple under the Parthenon, it is a "Hundred-Footer," while the "Basilica" is over half again as long. Though it is Doric on the exterior, some Ionic capitals have been found that belonged to its cella. Its pediment, partly preserved, is too shallow ever to have contained statuary. The perfection of its technique suggests a date about 510. Paestum as a whole represents the sturdy perfection of the archaic Doric style. In the fifth century this is infused, in the so-called "Temple of Poseidon," with an Attic grace.

For our last example of archaic lyricism, abandoning for better or worse the sixth-century conventions and looking forward to the earliest classic phase, we return to the motherland and to the island of Aegina. Here, in 1811, on a rocky mountain in the northeast corner of the island, falling steeply to the sea, two friends of Lord Byron, the English architect C. R. Cockerell (shown in a contemporary drawing carrying on his investigations in a tall hat),

Fig. 4.23 Paestum, temple of Ceres, *ca.* 510. (Author)

and the Bavarian Baron Haller von Hallerstein, discovered within a yard of the surface some strikingly handsome pedimental sculpture. It was bought in 1812 by Prince Ludwig of Bavaria for 100,000 francs, drastically restored in Rome (1815-17), against Cockerell's will, by the fashionable classicizing Danish sculptor Thorwaldsen, and set up in 1828 in the Munich Glyptothek, where it now is. In 1901 Adolph Furtwängler (who was to die in 1907 of fever contracted here) reopened investigations on Aegina. On the very first day of digging he discovered some further remains (now in the National Museum in Athens) of an east pediment older than Cockerell's and Haller's finds. This earlier sculpture had been destroyed before 487 by the Persians (or by Aeginetan democrats, or by lightning) and replaced by the version now in Munich. The metopes of the southeast side were set in place again by the Greeks in 1959. Furtwängler found an inscription establishing that the temple had been dedicated to Aphaia, an obscure goddess, related to Artemis, "Mistress of Animals," whose cult went back at least to Late Mycenaean times. Furtwängler was able to reconstruct the temple floor from the masons' marks in series on the blocks.

The key to the interpretation of the pediments lies in the presence of Heracles in both the earlier and the later east pediments, which probably portrayed his expedition to Troy to punish Laomedon, who had cheated him of his fee for building the citadel walls. The other pediment, then, probably treated a related theme, Homer's Trojan War, including cer-

Fig. 4.24 Aegina, temple of Aphaia, later east pediment, *ca*. 485, **Heracles drawing the bow**. Munich, Blyptothek. (Clarence Kennedy)

tain heroes from Aegina. From the later east pediment the most famous piece is the bowman Heracles (Fig. 4.24), himself as tense as a drawn bow. Thorwaldsen did him little essential harm, and centuries of bird droppings had protected his lower limbs from the weather. He is recognizable from the head of the Nemean lion, which he wears on his head like a helmet. Originally he held a bow of metal (restored in the photograph), had lead hair, and was brightly painted. The figure is freer than earlier archaic work. We are in a different world from the Heracles of the Selinus or even the Sele metopes. It is no longer the world of archaic conventions, enormously attractive, but somehow remote. The world of the Aegina Heracles is suddenly *our* world. The figure is carved entirely in the round, and with true Greek perfectionism the back, which was never intended to be visible, is as carefully finished as the front. The tension of the arms drawing the bow, the sharp contours (derived from bronze technique), and the realistic modeling all bespeak a new spirit, transitional between the archaic and the classical: it synthesizes naturalistic form, geometric design, and refinement of detail. Aeginetan sculptors were briefly famous just before and after the Persian War; their cultural debt (like ours) was divided between Spartan solidity and Attic grace, as the Heracles shows. But Aegina's cultural primacy was brief. Aeginetans were better at piracy and athletics than at poetry: when one of their athletes needed a poet to celebrate a victory he borrowed Pindar.

Between the Gorgon amphora from Eleusis and the Aegina Heracles, the lyric age of Greece spans a little less than 200 years. As we have described selected examples of its vase painting, its architecture, its sculpture, its coinage and technology, we have seen it develop from stark, sturdy simplicity (the Delian lions, the columns of the Heraion at Olympia, the Cleobis of Delphi, Theran pottery) through religious solemnity (the Corcyra Gorgon) and naïveté (the Selinus metopes), to humor (the François Vase, the Acropolis Bluebeard, the Cercopes metope from the Sele) and cosmopolitan sophistication (the Brygos and Arkesilas cups, the Peplos Korê, the Siphnian Treasury frieze, the temple of Zeus at Cyrene, the Aegina pediments). Here are great riches. It would be a mistake to see in this age, as some earlier critics did, a primitive forerunner of the perfection of classicism. This is the lyric age that produced Sappho and

Pindar, as well as the masterpieces we have been surveying. Archaic Greek art, like early Greek lyric, is increasingly naturalistic in content, and precisely, exactingly conventional in form. The artists of such an age, with their zestful vitality and strong sense of geometric design, need to apologize to no one—not even to Phidias and Pericles.

ADDENDUM

The plan of the book, which draws inferences as to dating from archaeological observations in the field, makes it undesirable to begin a chapter with a chronological synopsis, but for convenience the monuments and artifacts discussed are listed below in a time sequence. All date are approximate.

BC

675	Eleusis, Proto-Attic amphora
660-650	Delos, Nicandre statue
645-640	Olympia, Heraion
631-571	Thera, Temple of Apollo Karneios; Cyrene founded and refounded
627-585	Corinth, *diolkos*
625-600	Delos, Lion Terrace
620	Attic black-figure begins
615-590	Delphi, Cleobis and Biton
590-580	Corcyra, Gorgon pediment
570	François Vase
570	Athens, Acropolis Bluebeard
570-560	Sele, archaic metopes
570-530	Selinus, Temple C metopes
560	Arkesilas cup
550	Paestum, "Basilica"
550-527	Athens, Pisistratid coinage and building activity
550	Larisa-by-Hermos, archaic palace
540	Selinus, Temple G begun
530	Attic red-figure invented
530	Athens, Peplos Korê
525	Delphi, Siphnian Treasury
513-505	Delphi, Alcmaeonid temple
510	Paestum, Temple "of Ceres"
510	Sele, Heraion metopes
509	Delphi, Athenian treasury
490	Brygos Painter cup
485	Aegina, Temple of Aphaia, later east pediment
480ff	Cyrene, Temple of Zeus

5 The Classical Age: Greece and the West

(480-400 B.C.)

International archaeology, especially in the last eighty or ninety years, has thrown floods of light on the picture given us in Greek literature of the fifth century before Christ as the greatest, the most classical—a term which will need defining—and the most tragic of ancient centuries. Germans have made plain to us the setting of the first Olympic games; Americans, Greeks, and Danes have painstakingly measured, interpreted, and even restored the architecture and sculpture of the Periclean age and after; Italians and Germans have studied the temples and the art of Magna Graecia. The result is a clearer view than ever before of the material, social, political, religious, and artistic life of the classical age. Archaeology reveals that age as one in which Ionian elegance was wedded to Dorian strength: in which craftsmen put quality before quantity, and architects and sculptors showed an intelligent, controlled passion for clear, simple, generalized ideas. In Athens especially and in Athens especially on the Acropolis, archaeology has shown us how the unique blend of self-confidence, imperial wealth and ascendancy, a noble artistic tradition, a great leader, and craftsmen who loved and understood their materials and their work combined to produce the tragically brief flowering of the classical age.

Fig. 5.1 Olympia, model, by A. and E. Mallwitz, of Altis from southwest. Note how temple of Zeus stands out (right center). The windowed building, lower left, is Phidias' studio, above it, the palaestra. Round building, r. of palaestra, is Philippeion; behind it, the Prytaneion. Along north side, below Hill of Kronos, the Heraion, exedra of Herodes Atticus, treasuries, with Metroon in front. The vault of the stadium entrance is just visible behind the Echo Stoa (upper r.). On right edge, Victory of Paeonius, on its column; below it, Bouleuterion apse. Center, Pelopion; bottom, a corner of the Leonidaion: Many of these buildings will be discussed in later chapters. (DAI, Athens)

Treatment of so richly documented a period as the fifth century must be selective. We begin with Olympia. The first hint in modern times of the riches the site concealed came in 1829. In that year the French sent an expeditionary force to help the Greeks in their struggle against the Turks for independence. The French task force had a scholarly branch, the *Expédition scientifique de Morée*. Operating from a camp in the pines under the Hill of Kronos, the French were lucky enough to find almost at once fragments of metopes from the great temple of Zeus, depicting the labors of Heracles. These metopes are now in the Louvre; later excavators operated under an agreement with the Greek government that all the finds should be left in Greece, so that most of the justly famous sculpture from Olympia is now to be seen in its local museum; a few pieces are in the National Museum in Athens.

When the Germans opened their dig at Olympia in 1875, the site was a vineyard, there was no communication with the outside world, and when in the second season carts for hauling the excavated earth were imported from Corfu, they had to be brought over unfinished roads. Digging had to be done after the vintage, since the labor force was recruited from local field hands. (The ancient games themselves were held in August, a time of rest for farmers.)

Five campaigns enabled the Germans, with the help of Pausanias' invaluable ancient guidebook, to clarify the whole plan of the Altis, the sacred precinct of Olympia (Fig. 5.1). They found, built into the walls of postclassical huts, or lying where they fell, or scattered at random about the site, pieces of sculpture, of every degree of fragmentation. One of these was Paeonius' famous Victory, represented as hovering near the earth, thrusting firmly into the wind and full of passionate movement, a *tour de force* in which marble is made to appear weightless. She commemorated Athens' defeat of the Spartans at Sphacteria, near Pylos, in 424. Most of the sculpture, however, the excavators could identify as coming from the metopes and pediments of the temple of Zeus.

The French had already established that the metopes portrayed the twelve labors of Heracles, presumably six at each end of the temple. Since the metopes would have had to be put in place before the temple roof went on, they had to be earlier than the pedimental sculpture, and indeed their severe style is appropriate to a date between 470 and 460. Seeking a more precise dating, the Germans noted in Pausanias that the Spartans hung a dedication (whose inscription they found) on the east pediment to commemorate a victory which we know they won in 457; therefore the pedimental sculptures must have been finished by that year. It was the year before Aeschylus died, and the sculptures have the rugged power of his tragedies.

Six of the metopes were peaceful in tone, showing the hero at rest after his labors; six showed him in more or less violent action: cleansing the Augean stables; subduing Cerberus, the three-headed dog of Hell; holding up the world for Atlas, who gets for him the golden apples of the Hesperides; slaying the triple-bodied monster Geryon; taming the horses of Diomedes; threatening Eurystheus cowering in his jar (as on a Sele metope) with the Calydonian boar.

The two sets of metopes ought to offer either comparison or contrast with the mood of the pedimental sculptures above them. The Germans knew that the east pediments of classical temples usually bore calm, stately subjects. Pausanias describes the subject of the east pediment. It was Zeus presiding over the sacrifices that preceded the famous chariot race of Pelops and Oenomaus for the hand of Hippodamia, which Pelops won by cheating. (He removed the linchpins from the axletree of his rival's chariot.) On the east side of the temple the Germans in fact found, lying approximately where an earthquake had felled them, fragments of the Zeus, the chariots, and some of the figures Pausanias mentions. At the southeast corner they found the Eurystheus metope, one of the violent ones. Therefore the effect intended was contrast, and the violent metopes go with the stately pediment. Beyond the temple's other end the excavators found the pedimental masterpiece, the majestic, serene Apollo (Fig. 5.2). With the help of Pausanias' description, they restored him in the museum, holding firm control over the fighting Lapiths and centaurs on either side of him.

Besides using the evidence of findspots plus Pausanias, the archaeologists could place the pedimental figures by noting their dimensions and shapes (kneeling figures midway between apex and corner, prone figures in the corners), and they could infer which way the figures originally faced by assuming that the unfinished side had faced in, while the weathered side faced out. The over-all assumption, safe for classical architectural sculpture, was that symmetry (but

Fig. 5.2 Olympia, Museum, Apollo, from west pediment of temple of Zeus. (Alison Frantz)

without rigor) was the effect the sculptor aimed at, with the figures balanced in number and attitude on either side of the central figure, Zeus on the east, Apollo on the west. These are the inferences that produced the reconstructed pediments now on display in the Olympia Museum.

The temple itself is one of the most impressive ruins of the ancient world, with its massive column-drums lying in gigantic slices where the earthquake toppled them. The columns were thirty-two Doric feet high, the space between them sixteen feet; the triglyphs were spaced eight feet apart on centers, the lion's head waterspouts were four feet apart, the marble roof tiles were two feet wide; lead plates were set into the temple's upper step, to mark the space between columns accurately. This precision, this meticulously proportionate use of modules, is one of the things we mean by "classical."

Pausanias saw in the cella the gold and ivory statue of Zeus enthroned, forty feet high, a masterpiece of the Athenian Phidias, friend of Pericles, sculptor in charge of the Parthenon, and the most famous artist of his age. The Zeus is lost; the bedding for the pedestal remains, and in front of it a large sunken rectangle in the cella floor which once contained a pool of oil, its function to reflect the statue and perhaps counteract the humidity and keep the ivory from cracking.

West of the temple is a Byzantine church built on the ruins of a classical building. The Germans noticed as long ago as 1876 that its dimensions matched those of the temple cella, and deduced that it might occupy the site of Phidias' workshop. This brilliant deduction was confirmed in 1955-56, when further excavation in the area of the church revealed a pit for bronze-casting, the slag from it, earth pigments, lumps of modeling plaster, bits of worked bone, ivory, lead, bronze, iron, and obsidian (our first evidence for the use of the latter for decoration in classical times), and such sculptors' tools as the spatula and burin. The pottery (a fragment by the Kleophon painter) confirms a late date —after 438—for Phidias' gold and ivory statue of Zeus. Most interesting and important of all was the discovery of a whole series of terracotta molds, over which thin sheets of gold could be hammered to make the statue's drapery. Some of these are marked with serial letters on the back to indicate their place in the pattern. South of the workshop another long, low building proved to have housed subsidiary workrooms, late fifth century in date. There the most interesting find was the core of an elephant tusk from which the ivory for repair of the statue had been cut.

Naturally the great interest of Olympia apart from the temple of Zeus is in the stadium where the footraces were run. (The hippodrome, for chariot races, was long ago silted over and destroyed by the floods of the Alpheus River. Simply in the ten-year lapse imposed upon the new excavations by the war, the river deposited a layer of silt a meter thick on part of the site.) The vaulted passage that connected the stadium with the Altis was excavated as long ago as 1878, and thought to be Roman; not until the new excavations did its level and the bonding of its walls prove it to be a rare example of Hellenistic vaulting, of the third or second century B.C. In 1880-81 the excavators found the stadium starting blocks, of marble, with grooves a few inches apart. There were similar blocks at the far end, 192 meters or 640 feet away. Since the stade, the unit of distance for Olympic footraces, was 600 Greek feet, this implies a "foot" of just over thirteen inches, a unit of some importance for settling the modules and proportions of temples. Since the Greeks were an individualistic race, their foot unit varied from city to city, and Athens, for example, did not use the same unit as Olympia.

The nineteenth-century excavators did not have the funds for moving the 70,000 cubic meters of earth that would have been required to uncover the whole stadium, but the task has been undertaken since (1937-42, 1952-60) and proved well worth the trouble and expense for what it revealed about the stadium plan, and because of the intrinsic interest of the finds. The excavators found that the stadium evolved through five phases. In the first two (sixth and fifth centuries), it opened directly onto the Altis, so that the races were held in sight of the great temples, establishing the closest possible link between the games and the gods in whose honor the contestants vied for the crown of wild olive. In the fourth century, as athletics grew more and more professionalized, and Philip of Macedon built the Echo Portico on the east side of the Altis, the stadium was closed off from the sacred precinct forever. The seats were set in graded earth, taking advantage on the north of the slope of the Hill of Kronos, but artificial and expensive on the south. The ends were square, not curved as in Roman and modern stadia.

Even more interesting were the finds from the stadium.

Apparently victors in battle hung trophies of armor on the embankments above the track. As the archaic ones grew to look more and more old-fashioned, they were discarded, and the embankments raised above them. The result is the finest collection of archaic armor known anywhere: helmets (including one dedicated by the great Miltiades, victor over the Persians at Marathon in 490), breastplates, greaves, and shields. The bronze arm-straps on the backs of the shields were decorated in relief with scenes that add up to an anthology of Greek myth, a notable addition to the repertory of armorial devices of noble clans; they shed—because the shields were dedications for victory—some new light on Greek history. The armor is an interesting index to the progressive refinement of archaic Greek life, until the fine edging and delicate engraving prompt us to call this not armor but military millinery.

Both the earlier and the more recent excavations unearthed numerous inscriptions—over 500—that connect archaeology vitally with literature when, as in two cases, the persons named are the heroes of odes of Pindar; and with history, as when the Hellenistic diplomat-historian Polybius is mentioned. One, written on a rough 316-pound block of red sandstone, records that a certain Bybon threw the block over his head with one hand. Some bases belonging to statues of Zeus, at least a baker's dozen of them, were dedicated from the fines of athletes who had cheated. Time's irony has spared few of the statues, but there must have been a forest of them in the Altis in its fifth-century prime (see the model, Fig. 5.1). The new excavations did turn up parts of three fine groups in terracotta, which had been acroteria or ridgepole ornaments of smallish buildings, perhaps of treasuries. There are an archaic warrior; Zeus carrying off Ganymede to be his cupbearer in Heaven ("the finest boy's head in all Greek sculpture," says its proud excavator); an exquisite head of Athena; and, in solid bronze, the taut, fiery beauty of a small-scale chariot horse, all in the severe style of 490-460.

On the western side of the Altis, excavation revealed the gymnasium and palaestra, for the athletes to train in; they arrived a month before the games. The amenities included a practice track shaded by a portico from the hot July and August sun, storage rooms for oil, sand, and apparatus, and rooms with benches for the gossip of spectator-sportsmen. There was a hostel (the Leonidaion) for distinguished vis-

itors, a council house with double apsidal ends reflecting the
building techniques of an age far earlier than the fifth century, and hot baths with radiant heating, reflecting the decadence of an age far later, but still not Roman—about 250
B.C., the earliest such baths known in Greece.

Archaeology, by nearly ninety years of patient, intelligent
work on temple and sculptures, stadium and palaestra, inscriptions and armor, has made extraordinarily real for us
the setting of the ancient Olympic games, where champions
from the whole Greek world contended in chariot and foot-
race, pentathlon and race in armor. The ancient Olympics
were conducted under a Truce of God. War in our time has
passed over the Altis, but spared its treasures—packed in
sand in the museum—and even added to them, for excavation continued during the Nazi occupation. A site that had
endured Nero proved impervious too to storm-troopers. And
when German scholars took up the work again after the
war, in amity with their Greek colleagues, the spade proved
in the long run mightier than the sword. And thanks to
the work of the spade, when one visits Olympia now in
August at the time of the great fair, with the noise, the
singing, the lamplight, the hucksters asleep in their stalls,
the donkeys braying all night long tethered in the dry, pebbly
bed of the Alpheus, the gap between the fifth century and
now seems not so great after all.

The glory of Olympia and of the fifth century in general
is its architectural sculpture. Free-standing statues are rare,
and full-scale bronze sculpture rarer still: until the late
1920's the Delphic charioteer stood practically alone. Therefore it was thrilling when the announcement came that
chance and the sea had yielded up another. In April, 1926,
fishermen from the island of Skiathos sweeping the Bay of
Artemisium north of Euboea got their nets inextricably
fouled at twenty-five fathoms on an object which proved to
be a bronze statue. Unable to dislodge it after repeated div-
ing, they broke off an arm to prove their good faith and
carried it triumphantly back to Skiathos. In September, 1928,
sponge-divers, with no more equipment than a stone to
weight them, contrived to dislodge the torso. Fortunately
the authorities got wind of it in time, and the statue is now
a treasure of the National Museum in Athens (Fig. 5.3). It
is still known as the "Zeus" of Artemisium; however, as long
ago as 1931 careful analysis of the right hand suggested

Fig. 5.3 Athens, National Museum. Bronze god found in
sea off Artemisium. (Alison Frantz)

that it was curved not to clutch a thunderbolt, the attribute of Zeus, but to balance a shaft, like Poseidon's trident. But the superb figure has no need of an attribute for us to know he is a god. The superb vitality, the perfect balance (the spread of the arms matches the superhuman height to within a centimeter), the amplification of the essential planes (as when the crook of the right arm matches the bend of the left knee), the refinement of detail (as in the treatment of the beard in flamelike locks) are all characteristic of a period of Greek sculpture that has neither the hieratic stiffness of the archaic nor the sunny realism of the ripe classical, but is a blend of both. Art historians call it the severe style, and careful comparison with similar figures on painted vases proves that it is at home in the years between 460 and 447. No one knows, though there are many guesses, where it came from nor where it was going when its ship was wrecked; what matters here is that it makes the perfect transition between the Apollo of the Olympia west pediment and the festal procession on the Parthenon frieze.

Such works of art as the Parthenon are not created in an economic vacuum. They cost money, and archaeology can tell us where it came from. Excavation on the Acropolis, after the Greek War of Independence, turned up between the Parthenon and the Erechtheum a number of fragments, eventually mounting to over 100, of lists of place names with amounts attached. These proved to be the audited accounts of the quota (one sixtieth) levied by the treasurers of Athena, out of the total tribute, based on cultivable land or commercial prosperity, annually paid to Athens by the citizens of her Empire. Pericles used any surplus to beautify the Acropolis. He was criticized for it; the critics are dust, the beauty is still there—or in the British Museum. The accounts cover the forty years 454-414; thereafter the empire's expenses were defrayed by a 5 per cent tax on seaborne commerce. The accounts, originally inscribed on four sides of a series of marble slabs (*stelae*), the first one nearly twelve feet high, were reconstructed, wrongly, in the last century. In 1927-28 two American scholars took them apart in the Epigraphical Museum and built them up again correctly (Fig. 5.4). They have written four stout volumes about them, a monument of epigraphical learning. Their labors produced an accurate map of the Athenian empire, a gazetteer of 265 cities. The amount of a city's

Fig. 5.4 Athens, Epigraphical Museum, tribute list of 440/39, as joined by Meritt. It includes the lists for Ionia, the Hellespont, and Thrace. (Kirchner, *Imagines*, No. 34, by permission of Gebrüder Mann, Berlin)

quota is a gauge of its relative importance: thus Aegina pays 600 times as much as the barren Aegean island of Rheneia. (But Aegina was an enemy, and Rheneia's temple lands may have been tax-exempt, so the matter is complicated.) Only 50 per cent to 65 per cent of the tributary cities paid in any one year: the average annual revenue was under 400 talents—$500,000, with a purchasing power far greater. By the twelfth year bureaucrats had arranged the list geographically: Ionia, the Hellespont, Thrace, Caria, the Islands. In 425/4, after Pericles' death and under the stress of war, the assessment was doubled or tripled; unfortunately the inscription is fragmentary, experts still disagree, and the ordinarily accurate historian of the war, Thucydides, is silent.

However interesting these details may be in themselves, the important point is the use of the surplus to beautify the Acropolis. The nineteenth century stereotyped the Athenians into impractical dreamers. On the contrary, they kept meticulous building accounts, which survive, for the Parthenon, its cult statue, and the Erechtheum, and archaeologists have found, too, the specifications for the great west gate, the Propylaea. The accounts show that citizens, resident aliens, and slaves all worked side by side, and that all received equal pay for equal work. The achievements of Periclean Athens cannot be explained or dismissed by a scornful reference to "slave labor."

One other inscription bears on the great fifth-century Acropolis building program. In 1959 an American scholar recognized in a schoolhouse in Troizen, thirty miles east-southeast of Argos, where the Athenian women and children took refuge from the Persians in 480 B.C., a stone that purports to be in an early third-century copy the decree putting into execution Themistocles' evacuation plan for Athens and his battle plan for Artemisium and Salamis. The Persians sacked and burned the Acropolis. When the Athenians returned after the victory of Salamis, they at first vowed to leave the temples in ruins as a memorial to Persian *Schrecklichkeit*. It was only later, in 447, after the final peace with Persia was signed, that Pericles decided to use the tribute surplus for a public works program: Phidias as over-all designer, Ictinus as architect, and Callicrates as contractor began work on the most famous of all Greek buildings, the Parthenon, the temple of the maiden goddess, Athena, Athens' patron saint.

Since the emphasis of this book is on the history of archaeological discovery, not on the appreciation of art, discussion of the Parthenon here may best emphasize three matters: the work of Lord Elgin's agents, Penrose's analysis of the architectural refinements, and the painstakingly scientific repairs of the 1930's.

Lord Elgin, British ambassador to Turkey, had originally intended simply to have drawings and casts made, a task rendered difficult enough by Turkish objections to scaffolding, which, they said, would make visible to infidels the harem ensconced in the Erechtheum. Besides, "mercenary and insolent janissaries" stood perpetual guard over the draftsmen. At the time (1799) the Acropolis was covered with Turkish houses, the Parthenon boasted a minaret, and a small mosque encumbered the cella floor. It was not long since the Turkish officer in command had been the chief of the black eunuchs, a native of Borneo. However Greek patriots may fulminate at Elgin's "depredations," the fact was that under Turkish rule the marbles were deteriorating rapidly. For example, a drawing of 1674 shows twenty figures in the west pediment. The Venetian mortar that blew up the Turkish powder magazine in the Parthenon, on the evening of September 26, 1687, destroyed some of these, and knocked down a number of columns. Twelve pedimental figures were left in 1749, only four in 1800. When the Sultan, pleased at the British defeat of Napoleon in Egypt, gave Lord Elgin a free hand to remove "miscellaneous marbles" from the Acropolis, the ambassador could justify himself as a philanthropist interested in preserving priceless art, quite apart from his wanting Greek marbles to decorate a house he was building in Scotland, and quite independently of his later argument that to have the marbles in Britain would be "to the advantage of manufactures, whose progress depends upon progress in the arts." Lord Byron, a philhellene, disagreed, remarking, *"Quod non fecerunt Goti, fecerunt Scoti,"* which might be rendered "Scots rushed in where Goths did fear to tread." Metopes were lowered from the temple by a ship's carpenter, "with a windlass cordage, and twenty Greeks." When the Venetians had tried this with the pedimental sculpture in 1687, a priceless figure had fallen from the sling and been smashed to bits; the operation was then called off "for fear of loss of life." It took a gun-carriage and sixty men to get each metope down the Acropolis ramp; only the difficulty of transport caused Lord Elgin to satisfy himself with a single Caryatid from the Erechtheum porch;

what he really wanted was to dismantle the whole porch and carry it off bodily. The precious, cumbersome marbles suffered every vicissitude en route from Athens to London. One consignment was shipwrecked; Lord Elgin himself suffered imprisonment in France for three years, and it was not till 1814 that the sculptures were finally displayed in London, in a special museum in Park Lane. Flaxman and Canova, to their eternal credit, refused to restore them. Sculptors and architects, used to nothing but Roman copies, were ecstatic; the drapery was imitated in a portrait of Macbeth, and milliners capitalized on the craze: the *Times* advertised a "Grecian volute headdress." Meanwhile Lord Elgin's finances suffered a reverse, and he offered to sell his marbles to the British government. After much Parliamentary debate they were bought in 1816 for £35,000, and installed in the British Museum.

Meanwhile, the architectural refinements of the Parthenon itself engaged attention. They were first noticed in 1814 by Allason and "Grecian" Cockerell (of Aegina fame); the first accurate measurements were taken by F. C. Penrose in 1845. What interested him was systematic deviation from ordinary rectilineal construction: curvature, inclination of columns, entasis (swelling) of columns, optical corrections. He found that the Parthenon architects were aware of the tendency of any curve in proximity to a straight line to distort that line into an apparent reverse curve. Therefore, Penrose found, the architects caused the Parthenon's stylobate, or upper step, to curve upward from the horizontal (like a slightly billowing handkerchief pinned at the corners) by precisely 228 millimeters, or 1/1,000th of its length, the curve of a circle with a radius of three and a half miles. On the long sides the curve was a little more pronounced. The columns were slightly cigar shaped, attaining their maximum entasis (eleven sixteenths of an inch) two fifths of the way up. The door jambs showed entasis, too. The corner columns incline so slightly that their upward lines, projected, would converge a mile and a half in the air. The architraves curved to correspond to the stylobate. The curvature was achieved by countersinking the corners of the stylobate into the old foundations, which proves that the effect was not accidental, but designed. The same loving care was lavished throughout the building. The metopes were graded in size, the widest in the center of each side. The processional frieze was carved as carefully as though it were to be seen at eye level, and not from thirty-nine feet below by craning the neck. The back of the pedimental sculpture, unlike that at Olympia, was carefully finished, though it would never be seen. These refinements were worked out as the masons went along, not always with complete success: the pedimental space at the west end was miscalculated, and some figures had to be hacked to set them closer. And in the Parthenon the Athenians showed themselves, as Pericles called them, "lovers of beauty with economy," for the temple was planned to reuse as far as possible the valuable blocks from its predecessor destroyed by the Persians.

All this time, though the Turkish accretions were removed, the fabric of the Parthenon remained very much in the state in which the 1687 bombardment had left it, though all but six of the fallen column-drums of the north flank were extant. Finally, between 1922 and 1933, the Greek government entrusted N. Balanos with the re-erection of the columns and the discreet repair of the building. All the drums belonging to the same columns, Balanos found, had been marked in antiquity with an identical letter in red, and red strokes, I, II, III, etc., indicated the order of the drums. Complicated and ingenious scaffolding held up the architraves while the columns beneath were repaired. Where drums were missing, cement proved to provide a better match than new marble, which would not weather like the old, while all artificial patinas were washed off by the rain. New drums were therefore built up with cement on iron reinforcing rods, and ancient marble flutes readjusted on the cement core. New architrave blocks were slid into place on oil. New sections of capitals were fitted in with mortise and tenon joints. Capitals were turned 180° to put the handsomer unweathered sides facing out. Following what he found to be the ancient example, Balanos reinforced some front architrave blocks with iron bars, discreetly cut into the back of the block and hidden by the architrave backers. Where marble was used, it was cut as far as possible from the same quarries as those used in antiquity. The lintel and jambs of the great west door (its twin on the east would have admitted 440 square feet of light into the cella with its cult statue) were replaced, the east pediment was braced, and some fragments discovered in the nineteenth century were restored to it. By 1930, the centenary of Greek independence, the north flank was ready, and by 1933 all had been done that could be to the worse-damaged south flank. Short of actual resto-

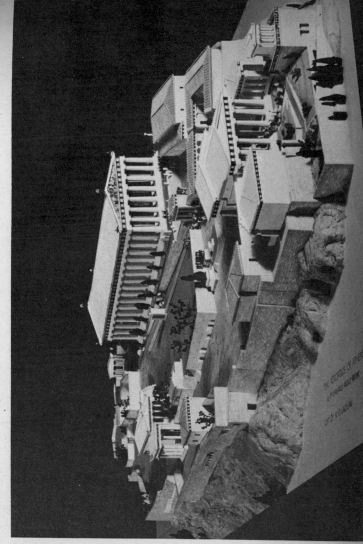

Fig. 5.5 Athens, Acropolis, model, from northwest. Panathenaic procession winds its way up ramp, through Propylaea, and approaches Parthenon. (Royal Ontario Museum, Toronto)

ration, which would have been a mistake, the Parthenon is now as complete as it can ever be, and handsomer than it has been since 1687. For this the world owes Balanos a great debt.

The glory of the Parthenon is not only its architecture but its sculpture, which it is not the business of this book to describe or evaluate in detail. Thanks to Lord Elgin, most of it, including 247 of the surviving 420 feet of the frieze, is not in Athens but in London. It was hidden in a subway during World War II, remained there until 1948, and was then replaced in the British Museum at eye level, where we can appreciate its detail better than anyone since its sculptors carved it *in situ* 2400 years ago, though the grime of London has taken a sad toll from the beauty of the stone.

Archaeologists have fixed the date of the sculpture within narrow limits. We have ancient evidence that the work began in 447. The metopes must have been carved first, since they had to be slipped into their slots before the roof went on. The frieze must also have preceded the roof. We have building accounts for the pediments in 438/7 and in 434/3. The metopes, then, are early, the pediments late; the frieze falls between, overlapping both; the whole was finished in fifteen years. Phidias could not possibly have done all the carving himself, and indeed between seventy-five and eighty different hands have been distinguished in the frieze, but the over-all design bears the mark of one distinctive hand, and that must have been Phidias'.

The metopes, now in ruinous condition, were in high relief. Working round the compass to describe their subjects, we may note that they were canonical examples of impiety, violence, pride, and folly: the sack of Troy, gods against giants, Lepiths against centaurs, Greeks versus Amazons.

The frieze begins in the southwest corner. It contains the figures of over 400 people and 200 animals, and represents the Panathenaic procession bringing, as it did every four years, the new sacred robe or peplos to Athena. In the new Royal Ontario Museum model (Fig. 5.5) the frieze figures have been made three-dimensional and the actual procession reproduced. Parallel lines of horsemen, chariots, elders, musicians, tray- and pitcher-bearers (Fig. 5.6), and sacrificial animals converge upon the east front, where, in the presence of the gods—Hephaestus has a thick ankle and a stick; Eros holds a parasol over Aphrodite—of citizens, and of magistrates, the maidens who wove the peplos present it to the goddess.

Fig. 5.6 Athens, Acropolis Museum, four boys carrying water pots, from Parthenon north frieze. (Alison Frantz)

The center of the east pediment was ruined, probably in the fifth century A.D., to make a Christian apse, but we know its subject from Pausanias: it was the birth of Athena, full-armed from the forehead of Zeus. The bizarre subject is reproduced in vase-painting: Hephaestus stands with the ax with which he has just cloven the skull of the father of gods and men, in the presence of gods and goddesses (showing various degrees of surprise), perhaps the three Fates, and the chariots of the sun and moon. The Dionysus or Theseus of this pediment is strikingly paralleled in Michelangelo's Creation of Adam on the Sistine Chapel ceiling.

The west pediment was badly damaged by the 1687 explosion, but its details have been ingeniously conjectured from reliefs on a wellhead in Madrid. The subject was the contest of Athena and Poseidon for Attica. The sacred olive was the focal point; the contestants' partisans look on: there are Iris, the gods' rainbow-messenger, the river-god

Ilissus, chariots and horses. The whole scene vibrates with excitement; the art of placing and interrelating figures organically in a pediment has come a long way since Corcyra and Aegina.

On the Parthenon the relevance of sculptured subjects to the temple and of pediment, frieze, and metopes to each is closer than elsewhere. The Acropolis itself is the scene of the contest on the west pediment; the anniversary of Athena's birth on the east pediment is the occasion for the procession in the frieze; the peplos represented in the frieze bore, woven upon it, the battle of gods and giants of the east metopes. Gods in the round occupy the pediments, heroes in high relief the metopes, men and women (the human world on a sacred building, a bold innovation) the frieze. The frieze is perhaps our best surviving example of ripe classicism in Greek art. In it, the gods are benevolent and cheerfully served, the subject is treated with sunny realism, the style shows linear economy and a pattern symmetrical without being stiff. Content and style reflect men: Pericles' statesmanship, Phidias' taste. We may take the dramatist Sophocles, who was the contemporary of both, as symbolizing the spirit of the frieze. One feels that the frieze figures were, like him, active citizens, men about town, lovers of food, wine, and company, both sophisticated and devout. The frieze depicts men who were both human and humane. It is the tragedy of Western history that the cultures that produce such people and such art have always had so brief a time of flowering: the age of Pericles lasted little more than twenty years.

Not the Parthenon but the "Theseum," overlooking the Agora, is the most perfectly preserved temple of the age. American archaeologists, especially since 1939, have added much to our knowledge of it. Excavation south of the temple has uncovered so many pits for bronze-casting that an inference is clear: this was a bronze-caster's quarter: their patron was the smith-god Hephaestus, and this temple must have been his, a Hephaisteion, not a Theseum. One of the finds from this quarter was a bronze shield, a dedication of the Athenians after their victory over the Spartans at Sphacteria, the victory commemorated by Athens' allies in the Nike of Paeonius at Olympia.

In 1939, too, the Americans excavated the temple footings. They found ancient graves and other deposits of pottery ranging in date from Sub-Mycenaean to about 450, but none later, and also more modern graves, for the Turks allowed Protestants to be buried here, among them Haller von Hallerstein, the excavator of Aegina. (Catholics were buried in the grounds of the Capuchin convent by the Tower of the Winds.) The excavators also found that the stucco on the inner walls of the cella had been intended to receive paintings, for the walls were sealed behind with lead to keep out dampness. But the project was abandoned when it was decided to equip the cella, in the newer fashion, with an interior colonnade that would block frescoes from view. Besides this, American archaeologists and Greek technicians in the summer of 1953 carefully cleaned the east frieze, revealing a battle of Greeks and barbarians of very high artistic quality. Fourteen years earlier, the American excavators in the Agora had turned up fragments of sculpture, now in the Agora Museum, of a size and style to fit the temple's east pediment, which faced the Agora. Acrobatic work high up in the pediment itself, examining the cuttings, made conjecture about subject and arrangement possible. It was a peaceful subject, appropriate to an east pediment; probably Heracles, in the presence of his patroness Athena, ending one of his labors by bringing the golden apples of the Hesperides to Zeus. To the roof ornament or acroterion above has been plausibly assigned a pair of figures, one woman (a Hesperid?) carrying another on her back, the earliest life-size marble acroterion in the history of Greek art. Much later, in the third century B.C., the Hephaisteion area was landscaped, perhaps to represent the Garden of the Hesperides: the Americans found the rectangular holes for planting, some with flower-pots still in them, in formal rows on three sides of the temple. Modern landscaping (Fig. 5.7) attempts to reproduce the original.

The metopes, too, portrayed the labors of Heracles, including that favorite theme, which we saw also in the Sele and Olympia metopes, the unloading of the boar upon Eurystheus cowering in his jar. As on the Athenian Treasury at Delphi, Heracles receives in the pediment the reward of apotheosis for completing the labors portrayed in the metopes below.

The pottery dates the temple after 450; the sculptural style suggests dates interlocking with the Parthenon, with influences working both ways; the cella colonnade is experimental. All this points to a date between 449 and 444, after the peace with Persia and revenue from the empire made

Fig. 5.7 Athens, Hephaisteion, from southwest, with pomegranate and myrtle shrubs set in the ancient planting holes (ASCS, Athens)

temple-building feasible. The American archaeologists have noted similarities of dimension, materials, and technique that would assign three other temples to the Hephaisteion architect: the strikingly placed temple of Poseidon overlooking the sea atop the rocky promontory of Sunium (where another column was re-erected in 1959); the temple of Ares in the Agora (see page 241), whose cornice-blocks are interchangeable with those of the Hephaisteion; and the temple of Nemesis at Rhamnus in north Attica, left unfinished at the outbreak of the Peloponnesian War in 432. Of the four, modern archaeology has been able to tell us most about the Hephaisteion, because it is the best preserved. It owes its preservation to its having been made over, perhaps in the fourth century A.D., into a Christian church. Archaeologists debit the Christians with the disfigurement of the Parthenon east pediment, but they credit them with the present state of the Hephaisteion. The church was dedicated to St. George the Untiring, himself, like the Heracles of his predecessor's temple, a slayer of monsters.

The Hephaisteion belongs to an early stage of a great building program that later produced the Propylaea, or entrance gate to the Acropolis. The Propylaea was begun in 437, to employ such masons as were no longer needed on the nearly finished Parthenon. Recent work upon it by a Danish architect, published in 1956, emphasizes two things: it was conditioned by previous buildings on the same site, and its virtues and defects are due, it is claimed, not so much to its architect, Mnesicles, as to the craftsmen who worked out its problems empirically as they built. The entrance was oriented on the colossal statue of Athena Promachos, which stood northwest of the Parthenon (the point of Athena's spear could be seen by ships approaching from Sunium). But a cutting in the rock shows that an earlier entrance, differently oriented, determined the location of Mnesicles' passageway. He was not a free creator: his job was to reproduce, with additions. Both for Mnesicles and for his craftsmen convention was the blueprint. From the west (Fig. 5.8) the building looks as though it had external unity, a central passageway between symmetrical wings. But the wings are not in fact symmetrical. The dimensions of the northwest wing, the so-called Pinacotheca, or picture gallery, may be predetermined by an archaic apsidal building (like the Bouleuterion at Olympia) underneath it, while the southwest wing is a mere façade only four meters deep; its southward extension was blocked by a Mycenaean wall forty-four feet high, and by the bastion on which was to stand a new temple of the Wingless Victory. The decision to build the Nike temple must have been made after the Propylaea was started, for the communicating stairs are makeshift, and have a gate post on one side only.

The central block, which has interior Ionic columns, is deeper on the west than on the east, because Mnesicles was bound by the dimensions of an earlier building, but he made a virtue of the necessity by providing benches in the western room where pilgrims might rest while waiting for the Acropolis gates to be opened.

To judge from the analogy of later building-inscriptions, Mnesicles probably provided his masons not with detailed plans, but with general descriptions of the work to be done. The exact measurements of the superstructure were perhaps not determined until after the euthynteria or leveling course had been laid. In fact, once the ground plan was marked out on a site, a Greek building more or less built itself. That the west front of the Propylaea is related in scale and appearance to the Parthenon is probably due less

Fig. 5.8 Athens, Propylaea, model, with end of Panathenaic procession. Left, picture gallery; r., Nike temple,
with sculptured balustrade. Behind Nike temple, Mycenaean
wall reduces south wing of Propylaea to shallow façade.
(Royal Ontario Museum)

to Mnesicles' planning than to the fact that his masons had worked on the Parthenon. Again, the west porch and the central building are on different levels, and the join between them at the roof line is totally without artifice, as though Mnesicles had never faced the problem, but left it to his masons to work out when they came to it. Some of the blocks have complicated cuttings. This looks extravagant, but a mason knows that it is really cheaper than splitting the block. The masons were careful workmen: they might spend from 50 to 110 working days on a single column, cutting the taper in the masons' yard, the inclination and the entasis during erection, last of all the fluting. To produce the entasis, they probably used an immensely long ruler (thirty feet or more) of pliant wood marked with red lead. Their only other instruments were the cord, plumb bob, level, and square. They had to work with column-drums not of uniform thickness, since this would be determined by the strata of marble in the quarry. Work under these conditions is much more creative than following a mechanical drawing, and a successful result depended on the traditional training in his craft of the artisan, who had a much freer hand than now (though good craftsmen today show a fine scorn of architects' blueprints). Greek architectural refinements, this late research suggests, come not as much from architects' drawings as from accurate execution by skilled craftsmen of principles that applied to every building. The architects were the organizers, and they deserve great credit for that, but the real artists were the masons: perhaps this is why not many ancient architects' names survive.

If it was the new Nike temple that blocked the symmetrical southward expansion of the Propylaea wing, that diminutive Ionic building must be dated 427-24, rather in the hope than in the possession of victory, for the Athenians were then locked in a death struggle with Sparta, with victory assured to neither side. But archaeologists have found remains of Mycenaean and archaic sanctuaries below the temple: it may have been the sanctity of these that limited Mnesicles. In that case the Nike temple need not be dated so early. Whatever its date, it suffered strange vicissitudes: the Turks dismantled it completely in 1685 and re-used its blocks in fortification walls. The liberated Greeks rebuilt it in 1835 with more enthusiasm than accuracy; Balanos, and, on his retirement, Orlandos dismantled and rebuilt it between 1935 and 1940. Its chief interest for us lies in what modern

American archaeologists have been able to tell us about its sculptured balustrade, the slabs of which were found in and after 1835, and are now in the Acropolis Museum. Considerations of subject, style, the spacing of dowel holes, the angles at which slabs were mitered to meet, and cuttings for water channels have made it possible to reconstruct the order of the parapet sculptures. They began in the northeast corner, where, as a pilgrim ascended the little stair from the Propylaea, he found a Nike in relief ascending the stair beside him. As on the Parthenon frieze, the figures on two sides (north and south) move symmetrically toward a central point (here on the west) where a ritual act is performed in the presence of Athena. Each long face portrayed four trophies, decorated with armor by Victories, and each face had a central sacrificial altar in relief, flanked by attendants. Most interesting of all, each long side was apparently assigned to two sculptors, some of them masterly, whose hands can be distinguished. The masterpiece is the Sandal-binder from the south face (Fig. 5.9), poised marvelously on one foot, her drapery, as a poetic German writes, "in whispering harmony with the melody of a beautiful body," the catenary folds radiating fanwise from the left shoulder and dipping lower and lower till they overlap the vertical folds of the chiton at the bottom, which serve as a foil, a plumb line to remind us of the vertical, and of the fact that the Nike's lovely stance is off balance. This art justly reminds its best critic, Rhys Carpenter, of a flower just in blossom, not yet full blown. Though it is timeless, archaeologists are sticklers for dates. History would suggest, for such emphasis on victory, a date between the Peace of Nicias in 421 and the resumption of hostilities in 415. But the style points rather to a date toward 407, when, under the arrogant Alcibiades, the Athenians were boundlessly but unreasonably optimistic.

Alcibiades apparently was responsible for the continuation of the work on the jewel of the Acropolis, the temple called the Erechtheum, for inscriptions record the details (in up to 2650 lines for a single year) of work resumed on the temple in 409, when he was in power. The temple had been begun probably in 421 during a breathing space in the Peloponnesian War, and work abandoned when the tide turned against Athens in the years after 415. Some of the inscriptions are in Athens; one, now in the British Museum, was discovered by the English traveler Chandler in 1765, and carried down from the Acropolis "by the strongest horse in

Fig. 5.9 Athens, Acropolis Museum.
Sandal-binder from Nike temple balustrade. (Alison Frantz)

Athens, while the Turks were at their devotions."

The inscriptions are noteworthy for their meticulous detail, and for the evidence they give about division of
labor. Expenses are recorded for such items as sacrifices,

paper, whitened boards for recording the accounts, gold leaf, lead, struts, gutters, and oiling; wagons and mules. Among the artisans are woodworkers, gilders, masons, carriers-up of paint pots, workers of block-and-tackle, dismantlers of scaffolding, wax-modelers, painters, and sculptors (who were paid up to sixty drachmae per figure; a drachma was a day's wage for skilled labor).

This division of labor reflects the refinements of the building, which American archaeologists had an opportunity to study while Balanos was repairing it (1902-09). It was complicated to begin with by the requirements of piety. Built on the site of the Mycenaean palace, it occupied the holy spots where Poseidon struck his trident, and Athena caused the sacred olive to spring up (a spindly olive, planted in 1917, struggles to grow on the west side). From the architect's point of view, the trouble was that these holy spots differed in level by over ten feet. His solution to the problem produced the most unusual building in the history of Greek architecture, on two levels (Fig. 5.10), with four porticoes, four entrances, and four rooms, of which the central two have different floor levels. Space was limited on the south by the footings of the ruined Old Temple of Athena. What would have been the west porch in a normal temple had to be shifted round to the north to avoid the sanctuary of Cecrops, the mythical first king of Athens, so holy that no rainwater was allowed to drip on it from the temple roof; then, to balance the North Porch, the architect conceived the most extraordinary innovation of all, the Caryatid Porch, in which six maidens, sisters to the peplos-weavers in the Parthenon frieze, support the roof with the proud dignity with which Mediterranean women still carry burdens on their heads. All but one are in marble; the second from the west is a cast; the original has been missing since 1803, when Lord Elgin had it shipped to London. The Greeks under the Turkish occupation believed that the maidens had been turned to stone by enchantment, which would pass when Greece was free. No two maidens are alike—one, for example, has pierced ears—and they are irregularly spaced. Their hands are broken away; complete exact copies found in 1954 at Hadrian's Villa at Tivoli, near Rome, show that they held *paterae*, sacrificial saucers. Their hair style, thick at the back of the neck, is functional; without it, they could not support the weight of the architrave. The architrave is enriched with rosettes, but they are not all finished, mute

Fig. 5.10 Athens, Erechtheum from west, showing levels. At left, North Porch; center, sacred olive replanted; right, Caryatids. At r. edge, northeast corner of Parthenon. (Alison Frantz)

evidence to Athens' financial crisis and the loss of the Peloponnesian War.

The differences in detail among the Caryatids are refinements, which American archaeologists have assiduously studied throughout the building. The columns, doors, and windows are all inclined slightly inward; the columns of the North Porch show the subtlest entasis; there is beading round the top of each flute; the eye of the Ionic volutes (spiral scrolls) is countersunk to receive a flat bronze disk; the volutes are deep-cut for *chiaroscuro*; their outer face is set with forked bronze pins to hold garlands for holidays. The bottom column moldings, a guilloche or ropelike plaited pattern of interwoven fillets, were set with colored glass, blue, red, yellow, and purple. The moldings have mitered corners; the *anthemia* (moldings under the architrave) show nine different lotus-and-palmette patterns. The frieze, of dark Eleusis stone, had its figures doweled against it in contrasting white marble, giving the effect of Wedgwood jasper ware. The sumptuous surround of the North Porch door is enriched with bead-and-reel, rosettes, and tongue-and-dart patterns, but the rich volutes under the lintel are nonfunctional, since the lintel (coarser work, a piece of Roman repair) is carved in a projecting wall-block. Painted meanders framed each wooden ceiling-coffer; the marble ones had egg-and-dart surroundings, and metal rosettes centered in each. The space between the egg-and-dart moldings of the Porch of the Maidens was pierced on the south to let water run off; the roof joints were sealed with lead. The marble coffer-blocks were cut away above to reduce the bearing weight, which was unusually heavy, for the marble beams of the North Porch have the remarkable span of nineteen feet. In the North Porch roof a hole was piously left to admit sun-light onto some mysterious marks in the bedrock below, probably believed to be the marks of a thunderbolt, for the "sea" miraculously produced by Poseidon's trident was probably in the narrow west portico. If the columns on the west side had been built up from ground level, they would have been grotesquely out of proportion; the wall was there-fore carried up to the appropriate height below. Three of the columns are Roman work; when a hurricane struck in 1852, these were the only parts of the building that did not withstand it.

The hand of man has been crueler than nature to the Erechtheum. The Byzantines knocked out the inner cross-walls to make a church, of which the Porch of the Maidens was probably the baptistery. For nearly 400 years from 1458 the Erechtheum was a Turkish house, complete with harem; from 1676 it was also a powder magazine. Used as Greek headquarters in 1826-27, it suffered ruinous Turkish bomb-ing; the North Porch collapsed, killing eleven people, whose bodies were still in the rubble in 1832. It was not until 1837 that clearing began.

To discover the elegance of the building well repays the trouble spent upon it. It is a precious jewel box, a reliquary. Many of the refinements would never be noticed; they point up the fact that a Greek temple was built not to edify a congregation, but to honor a god. The Erechtheum especially, with its sumptuous decoration, breaks with the archaic tradi-tion of austere restraint on which Pericles had insisted; it marks a transition toward the more baroque architecture of the fourth century and Hellenistic times.

Excavation in the Agora has revealed its fifth-century plan and produced significant fifth-century finds. For example, one set of objects casts light upon the peculiarly Athenian in-stitution of ostracism, a kind of political safety valve. If any citizen proved unpopular enough to be blackballed by 6000 of his fellows, indicating their preference by scratching his name on a potsherd, he was forced into a ten-year exile, after which he might resume his full civic rights. The thousand-odd ostraka from the Agora include all the victims' names (some amusingly misspelled) recorded in literature, including Aristeides "the Just," Themistocles, Pericles, and Alcibiades, plus many more. Among them are some which give evidence of sharp practice, and help to remind us that the Athenians were more subject to human frailty than the nineteenth-century believed. On these the names were professionally painted on the sherd, hardly a spontaneous procedure, and one which suggests that people with a grudge were present with baskets of previously prepared sherds, ready to help the undecided make up their minds.

The fifth century saw the Persian sack of Athens. Besides the evidence of the destruction of buildings, the Agora dig turned up a Persian Daric, one of the rare gold coins to be found, and a number of Persian arrowheads.

The excavators date about 470 the definitive phase of the Tholos (see plan, Fig. 5.11), a round building with a kitchen attached. Socrates must have eaten and slept in this building when he served as Committeeman for the day. A fifth-century house, near the southwest corner of the Agora, was found to contain hobnails and bone rings—the eyelets for sandal laces. It was obviously the shop of a shoemaker. The excavators found his name incised on a pot. It was Simon, and he takes his modest place in intellectual history when we discover from Diogenes Laertius, a late (A.D. 250-300) biographer of philosophers, that he was a friend of Socrates. Socrates' contemporary, Sophocles the playwright, has his name recorded in an inscribed list, discovered in the Agora in 1937, of competitors in the dramatic competition of 448/7. Socrates' pupil Alcibiades was involved in 415 in a drunken prank, which his enemies exaggerated into a prof-anation of the Eleusinian Mysteries; he was deprived of civil rights and his property confiscated. The excavators found near the southeast corner of the Agora numerous fragments of the inscribed sale list of his furniture. The items inventoried are so ordinary that we must suppose either that rich Athe-nians lived very simply, or that his friends abstracted the best pieces before the authorities arrived. The inscription should have been set up in a context appropriate to the Mysteries, and the excavators inferred, rightly, as it turned out, that its

Fig. 5.11 Athens, fifth-century Agora, plan. Tholos, bottom center. (Agora Excavations)

findspot marked the site of the long-sought-for Athenian Eleusinion, from which the faithful used to set out on their long procession along the Sacred Way to the mother sanctuary in Eleusis. Another Agora inscription is a casualty list of the barbarian bowmen who fell for Athens early in the Peloponnesian War. And on a list of about 460 is carved the name of a casualty who over forty years before had been the toast of Athens for his good looks: the same name was found painted on a sixth-century Agora vase of the kind that middle-aged admirers used to present to handsome Athenian boys.

Among fifth-century buildings one of the most interesting, the Stoa Poikilê (Painted Porch) could not be excavated, since it lay north of the electric railway, outside the American zone. But west of the Stoa of Attalus the Americans found, in reuse in a wall, limestone architectural members which they dated about 460, and which very probably belonged to the Stoa Poikilê, for inserted in them were the iron pins that could have held the grid of scantlings on which the famous paintings, by Polygnotus and others, of battles mythical and historical that gave the Porch its name could have been hung. The Stoa became in Hellenistic times the haunt of philosophers, including Zeno the Stoic, whose philosophical school took its name from the Porch where he held forth.

Another fifth-century building was found in the southeast corner of the Agora in 1953, the last season of large-scale excavation. Since within it were found remains of two furnaces, and water-basins lined with hydraulic cement, and on its floor lay ten bronze disks struck by a chisel from a rod, suitable for use as the flans or blanks for coins, the excavators inferred that they had hit upon the Athenian Mint, a building of great historical interest, since the "owls" struck there were the standard coinage of the whole Levant for over 200 years. The inference was strengthened by an inscription found nearby bearing a decree having to do with coinage.

In 1954 an inscription turned up southwest of the Tholos, containing directions that it be set up "in front of the headquarters of the Generals." Thus another important civic building, the Strategeion, was identified: a large structure of fifth-century date, close to the findspot of the inscription, with a T-shaped courtyard for semipublic meetings, and several smaller rooms, including a dining room, opening off, which could be used for more private sessions. Here met the only Athenian officials not chosen by lot, the board of ten annually elected generals, the most famous of whom was Pericles, who directed the state in its palmiest days by virtue of repeatedly holding this office.

Late in the century (425-410) is dated the building the ex-cavators call South Stoa I, a long double-aisled colonnade fronting a row of sixteen square rooms. Their doors were set off-center, perhaps to allow room for dining couches (Fig. 5.12); each room would thus have accommodated seven. The stoa may, then, have been a restaurant, serving over 100 at a sitting. It may have been used by the dikasts (jurymen) from the adjacent large building to the west, identified as the Heliaea, or People's Court.

The final fifth-century building worthy of mention lies on the Acropolis north slope, outside the Agora proper, but connected with it by a monumental stair. It is the Klepsydra, or fountain house. Over 2800 potsherds were found in it, bits of the pitchers broken by the women at the well. Since the latest of them are early first century, the inference is that the Klepsydra went out of use after Sulla sacked Athens in 86.

In Attica, one of the most fascinating fifth-century com-plexes to be excavated in recent years was discovered by accident in the mid-forties when some men requested per-mission to build a wall near the little old church of St. George at Vraona, ancient Brauron, some twenty-two miles east-southeast of Athens. The request was referred to the Greek Archaeological Service, who dug trial trenches by the church to see if there were any antiquities there, and were more pleasantly surprised than the would-be wall-builders to find that there were. The terrace on which the church stood proved to be ancient, part of the acropolis of Brauron; north of it (see plan, Fig. 5.13) the excavator, Dr. John Papadimitriou, found the wall and five steps of a building, partly under water, for the site was subject to flood-ing and was not successfully pumped out until 1958. The steps reminded Papadimitriou of a passage in Euripides' play about Agamemnon's daughter, the *Iphigeneia in Tauris,* which mentions the "holy steps" of a temple of Artemis at Brauron. The play had its première in 413; Papadimitriou argued that the reference was topical, that he had found the temple, and that it had been fairly new in 413. The dis-covery of an inscription, mentioning the temple, and of

Fig. 5.12 Athens, Agora, South Stoa I, reconstruction drawing of a room arranged to hold seven dining couches. (Agora Excavations)

a kylix, red-figure outside, white-ground inside, both of appropriate date, soon proved him right. Brauron has turned out to be rich in inscriptions, mostly inventories of objects dedicated to the goddess: archaic statues, rings, earrings, cloaks. One inscription, ninety-four lines long, is dated 416/5, about the right date for the temple. Some of the inscriptions are twins to others found on the Athenian Acropolis, near the site of the Athenian Brauronion, the sister sanctuary to the one at Brauron; it lay on the south edge of the holy hill, just southeast of the Propylaea. But the cult of Artemis at Brauron proved to be older than the one in the city; Papadimitriou found sixth-century roof tiles from an earlier temple, and several *bothroi* (sacrificial pits) containing Geometric sherds and bronze and gilt rings. Furthermore, a cave southeast of the temple, explored in 1956, contained Mycenaean and later pottery and might have been revered as Iphigeneia's tomb. She was to have been sacrificed

Fig. 5.13 Brauron (Vraona), sanctuary of Artemis, plan. Left center, the temple; upper right, "bears'": dining room. (*Ergon*, 1960, p. 27, Fig. 36, by permission)

(to obtain for her father's fleet fair winds for Troy) at Aulis, only forty miles northwest (where another fifth-century temple of Artemis has been recently excavated), and still another temple at Halae Araphenides (modern Loutsa), only an hour's walk northeast, was dedicated to Artemis Tauropolos, whom Iphigeneia served as priestess in the far-away Crimea, as described by Euripides in his play. Reliefs found at Brauron portray her and her brother Orestes, whose recognition of her in the Crimea, when he had believed her dead, is the moving climax of the drama. Papadimitriou believes that the play was first performed at Brauron, or at Halae, where the Rural Dionysia were staged.

Brauron has produced hundreds of terracotta figurines, of the goddess, her votaries, and sacrificial animals; they fill drawer after drawer in the storehouse on the site. Perhaps most interesting of all was the discovery, in 1950, in the hundred-foot stoa north of the temple, of a number of charming marble statues and heads of little girls between the ages of five and ten. Inscriptions refer to them as *arktoi*, "bears." The late lexicographer Suidas explains that they were the acolytes of Artemis Brauronia, the "Mistress of Animals," whose cult arose from her demand that the young girls of Attica serve her to atone for the killing of a bear. In 1958, in the northeast corner of the stoa, Papadimitriou found a room with low benches and diminutive tables, where the "bears" presumably ate. The stoa was therefore probably their dormitory. In 1961 a join was made between the presumed head of a "bear" and the torso of what is unmistakably a small boy, so that the assumption now is that small brothers and sisters together served the goddess. Some of the columns—poros, with marble capitals—of their dormitory have been re-erected, and some of their likenesses are on provisional display in the National Museum in Athens. They are among the most enchanting exhibits of that rich treasure-house.

Space permits no more than the bare mention of other fifth-century buildings in and near Athens on which recent archaeological activity has cast light: at Eleusis, the Prytaneum (state dining-room), the House of the Heralds, and the Telesterion or Hall of the Mysteries, enlarged in the Periclean age; in Athens, the Pnyx or assembly place, re-oriented in 404 to turn its back on the traitorous sea; on the south slope of the Acropolis, the shrine of the Nymphs; the fifth-century phase of the Theater of Dionysus and the covered Odeon of Pericles adjoining it; the new rectangular grid evolved for the Piraeus by the famous city-planner, Hippodamus of Miletus. To theaters, city plans, and stoas we shall revert in later chapters; the rest of this chapter must be devoted to what archaeology has to tell us about fifth-century architecture and sculpture in the Peloponnesus and the West.*

The temple in the Peloponnese of which we know most because of modern archaeology is that of Apollo at Bassae (Fig. 5.15). It stands solitary in a heroic landscape, 4000 feet up in the stark Arcadian mountains, until 1959 inaccessible by road. Its first visitor in comparatively modern times

---

* One remarkable structure from elsewhere demands mention: the palace at Vouni, near Soli in Cyprus, excavated by the Swedes in 1927-28. Its earlier phase (Fig. 5.14), dated 500-450, had forty-six rooms, its later (450-380) a hundred. Its excavators ingeniously reconstruct its history. The Persians let a Quisling build the palace to guard Soli after they took it. The Athenian Cimon expelled him in 449; the new occupant, a philhellene, rebuilt the palace in Greek style and ruled until the King of Soli overthrew him forever.

Fig. 5.14 Vouni, Cyprus, fifth-century palace, ground plan, model. (Swedish Cyprus Expedition, III, Fig. 121 by permission of Professor Einar Gjerstad)

Fig. 5.15   Bassae, temple of Apollo.

was the French architect Bocher, who rediscovered it in 1765 while on a tour to relieve the tedium of designing villas on the island of Zante. Returning to the spot a year later, he was murdered by brigands. Haller and Cockerell, fresh from their triumphs at Aegina, worked there in 1811, and Cockerell discovered the first slab of the sculptured frieze, serving as the roof of a foxhole. The Turks were bribed, the twenty-three frieze slabs carried to Zante, and sold at auction to the British Museum for 60,000 Spanish dollars.

One of the recent valuable observations of American archaeology is that the moldings of classical Greek buildings fall into datable sequences; this technique has been used to date the Bassae temple about 420. Pausanias, who never mentions the frieze, attributes the temple to Ictinus, the architect of the Parthenon. New excavations in 1959 revealed the footings of an archaic temple beneath the fifth-century one, together with such copious deposits of worked iron that the temple area of Bassae obviously attracted iron-smiths as that of the Hephaisteion on Athens attracted workers in bronze. The narrow ridge on which the temple lies forced its orientation north and south instead of east and west as usual. The cella has Ionic interior buttresses, except the two diagonal ones at the south end, which, probably had Corinthian capitals, the earliest known. Since the exterior columns are Doric, the temple uses all three orders. Since it was dedicated to Apollo the Healer in time of plague, it has been conjectured that the pious slept in the cella bays, hoping to be cured.

The architecture is limestone, the frieze marble. The sequence of the slabs has posed a fascinating problem, which the brilliant dean of American architectural historians, W. B. Dinsmoor, has worked out entirely by objective structural evidence. He noticed that the frieze slabs in the British Museum have cuttings for clamps, some of which, by a painstaking process of long-distance elimination, can be made to match the corresponding cuttings in the frieze backers lying on the ground at Bassae. He noticed, too, that some backers were thick, some thin. He conjectured that the thick ones fell over the buttresses, the thin ones over the niches. Once he had established the sequence of backers, he could use the evidence of the clamp-cuttings to arrange the frieze slabs in sequence. It helped to notice that some of the slabs had been pared down in antiquity, because they had been carved all the way to the edge, without allowing for overlap. These amputated slabs must have fallen at the corners. He was the first to measure the cella accurately (4.21 x 10.942 meters). Fitting the frieze slabs, which varied in length, into these dimensions, and combining this with his other evidence, he emerged with a sequence of eight slabs on each long side, three on the south, and four on the north.

Only when Dinsmoor had published his final results (in 1956) could the frieze be evaluated as an artistic whole. It has two subjects, both canonical, and both Athenian: the battle of Athenians and Amazons, beginning with the second slab on the east and running round the south side to end with the second slab from the south on the west side; and the battle of Lapiths and centaurs, occupying the other eleven slabs. Nine hands have been distinguished at work, and each of the three most important slabs is by a different master, all probably Peloponnesian, to judge by the sturdy, rugged style. If the Parthenon frieze has the sunny realism of Sophocles, the ninety-three figures of this one show the combination of daemonic passion with the note of pity, tenderness, humanity, and the horror of war that we associate with Euripides. The daemonic is *fortissimo*, emphasized with flying drapery and extravagant gestures and played out against a background originally blue, with accessories picked out in red, yellow, violet, and green, or added in metal. A centaur, stabbed in the belly, bites one adversary and kicks another. Victors seize the vanquished by the hair, rip their clothes bodily from them, kick them in the groin, apply the hammerlock, knee them in the back, strangle them,

541

Fig. 5.16 Bassae, temple of Apollo, south frieze, Theseus and Amazons (London, British Museum) drag them from altars where they have sought sanctuary. But the note of tenderness is there, too, though muted: an Amazon pleads for the life of her Athenian enemy; Apollo, with Artemis in a stag-drawn chariot, comes to the rescue of Hippodamia, who has taken pitiful refuge at a cult-statue; the wounded are helped tenderly from the field. And these are not lay figures: the sculptors have distinguished them with minor details: a beard, a crested helmet, a horse, a long dress, sandals, earrings; two of the Lapiths carry children in their arms. The masterpiece (Fig. 5.16) fell in the middle of the south side, where an Amazon intervenes between Theseus, with lion skin and club (he was the Attic Heracles) and the Amazon Queen Hippolyta, mounted to the left. The note of humanity is here: at the right, a Greek lifts a fatally wounded Amazon tenderly off her stricken horse. It was the note of pity that Goethe caught when he wrote that to look at this sculpture made one two thousand years younger and better. In the temple of Bassae, with its Attic myth and its Peloponnesian sculptors, we see the unifying effect of art triumphing over the divisive forces of politics and war.

Their victory over the Carthaginians at Himera in 480 brought the Western Greeks two long generations of prosperity, the archaeological evidence for which is a series of splendid temples and sculpture, a selection from which is presented here.

Among the most spectacular temples are those at Agrigento, Greek Akragas, on the southwest coast of Sicily, planned on the initiative of Theron, tyrant of the city, one of the victors of Himera, patron of Pindar. Theron in the west anticipated by a generation the kind of projects for beautifying a city that Pericles was to carry out in Athens. The most massive of these, still striking even in ruins, was the temple of Zeus, whose columns rose 120 feet in the air, as tall as a modern ten-story building, beside the sea-gate of the city. Built by the labor of Carthaginian war captives, it was one of the three largest temples of the whole classical world, measuring over 150 by 350 feet, and containing, by German archaeologists' calculations, 65,000 blocks of limestone; the column-drums were over thirteen feet in diameter; its foundation courses went down twenty-nine feet. When American amphibious forces occupied nearby Porto Empedocle in July, 1943, few of them knew that the harbor moles were built of limestone blocks robbed from the temple of Zeus in the eighteenth century. Long before that it had been in ruins; its last upright wall fell in 1401, so that when the ubiquitous Cockerell visited it in 1812 he found nothing standing. Not till 1894 was a successful reconstruction drawing made. In that year the German archaeologist Robert Koldewey (who later excavated Babylon) studied, with notable results, the gigantic figure, over twenty-five feet long, its arms held palms up beside its head as though to support a mighty weight, which lay reconstructed out of twelve courses of limestone in the middle of the cella. Koldewey noticed other blocks, parts of similar figures, in other places on the site; one of them was a top course with the lower arm and hand worked in the same block as a wall course. He noticed also that the torso blocks lay as though they had fallen forward from the temple's outer face. Thus a quick eye and a creative imagination enabled him to produce his now generally accepted reconstruction (Fig. 5.17), in which the temple walls are solid behind the engaged columns, and the colossal figures, called Telamones, stand upon consoles between the columns, and appear to support the architrave. The support is only apparent, for Koldewey found architrave blocks grooved on the underside to receive reinforcing iron bars, which ran from column to column: the architect did not trust his grandiose figures to be functional.

The temple was still unfinished when the vengeful Carthaginians overwhelmed the city in 405. Two other fifth-century temples, almost twins, traditionally called the temples of Juno Lacinia and of Concord, also lie near the south wall of the city, east of the temple of Zeus. Of these the temple of Concord is almost as perfectly preserved as the Hephaisteion in Athens, and for the same reason: it became a Christian church. The stairs that gave access to the attic still survive, and the mellow golden-brown patina of its weathered stone, set among olive trees overlooking the sea, makes it one of the most attractive buildings of the ancient world.

Theron, tyrant of Akragas, had a son-in-law Gelon, who was tyrant of Gela and later of Syracuse. Gelon had a brother, Polyzelus, whose fame rivals Gelon's own because he commissioned one of antiquity's most famous works of art, the bronze Charioteer in the Delphi Museum (Fig. 5.18). The French excavators found it in 1896, together with the in-

Fig. 5.17 (above) Agrigento, temple of Zeus, telamones.
(Koldewey-Puchstein, 1899. Fig. 143) Fig. 5.18 (opposite)
Delphi, Museum. Bronze charioteer. (Émile Séraf)

Fig. 5.18 Delphi, Museum. Bronze charioteer. (Émile Séraf)

scription of Polyzelus, who dedicated it probably to celebrate a victory in a Pythian chariot race in 474. In World War II it was taken to Athens for safety; directly after the war it was for the first time expertly photographed and studied. It proved to have been cast, by the lost wax process, in seven parts: head, torso, lower half, and the four limbs. The lips were soldered on in copper, the eyes are in white paste, with iris in brown and pupils in black. The victor's band, with its meander pattern around the brows, made it possible to cast the head in two pieces, so that the eyes could be inserted from the inside. The hair is engraved, not modeled, as though it were plastered to the head in the sweat of victory. The garment falls in twenty-one folds, like the flutes of a column, except that no two folds are alike. The veins and tendons are brought out, so that the total effect combines geometry and naturalism, and the detail makes the figure alert, alive, and unique. The statue commemorates an athlete in the spirit of an ode of Pindar, with which it is contemporary, and, like it, it is hieratic, forceful, controlled, finished, intellectualized, a splendid example of the severe style.

Another masterpiece of sculpture from the West, this time a three-sided marble relief, is the Ludovisi Throne (Fig. 5.19) in Rome's Terme Museum; its style links it with Locri in south Italy. It was found in 1887, when Rome's expansion as capital of a united Italy decreed the breaking up into a grid of streets of the Ludovisi Gardens, east of the Via Veneto, in what is now the fashionable tourist quarter. It was probably not a throne, but the windbreak for an altar. The front portrays Aphrodite rising from the sea, which has brought out the wave in her hair and made her garment cling gloriously to her breasts. On the sides are a young naked flute-girl on a cushion, her body all swelling, unbroken curves; and an older, slimmer woman, clothed, sacrificing with incense. Perhaps they symbolize profane and sacred love. Again the style shows the controlled excitement, here miscalled "severe," characteristic of Greek sculpture of the years around 460. Surrounded as it is in the museum by pale, soulless copies of Greek originals, this masterpiece strikes the visitor as the finest piece of classical art in Rome, and its probable place of origin underlines the fact that Magna Graecia in the mid-fifth century rivaled Athens, Olympia, or any site in the motherland as a center of sophisticated art.

Fig. 5.19 Rome, Terme Museum, Ludovisi throne. (Fototeca)

Paestum, too, flourished in the fifth century as in the sixth. The evidence is the sturdy classical Doric limestone temple "of Poseidon," now known from the votive deposit found in recent excavations to have been dedicated to Hera. The fever-ridden and brigand-infested site was, as we saw, little visited until the eighteenth century, and the temple was never scientifically studied until just before World War II. Friedrich Krauss, who knows it best, described it as the finest Doric temple in the world (Fig. 5.20). Its refinements rival the Parthenon. Krauss found that in precision of detail it marks a great advance over its neighbor, the sixth-century "Basilica." The corner columns are oval, not round, to correct optical illusion; the architrave curves imperceptibly upward to its center. The *antae* (corner pilasters) of the cella incline slightly inward. The errors in stone-cutting are limited to a thousandth of a meter; the proportions work out in multiples of nine. Such mature work belongs to the decade 460-450. All that architecture can express is said here, but it is architecture, not religion: the hieratic solemnity of the Gorgon pediment at Corcyra has vanished, and indeed the Paestan pediments are too shallow to have contained sculpture. Here architectural elegance is all; this is a tribute not to the awesomeness of the gods but to the competence of men, which is another of the things that classical humanism means.

Fig. 5.20   Paestum, temple of Poseidon. (Author)

Our final example of fifth-century art in the West, as archaeology expounds it, comes from Selinus: the metopes of Temple E, dedicated, as an inscription found in 1865 reveals, to Hera. This is the southernmost of the temples to the east of the Acropolis. Two of the metopes, from the west, or back, façade, were found by Angell and Harris in 1823, but they were not extracted from the earthquake-caused debris until 1877; only in recent years has a start been made in re-erecting the columns. In 1877, too, three more metopes from the east front were found; all are now in the Palermo Museum. The subjects are miscellaneous: on the east, Athena and a giant; on the west, Actaeon attacked by dogs for having seen Artemis naked; Heracles battling with the Amazon Antiope; and the masterpiece (Fig. 5.21): Hera, a new bride, unveiling herself before her husband, Zeus. The style is earlier than the Parthenon; given the time lag that has to be reckoned with in the West, the date is probably later. The material is local calcareous tufa (a chalky pumice), but Hera's head and limbs are done in white marble. In a ritual gesture of this divine marriage, the bride, grave and distant, lifts her veil to offer herself to the avid admiration of Zeus, who takes her possessively by the arm. The composition is simple but not awkward, the bodies sturdy but not heavy; Zeus' drapery falls stiffly from the waist, but the rigidity is redeemed by the swirling arabesque around his left wrist. His head is reminiscent of the god of Artemisium, and the metopes as a whole recall stylistically those of Olympia, reminding us that however far apart geographically the examples may be, Greek art of the fifth century is essentially one.

Archaeology has underlined the unity of fifth-century classicism in both architecture and art. In architecture, the temple of Zeus at Olympia, the Parthenon, and the Hephaisteion and the temple "of Poseidon" at Paestum are demonstrably related by their adhesion to the canonical Doric plan, while their refinements of detail give them individuality. The Erechtheum, the Apollo temple at Bassae, and the Temple of Zeus at Agrigento show more idiosyncrasy, but no one could mistake them for archaic, Hellenistic, or Roman. All were built in a spirit that our age has lost, of self-confidence born of prosperity and empire, a self-confidence that seems all the more tragic when we contrast it with Athens' fall be-

Fig. 5.21 Palermo, Museo civico, metope of Hera
unveiling herself to her bridegroom, Zeus, from Temple
E, Selinus. (Fototeca)

fore totalitarian Sparta, and the humbling of Sicily before the Punic barbarian.

The unity and the tragedy are found as well in the art that the archaeologist's spade has uncovered and his pen interpreted. It is in the otherworldliness of the Apollo of Olympia, the bronze god of Artemisium, the Hera of the Selinus metope; in the calm self-confidence of the Delphi Charioteer, in the sunny realism of the Parthenon frieze, the sprightliness of the Nike balustrade, the pathos and the humanism of the frieze from Bassae, the delight in sheer beauty of the Ludovisi Throne. What binds these masterpieces together is the intoxication of man's discovery of himself—for the Nike and the Aphrodite are women first and goddesses afterward—and the artist's delight in the intellectual expression of what he has discovered. This is what classical humanism means. But the humanist has intellectual resources that help him to face tragedy, too: to realize how evanescent is the victory of the Nike balustrade, how constant the pathos of the frieze at Bassae. Strong in the realization of their cultural tradition, Greek architects and artists had more than fragments to shore against their ruins. This archaeology has proved by those of its discoveries that it belongs to the fourth century.

6 The Fourth Century

From the overwhelming wealth of material remains of the fourth century turned up by the archaeologist's spade, I have chosen six topics: the sanctuary at Epidaurus of the healing god Asclepius; a set of theaters, especially the Theater of Dionysus in Athens; the continued expansion of the great international game sites; city planning; the Ionian Renaissance, which produced great temples and tombs, the wonders of the world, on the coast of Asia Minor; and the public-works projects in Athens of the only Greek rival of Pisistratus and Pericles, Lycurgus of Boutadae.

Some nineteen miles east of Tiryns, in the lee of mountains rising from the Argive plain, lies the sacred grove of Asclepius, his sanctuary at Epidaurus, where patients went to be healed. Its excavation was a by-product of the new Greek nation's pride in its past. In 1881 the Greek Archaeological Society commissioned P. Kavvadias to clear away the trees from the site of the theater, which was known from Pausanias and had been cursorily excavated in 1829 by the *Expédition scientifique de Morée*. Kavvadias' discovery that its orchestra (dancing-place) was unique in being circular aroused enthusiasm, and modest funds were provided, which produced a major and highly successful excavation, documenting a fascinating chapter in Greek cultural history. Taking time out only to excavate the Acropolis *korai* (1886-87) Kavvadias excavated at Epidaurus twenty-six buildings or complexes, including the theater, Asclepius' temple, a handsome but puzzling circular building (tholos) adjoining; the

Fig. 6.1 Epidaurus, sanctuary of Asclepius, reconstruction drawing. Plan centers on temple (C), dormitory (D), and tholos (E). Theater is 350 yards off plan to east. (Caton, *Asklepios*, fac. p. 3)

Outline Restoration
of Some of the Principal Buildings
of the Hieron of Epidauros

(Some emendations in this plate have been borrowed from the important work published by M. Cavvanias during the present year.)

PLATE I.—OUTLINE RESTORATION OF A PART OF THE HIERON OF EPIDAURUS (B.C.)

A South Propylæa, or possibly Temple of Hygeia. B Gymnasium ($). C Temple of Asklepios. D D East and west Abatons, the lower story of the latter and the steps leading down to it are shown. E The Tholos. F Temple of Artemis. G Family of late construction. I Large altar ($). J South Stoa(?). I Tholos near construction. K Greek Tomb. L Thесaurus and probable site of library. M Group of baths or houses. N The building with four quadrangles, probably a basari. O Roman building. P Roman baths. Q Supposed portice of Kotys. R Northeastern colonnade. S North-eastern quadrangle, a hestil ($). T Temple of Aphrodite. U Northern Propylæa on road from town of Epidaurus. V Roman building. W Northern boundary of precinct ($). X Stadium. Y Goal, or perhaps starting-place. Z Mouth of subterranean passage, communicating with precinct ($). α Temple of Asklepios and Egyptian Apollo, according to Cavvanias. β Supposed temple of the beautiful gate. γ Temple of Themis (?). δ Reservoir or bath. ε Position of ancient cemetery.

The great theatre is situated about 200 yards to the south-east of the building marked N.

NOTE. THIS BUILDING (N) IS SITUATED 150 YARDS MORE TO THE EAST THAN IS HERE REPRESENTED.

patients' dormitory, a hostel, and a stadium (Fig. 6.1).
He also found over 300 inscriptions, including the building
accounts for temple and tholos, and an engrossing record
of forty-three miraculous cures. He also built a carriage
road from Nauplia, a guest house, and a museum where his
bust now faces the entrance.

Of the temple only enough survived to reconstruct a
ground plan, but the building accounts found nearby, inscribed in fourth-century letters, provide details of vanished
glories. The temple cost 100 talents ($120,000 uninflated).
It had ivory-inlaid boxwood doors studded with gold nails,
and cypress and olive-wood ceiling inset with gold stars.
Its pedimental sculpture (centaurs and Amazons; only fragments survive) cost eight talents. The accounts cover, with
that meticulous detail more characteristically Greek than Ro-
mantics think, the quarrying, masonry, transport, timber, tile,
sculpture, metal work, ivory, and wages. Contractors had to
give bond; a tenth of their fee was held out (as now) until
their work was tested; and they were subject to fines for
delays, skimping, or exceeding their estimates.

Building accounts, foundation courses, and epistyle blocks
and ceiling coffers of almost unbelievably delicate workmanship also survive from the circular building or tholos southwest of the temple. Its footings are six concentric circles.
The outer three supported its outer columns (Doric), wall,
and inner colonnade (Corinthian). The inner three form a
kind of miniature labyrinth centering on what may have been
a pit for Asclepius' sacred snakes. One Corinthian capital,
now in the local museum, is so beautifully worked, and so
unweathered, that Kavvadias thought it might have been the
architect's model, never used on the building: on various segments of it various numbers of acanthus leaves are tried out
for effect.

North of the temple and tholos Kavvadias excavated a
long porticoed building, two-storied on its west end, where
the ground slopes down, and oriented on a sacred well, still
full of water. It was in this building that the cure-inscrip-
tions were found; this must have been the dormitory where
ailing pilgrims slept, dreamed of Asclepius, and were licked
by his sacred snakes or sacred dogs. The south face of the
dormitory must have had openings high up, for the inscription records one Aeschinas, an ancient Peeping Tom, who
climbed a tree to peer in, was blinded for his prying, re-
pented, and was cured. The cures included every ill that flesh

is heir to: barrenness, paralysis, dumbness, pockmarks, gall-stones, pink-eye, blindness, lameness, baldness, dropsy, worms, tumors, ulcers, lice, migraine, gangrene, tuberculosis, gout, arthritis. Unbelievers were doubly stricken, or paid the offended god a heavy fine in silver. A mother-in-law administers leeches to drink, a boy nine days drowned miraculously revives, a man erstwhile lame climbs to the temple ridgepole, a worried slave (in a particularly touching entry) has a pot he has broken mended. The kick of a horse cured arthritis, the lick of a dog cured tumor, the nip of a goose cured gout. The credulity is remarkable, embracing high and low alike: a Molossian princess gratefully records how she was cured of barrenness. Thankful patients would dedicate to the god models, of which hundreds were found, often macabre, of the part of the body cured.

Between the theater and the sacred precinct Kavvadias in 1893 excavated the largest building in the sanctuary, with twenty rooms in each of four quadrants on the ground floor, and walls thick enough to presuppose a second story. Such a building, with 160 rooms, can only have been a hostel for pilgrims, a sort of Grand Hotel; the fourth-century Leonidaion at Olympia closely resembles it.

South of the temple complex the lay of the land led Kavvadias to the stadium (1894). It has square ends and starting blocks, as at Olympia: their distance apart suggests a foot-unit different from the Olympian. He found stone seats only at the center of the long sides. On the south long side was the umpire's platform, with a table for the crowns to be awarded as prizes. A passage under the northern tier of seats leads to tholos and temple; one may imagine the cheering crowds escorting the victor to give thanks to the god. The atmosphere must have been like that of Lourdes, Fatima, Ste. Anne de Beaupré, or the modern Greek summer pilgrimage to the miraculous island shrine of Our Lady of Tenos. One can picture the crowds, the piety, the gold that flowed into the priests' coffers, the different dialects and costumes, and the night scenes as the afflicted made their way by flickering torchlight through the silent grove to the dormitory, there to await the dream, the snakes, and the hoped-for glad awakening.

The theater at Epidaurus is only one of many built in Greece in the fourth century: in Greece, as in our culture, the stately playhouse seems to come after the craft of the playwright has passed its prime. The Epidaurus theater is the finest and best preserved in the ancient world; recent repairs show it to particular advantage (Fig. 6.2). It is still used for summer outdoor performances of Greek tragedy and comedy, when the sanctuary comes to life again, furnished with lawns, flowerbeds, patios flagged with imitation marble, and an ugly cyclone fence around the ruins. Much of this is disliked by old Greek hands who remember a simpler era, but it probably faithfully reflects the atmosphere of Epidaurus in its prime. Filled, the theater now holds over 12,000 spectators; when it was new, it probably held 2000 more. Its acoustics are perfect, and remarkable: they may have been achieved by imbedding hollow jars, neck toward the orchestra, under the seats to create a system of infinite baffles. The bottom seats have risers six inches lower than those of the upper tier: this implies that the front rows were cushioned. The front and the two middle rows (above and below the transverse aisle) have higher backs, and arms at the ends of the rows. All the seats were hollowed out below so that spectators could draw back their feet and let others pass. The front-row seats had footstools, and a wide aisle behind. The orchestra, perfectly circular, still shows the footings for an altar in the middle, to remind us that Greek drama was a religious rite, sacred to Dionysus.

The buildings behind the orchestra have given rise to a great and, on the whole, pointless controversy over whether

Fig. 6.2 Epidaurus, theater, showing (right center) recently reconstructed retaining wall and entrance. (Alison Frantz)

classical Greek theaters had a high stage. Appeal in this argument is often made to classical drama, but here the problem
is that for the fifth century we have plenty of texts but
almost no theaters, for the fourth century plenty of theaters
but almost no texts. Those we have, however, show that
the chorus has become less important, the actors more so;
this should mean, in a building, less attention to the orchestra
and more to the stage. The stage at Epidaurus is twelve feet
high, and is not a Roman addition. It seems sensible, practical, and nonconfusing to raise the actors above the level of
the chorus in front of them in the orchestra. The raised
stage of the theater on the island of Thasos, recently redated
by its French excavators to the fourth century, seems to
clinch the matter in favor of an early raised stage.

One of the largest ancient theaters in Greece was excavated by the British in 1890-91 at Megalopolis in Arcadia,
thirty-six mountainous miles southwest of Argos. The site
had always been known: it was a made city, a spite-city
built at one go by the Thebans to keep an eye on Sparta
after her defeat at Leuctra in 371. When the British came
there, the site of the Agora was green with young grain, the
mayor was using the official standard of measure from it as
a pig-trough, and the Thersilion (assembly hall) was a plowed
field; to this state it has largely reverted, though the theater
was tidied up in 1959. Though the six miles of the ancient
town walls have been traced (in 318 they held a population
of 65,000), and major buildings excavated, the town plan is
quite unknown, and would repay excavation if the difficulties
could be overcome that always arise, in a country as land-
poor as Greece, over compensation for crops.

The Thersilion, a roofed and pillared building modeled
on the Hall of the Mysteries at Eleusis, had a south porch
that was ingeniously and economically used as the stage
building of the theater immediately south of it. Whether the
theater was actually used as such from the beginning is
doubtful, for blocks of seats are inscribed with the names of
various Arcadian tribes, which suggests that the structure
doubled at least as the assembly place for the Arcadian
League. The excavators, after consulting London theater
managers, calculated the seating capacity as 19,700. They
argued that in its fourth-century phase the theater had at
least a temporary raised stage in wood; their evidence was
some oblong sinkings, which they interpreted as slots for
the wooden posts of such a stage. These they found on the

under side of the reused foundation blocks of the later proscenium building of about 150 B.C. Grooves in the green-room floor were apparently used to slide scenery in for storage.

The most famous and most discussed of ancient theaters is of course that of Dionysus, on the south slope of the Athenian Acropolis (Fig. 6.3). Excavation and study since 1862 by Greek, English, and German scholars (including Dörpfeld, who had also helped Kavvadias at Epidaurus) have established that the stone-built auditorium that the visitor sees today belongs to the last third of the fourth century, having been commissioned by the puritanical orator, patriot, aristocrat, and financial genius Lycurgus, who administered the city after her defeat by Philip of Macedon at the battle of Chaeronea in 338. In seventy-eight rows it seated 14,000 to 17,000 spectators. The first two rows are thrones, of Pentelic marble, with footstools; they seated officials and priests. Put-holes around the central throne, for the priest of Dionysus, suggest that it had a canopy. A drainage channel borders the orchestra, with bridges at the aisles; letters on the edge of the open interspaces between the bridges probably refer to corresponding letters on slatted wooden covers that could be put down to keep the chorus from falling in. In this phase the scene building may have had a temporary

Fig. 6.3   Athens, theater of Dionysus, from above. (Alison Frantz)

stage between its projecting wings, as Dörpfeld claimed in 1924, though he did not cite his evidence. The statues of the Tragic Three, which Lycurgus set up in his theater, would in any case have been placed so as not to interfere with the spectators' view of the action. A stage, of course, may be said to mark the moment when drama becomes more entertainment than ritual. The late fourth century is such a moment, when Menander's bourgeois family comedy of manners held the stage. (His *Dyskolos, The Bad-Tempered Man,* was discovered in a Swiss antiquary's shop in 1957.)

Beneath the fourth-century building are scanty traces of earlier phases: of the theater of the great days of Aeschylus, Sophocles, Euripides, and Aristophanes nothing remains but ashes, nails, and a few stones. Yet these are enough to suggest that the original orchestra was circular, as at Epidaurus, that it had a long hall behind it, with a central platform perhaps used as a base for the *mêchanê,* the crane that permitted the apparition of gods, flying chariots, or (in Aristophanes) enormous dung-beetles. East of the theater are traces of a covered building, the Odeum of Pericles.

Post-fourth-century phases can also be distinguished. The Hellenistic theater certainly had a permanent raised stage. In Roman times a marble barrier was erected around the orchestra, to protect the spectators of beast fights or gladiatorial combats, and late in the Empire provision was made to convert the orchestra into a watertight basin for aquatic ballets.

Often in archaeology a find raises a problem, the pursuit of which leads to new finds. Research into theaters is a case in point; over a dozen have been investigated in Greek lands since the theater of Dionysus was first scientifically excavated. One of the best preserved of these is at Priene, twenty-five miles south of Ephesus in Asia Minor. This was a planned city, to be discussed in some detail later, founded by Alexander the Great in 334. The technique of the theater is Hellenistic, the date about 300. Since Priene is a small town, its theater is smaller than the others described; nevertheless it seated 6000. Its excavator, writing in 1921 under the influence of the then prevailing view that Greek theaters did not have high stages, argued that the Priene theater had no raised stage till 160. (In that year statues were set up that would have been in the way if the stage had not been raised.) But the architectural remains demand restoration as belonging to a flat-roofed colonnade between the orchestra and the scene-building. (This colonnade, called a *proskenion*, was also a feature of earlier theaters: the fact that a famous Greek prostitute was nicknamed *proskenion* led one scholar, not otherwise noted for facetiousness, to define it as "a decorative exterior concealing something plain.") The point at Priene is the flat roof: why should it be flat if it was not to be used, along with the three-doored stage building behind it, and what better use for it than as a stage, with one or more of the openings behind used for interior scenes? The fact that there are seats of honor at Priene in the fifth row as well as the first, with no real evidence that these are not of one build with the original auditorium of 300 B.C., is another argument in favor of the use from the beginning of the *proskenion* roof as a stage. But in the end what matters is not this detail, but the proof offered by Priene and many another small city that a Greek community did not consider itself culturally complete without a theater.* Thus the intellectual heritage of Athens, where Greek drama began, lived on after she became politically negligible.

Archaeology shows that throughout all the jockeying for power in the fourth century of individual cities and states, first Sparta, then Thebes, then Macedon under Philip II and Alexander, the great international game sites flourished.

At Olympia, (see Fig. 5.1) the evidence is in four buildings and one great statue. The earliest fourth-century building is the smallest and worst preserved of the three temples in the Altis. Miniature cymbals found in a level of ash west of it give a clue to the divinity worshiped in it: the clashing of cymbals (to drown out Zeus's birth-cry from the ears of his jealous father) was a part of the worship of the Great Mother, Rhea or Cybele. It seems appropriate that the mother should be worshiped in the son's precinct, so the temple has been identified as a Metroön. Appropriateness and piety yielded in Roman times to considerations of policy, when the temple was rededicated to Augustus. (Ruler cult is of course not an index to religiosity, but to how irreligious the worshiper is.)

---

* Mention should probably be made here of the theater at the oracle site of Dodona in Epirus, restored by the Greek Archaeological Service in 1959. At the summer festival of 1961, crowds of up to 22,000 filled it to overflowing; in antiquity, it was probably the largest theater in Greece.

An inscription identifies another fourth-century building, the second largest secular structure on the site, as the Leonidaion, donated by one Leonidas of Naxos, who may thus have shown his gratitude for being enriched in the marble trade. It is almost square, like the hostel at Epidaurus, and contains such a combination of large rooms, for formal occasions, and small ones, for bedrooms, as would be appropriate to a guesthouse. The rooms are arranged around a courtyard with a fountain in the middle, and were presumably luxurious, for distinguished visitors, since they were made over, centuries later, into the headquarters of the Roman governors of Achaea. Wheel ruts leading up to the building suggest that its guests were considered too distinguished to be allowed to arrive on foot.

Pausanias identifies the other two buildings: a tholos, called the Philippeion, and the Echo Stoa on the east side of the Altis, so named because of the sevenfold echo that reverberated from the buildings it faced. The Philippeion is a finely worked imitation of the Tholos at Epidaurus; the Stoa is in the same style. Less important than their architectural detail is what their existence implies. A pedestal found in the Philippeion once held statues of Philip, Alexander, and other members of the Macedonian royal family: here the form of a temple is used to house the statues of mortal men, something new in Greek life, and destined to bear bitter fruit, as the rededication of the Metroön to Augustus and the later adulation of Nero show. The Echo Stoa, from its style, is dated after the battle of Chaeronea, where Philip humbled Greece: its fine-wrought marble makes an ostentatious display of victor's condescension to vanquished.

Olympia's most famous fourth-century statue is the Hermes of Praxiteles, found, as we saw, in the Heraion. The work of Praxiteles, Lysippus, and Scopas, the three great sculptors of this century, can all be plausibly illustrated from archaeological finds of the last hundred years at Olympia, Delphi, and Halicarnassus. Hermes' stance (Fig. 6.4) is the characteristic and beautiful Praxitelean S-curve, though debate rages as to whether it is a Praxitelean original. The baby Dionysus in his left arm is of course his brother, whom he was represented as teasing, probably with a bunch of grapes. The god is rendered with fourth-century informality, with his unruly hair (originally painted red-brown) and his debonair handsome youthfulness. He is the glass of

Fig. 6.4   Olympia, Museum. Hermes, with infant Dionysus. Found in Heraion. Perhaps an original by Praxiteles. (Alison Frantz)

fashion, too, for his sandals were once gilded. It is hard to believe that this concept of divinity is the product of the same culture that made the Corcyra pediment, or even the superhuman Apollo of this same precinct. The same emphasis on the human dimension, but much more modest and bourgeois, is to be seen in the charming little terracotta figurines that archaeologists found by the hundreds in late fourth-century graves at Tanagra in Boeotia, of which the most typical show cloaked women in traveling dress. The one shown (Fig. 6.5), acquired by the Metropolitan Museum in New York in 1930, has brown hair, wears a tunic, a rose mantle with a bright blue border, and red peaked hat and shoes. She once held a fan, and she wears a ring. The drapery is very delicately handled, and there is a fine swing to her fashionable pose. She was a gift to the museum, and her precise findspot is unknown, as often, since collectors buy from art dealers who have clandestine sources, which they feel they must protect, but she is published as coming presumably from Tanagra.

At Delphi an earthquake destroyed the Alcmaeonid temple in 373. French archaeologists found the list of those who subscribed to rebuild it, from the king of Sparta to the humble contributions of women in Sicily, the Peloponnese, and the islands, whose pious obols hardly sufficed to pay the cost of carving their names on stone. From the subscription list and from the complicated accounts of the international commission in charge of rebuilding the temple, French epigraphists were able to learn precious details. Philip of Macedon's incursions into Greece interrupted the rebuilding, which consequently took thirty-five or forty years. Part of the expense was to have been defrayed from a 10,000-talent fine levied on the Phocians for robbing the shrine to pay mercenaries, but the culprits paid only 400. Another inscription found in excavating the temple records the per diem paid to experts from Athens and Corinth who came to replace the sacred silver and gold vessels, the gift of Croesus, the millionaire sixth-century king of Lydia, which the rascally Phocians had melted down. As at Epidaurus, contractors were subject to fine for not meeting deadlines, but at Delphi they were also paid extra, because the temple was rebuilt larger than had been originally planned. As many blocks as possible of the Alcmaeonid temple were reused, the rest reverently buried, and the excavators found them. Some of the new stone (the poros) came from quarries between Corinth and

Fig. 6.5 Tanagra figurine. (New York, Metropolitan Museum, gift of Mrs. Sadie Adler)

Sicyon; the inscriptions show that freight rates were pro-
hibitively high: transporting the stone across the Corinthian
Gulf and up the steep winding road to Delphi cost ten times
as much as quarrying it. Hence local limestone was also
used. It came from quarries two hours west of Delphi, where,
as on Naxos, one can still see where the wooden wedges
were driven in and wetted to swell and split the stone. The
builders' workshops lay beside the meeting place of the
Amphictyonic Council (the delegates from neighboring states
who governed Delphi) at the spot where their descendants
have their threshing floors, beside the new School of Fine
Arts.

Nature and man have been hard on the fourth-century
temple. A landslip has twisted the whole structure, top-
pling columns into the ravine; Byzantines in need of metal
pried up the peristyle pavement, and propped it up while
they got at the metal clamps in the blocks beneath. Little
is left but the plan, yet from the evidence of scattered architectural blocks conjecture has produced a model (Fig. 6.6)

**Fig. 6.6 Delphi, precinct of Apollo, model. 1, Sacred Way;
2, Siphnian Treasury; 3, Athenian Treasury; 4, Athenian Portico; 5, Temple of Apollo; 6, Statue of Agias, findspot; 7,
theater. (New York, Metropolitan Museum, Dodge Fund)**

not only of the temple, but of the whole sanctuary. The temple plan is unusual enough to be worth describing. Separate from the four walls of the cella was a smallish room that once contained marvels: the golden cult-statue of Apollo, the tomb of Dionysus, the omphalos, or navel-stone of the world, of which Delphi, like Boston, considered itself the center; a bench for those waiting to consult the oracle, and a stair down to an underground room that may have been the holy of holies, where the prophetess allegedly sat over a crevice in the rock that emitted vapors. There was in fact no crevice, and there were no vapors. Nevertheless, the pious believed that under their influence the prophetess uttered sounds that the priests translated into hexameter verse (often ambiguous) and submitted to the pious awaiting the god's answer to their questions. The temple walls bore the famous mottoes, "Know thyself" and "Nothing in excess," the latter more honored by the Greeks in the breach than in the observance, which is what makes them so interesting as a people.

In the same fill as the pediments from the Alcmaeonid temple was found a graceful group of three dancers, fourth-century work, which originally supported a tripod atop a high column with baroque decoration of vegetable motifs (Fig. 6.7). The precise date and occasion of the dedicating is unknown, but from the style, the maidens seem to have been carved not very long before the earthquake toppled them in 373. If the leaves on the column are silphium (asafoedita), then the dedicator was Cyrene in North Africa, which, as we saw, exported the plant, and the maidens are Graces, who enjoyed a special cult there. If their headdresses are those of priestesses, then they are Thyiades, who buried the dismembered Dionysus, god of vegetation, and woke him by ritual incantations every spring. If the leaves are acanthus, then perhaps the group is the Laconian Maidens by the Athenian Callimachus, inventor of the Corinthian column with its acanthus motif, and the dedicator was King Agis of Sparta, from the spoils of a war against Elis won in 400. But no one has yet satisfactorily identified the leaves. Less of a puzzle is the marble statue of an athlete (Fig. 6.8), which came from a base northeast of the temple with cuttings for nine figures. Verses inscribed on the base tell who they are: seven generations of a family prominent in Pharsalus. The dedicator was the Thessalian delegate, pro-Macedonian, to the Amphictyonic Council, (which administered the temple at Delphi) in the critical years between 338 and

Fig. 6.7   Dancing girls from acanthus (?)
column, restored. (Delphi Museum)

Fig. 6.8   Delphi, Museum. The athlete Agias, after an original by Lysippus. (Alison Frantz)

334, after Athens' fall. The athlete, Agias by name, was a famous pancratiast (boxer and wrestler with no holds barred), who won once at Olympia, three times at Delphi, five times each at Nemea and the Isthmus, as the inscription records. The statue is of special interest because it is a contemporary copy of a lost bronze original from Pharsalus by one of the three great sculptors of the time, Lysippus. The sculptor has succeeded in rendering the ideal athlete, indomitable and tense to win.

Less than a mile southeast of the main precinct lies another sacred area, nowadays called Marmaria, whose most interesting building is the Tholos, of the early fourth century. The French scholar Paul Bernard, working on the fragments of its metopes with techniques like those used by Dinsmoor at Bassae, has made (spring, 1961) a number of ingenious joins; the subject, as at Bassae, is the battle of Greeks and Amazons.

At Nemea, the third of the four great game sites, some thirteen miles southwest of Corinth (see map, Fig. 6.21), the three surviving upright columns of the temple of Zeus prompted Blegen to dig (1924-26). The temple was of special interest because its dimensions and style were so very close to those of a contemporary temple (of about 360) at Tegea, forty miles farther southwest, that the two temples might well be by the same architect. That architect was Scopas, more famous as the third of the three great sculptors of this century. The striking thing about the Nemea temple is that it had a mysterious crypt, below the rear of its cella, described by Blegen as "an open depressed area with an impracticable stair." The crypt is a puzzle because crypts in Greek temples are usually associated, as at Delphi, with the working (or manipulating) of an oracle, whereas no literary source mentions such a thing at Nemea.

While Nemea was the most rustic and simple of the game sites, its prize a simple crown of wild parsley, it must nevertheless have had, perhaps on a smaller scale than the others, the buildings appropriate and necessary to the games. It is a promising place for future excavation, but the land produces a profitable currant and grape crop, and is divided among eight or more owners, so that expropriation is complicated. Blegen did find the great altar of Zeus; a fourth century porticoed gymnasium, with bath and bathtubs (but without outlets for draining!); a stadium, 500 yards southeast of the temple, of sloped earth without stone seats; and a votive deposit and sherds going back through the archaic, Geometric, Corinthian, and Protocorinthian periods to early Neolithic. But a bouleuterion (council chamber) and hostel, for example, are still to seek.

The last great game site is Isthmia (see map, Fig. 6.21), near the southeast end of the Corinth Canal, where Broneer has been excavating for the University of Chicago since 1952. He was drawn to it because it was the only such site not yet excavated. Surveying the terrain with a practiced eye, and noticing roof tiles and column-drums in re-use in the wall of a fortress of Justinian there, he began to dig, and hit the footings of the fourth-century temple of Poseidon (plan, Fig. 6.9) on the very first day. It had been destroyed in 394, in the Corinthian War, and richly rebuilt in a rectangular, colonnaded precinct, but its earlier phases were even richer, as a splendid archaic libation basin in the Corinth Museum testifies. Broneer distinguished the archaic from the fourth-century blocks by noticing that the former were dressed smooth, the latter tooth-chiseled. Near the altar he found countless large pebbles, which he thinks were used for the ritual stoning of sacrificial animals. Among the finds were coins dedicated by the pious, including some counterfeits, a sufficient commentary on the attitude of some Greeks toward their religion. Some hinged pieces of bronze from the archaic fill are probably architects' instruments. Preliminary investigation of the theater revealed a Hellenistic *proskenion;* the presence of wood ash in the orchestra warrants the inference that the building was roofed, more properly an odeum than a theater. Behind it Broneer found caves in which ritual meals were taken, for he excavated a kitchen (the dishes left upside down to drain), and rooms with five or six dining couches each. He found fragments of victor lists (one man won ninety-four musical competitions), and a late phase of a precinct of the minor sea god Palaemon, usually represented in art as a boy on dolphin-back. According to legend his body was washed ashore near this spot, and the Isthmian Games instituted in his honor, the races starting from his tomb. Broneer found that one end of a stadium does indeed overlie the precinct of Palaemon, and the myth explains an enigma (Fig. 6.10): a set of grooves in a triangle, like a temple pediment laid flat, cut in the stone near the end of the stadium, in closest proximity to Palaemon's sanctuary. In the center of the triangle is a pit, deep enough for a man to stand in waist-high.

Fig. 6.9 Isthmia, main areas of excavation. Note triangular plan of "enigma" at northwest end of stadium. (O. Broneer)

Fig. 6.10 Isthmia, "enigma." Professor Broneer demonstrating the working of the starting-gates. (Author)

Within reach of the pit staples (originally sixteen) are set; from them grooves fan out to the base-line of the triangle. Broneer ingeniously proved that a man standing in the pit could control cords run through the staples; a jerk on the cords would drop the hinged barriers across the stadium starting-stalls. The triangle was therefore an interesting kind of starting-block, in which one man could control sixteen gates or stalls. Excavation continues at Isthmia: in the spring of 1961 Broneer uncovered the starting blocks of another stadium, and we may hope for still more surprises.

Skilled city planning and advanced techniques of fortification were among the engineering accomplishments of the fourth century. Two planned, fortified cities, Messene and Mantinea (Fig. 6.21), both in the Peloponnese, were, like Megalopolis, set up to help Thebes keep an eye on Sparta.

Messene, modern Mavrommati, twenty-five miles west of Sparta, had long been a thorn in Sparta's flesh. To this mountain fastness, in times gone by, Sparta's disaffected helots (serfs) had fled, and her repressive measures against them had rankled deeply. Thebes took advantage of this ill-feeling to strengthen Messene's walls against her hereditary enemy, and the result (Fig. 6.11) is one of the most impressive pieces of fortification in the Greek world, remarkable for the perfection of its masonry and the ingenuity

Fig. 6.11 Messene, circular court within Arcadian Gate, with stretch of circuit wall in background. Nineteenth-century photograph, taken on one of Dörpfeld's famous Peloponnesian tours. (DAI, Athens)

of its plan, which was first drawn by the French in 1829; Greek archaeologists excavated the walls in 1895, 1909, and 1925. The Arcadian Gate (see plan, Fig. 6.12) has a mighty monolithic door post nearly nineteen feet long, and a circular courtyard walled without mortar, with almost invisible joins. The circuit wall itself, fifteen feet high to the battlements, and six and a half to eight feet thick, was built in two faces of squared blocks with a rubble fill between. To compensate for its lack of height, escarpments before its outer face prevented the bringing up of scaling apparatus. Two-storied square or semicircular towers, of which thirty-three are preserved or conjectured, with loopholes and posterns, strengthened the wall at irregular intervals. On the average they are twenty-eight feet high and project thirteen feet. They straddle the wall so as to seal off its various sectors or curtains; even if an enemy succeeded in occupying the wall-walk between a pair of towers, he could be blocked from access to the rest of the wall.

In the town proper the theater and stadium had long been known; the Agora has been the object of special investigation since 1957 by the Greek archaeologist A. K. Orlandos. He dates it in the second half of the fourth century. On the east side a central Propylon leads into a vast peristyle, nearly 400 feet long. On the right of the Propylon is a small theater, on the left the Synedrion, where the Messenian Assembly met.

Mantinea's walls were built around 370, probably by the same engineers who worked at Messene, in the flat, marshy, treeless plain nine miles north of present-day Tripolis, in central Arcadia. It is one of the oldest digs in Greece: G. Fougères first hit upon it in 1868, while exploring for inscriptions, and excavated it in 1887-88, after he had gained experience at Delos, and while he was waiting for permission to dig at Delphi. He found it a melancholy, desolate spot, fever-ridden and subject to extremes of temperature. His hands and legs grew gangrenous from working constantly in water, but he found uplift in the view of Mt. Maenalus to the west, dark blue, with purple shadows, like a tossing sea turned to stone. He kept doggedly at it, working from dawn to starlight. The workmen in their heavy goatskin capes dug trenches fanning out from the mound sown with wheat that

Fig. 6.12   Messene, plan. The area in Fig. 6.11 is to the north; area labeled "Bouleuterion" has been center of recent excavation. (ASCS, Athens)

marked the theater (see plan, Fig. 6.13). Inscribed on its seats were names of local tribes, somewhat as at Megalopolis; there were five, and Fougères inferred that Mantinea had five quarters, like Sparta, each centering on a sanctuary, but all this remains to be dug.

One of the radial trenches hit upon the Agora, mostly Roman, but with a fourth-century bouleuterion. It had been built over a swamp, like the Roman Forum. This was one of the first agoras to be excavated, and Fougères was quick to note its importance to the Greek city-state: as club, bourse, market, promenade, sanctuary, and museum, where the townspeople could talk, buy, and relax under the benign eye of their gods and heroes.

Face down in the pavement of the Byzantine church near postern gate H, Fougères found confirmation of Pausanias' accuracy: three reliefs, Apollo, Marsyas, and the Muses, of the school of Praxiteles, which that indefatigable traveler had singled out in his description of Mantinea.

The circuit wall was accurately mapped by noting the breaches that marked its gates. It proved to mark an oval two and a half miles in perimeter, with 122 towers and 10 gates, each with a different plan, as though the engineers were experimenting, but each gate contrived to force those entering to present their shieldless side to the garrison on the wall. The structure in general is the same as at Messene, except that here the blocks were polygonal instead of squared, and the upper courses were of mud brick. The builders diverted a river to fill their moat.

Mantinea covered too great an area to be dug entire: trial trenches were all Fougères could afford. He therefore had to be, and was, ingenious about where he dug them, though Schliemann (who later apologized, in Byzantine Greek) accused him of being "unsystematisch." Tiles or cut stones on the surface were a clue, and so were crop marks: the stunted growth of grain—or, at Mantinea, hashish—over buried ancient walls was already a useful indicator to Fougères in the field nearly sixty years before Bradford put it to use for air photography (see *The Mute Stones Speak*, Fig. 1.2).

Once the line of the circuit wall was established, Fougères discovered that diagonals from gate to gate intersected in the Agora, whose off-center siting he thus explained. But the street plan was apparently not radial, but a rectangular grid, which he tentatively drew in on his map, adding the

Fig. 6.13 Mantinea, plan. (BCH 14 [1890] Pl. I)

caution that it is easy to mistake the lines of modern stone walls for ancient streets.

The excavation of Mantinea, though incomplete, was seminal. It showed that Arcadia was rather virgin than sterile soil, and led to the exploration of Megalopolis and Bassae; it was also the forerunner of the study of other fourth-century city plans elsewhere in the Greek world.

Over many of the archaeological sites dated in the fourth century looms the sinister shadow of Philip of Macedon. His destructive hand, paradoxically, preserved for us one of the finest examples of Greek city planning on a rectangular grid, for when in 348 he leveled to the ground Olynthus, on the peninsula of Chalcidice, thirty-six miles southeast of Salonika (Fig. 6.21), it was only sporadically resettled, and its ground plan (Fig. 6.14) therefore preserved to us intact, under the earth of its crumbled adobe house-walls. An American expedition under D. M. Robinson excavated here (1928-38); what was found made possible a reconstruction, from the ground plans and gear of over a hundred houses, of the life of a fourth-century Greek city ranking for interest with Priene and Delos in Greek lands, and with Pompeii, Herculaneum, and Ostia in Italy. Besides the house plans themselves, the evidence is drawn from kitchenware, vases, lamps, baths, *chaises percées,* mosaics, murals, querns, grain mills, mortars, olive-crushers, and over 3500 coins, of which very few are later than 348. The city plan was probably first laid out in 432, when the Chalcidice revolted from Athens and united to form one strong city at Olynthus. The city seems to have expanded from the south, where indeed there had been a settlement in Neolithic times. Between the South Hill and the northern grid is an open area, probably the agora, but at first thought by Robinson to be a common for military maneuvers, since he found no public buildings in or around it. The northern grid is one of the most complete ever excavated. Robinson found that the city blocks were planned on a module of 120 × 300 Euboean feet. (The Chalcidice was colonized from Chalcis in Euboea.) The houses, five on each side of each east-west street, had each a sixty-foot frontage. Each block was all of one build, since the houses in it have their walls bonded into one another. Only the sloping streets were cobbled. The drains run in alleys behind the houses, not in the streets: the Olynthians thought inhabitable houses more important than passable streets. A towered wall of mud brick, surprisingly unpretentious, surrounded the city. By estimating the number of houses and multiplying by eight (philoprogenitive parents, children, and slaves), Robinson calculated the population at 9,000 to 12,-000; variations in tribute paid to Athens suggest fluctuations in population.

A chance find in the fields on the East Spur of an inscribed deed of sale for a villa led to the excavation of Olynthus' best-known building, the Villa of Good Fortune, so called from an inscription in the pebble-mosaic floor of its reception room. It had two stories, as did most Olynthian houses: the evidence is surviving staircases or stairwells. On the ground floor its eight rooms were asymmetrically grouped around a wooden-pillared courtyard facing south, with a long corridor, called a *pastas*, typical of Olynthian domestic architecture, running behind it. At a corner, so as to have

Fig. 6.14   Olynthus, North Hill, air photograph, showing grid, house blocks, wall, and main north-south street. (*Die Antike* 11 [1935] p. 281 by permission of the University of Mississippi)

windows on two sides, was a dining-room with space for couches (for three to nine, not fewer than the Graces nor more than the Muses, the ideal size for a dinner party) around a central pebble-mosaic (again typical of Olynthus) representing Dionysus on a panther. In a mosaic in the ante-room, Thetis brings the armor forged by Hephaestus to Achilles. The unit of measure in the Villa is longer than in the houses to the west: it is the Attic foot. This should prove the Villa later than the town houses; one may reasonably suppose Olynthus to have shifted from the usages of the mother city to those of Athens, with whom, as imported Attic pottery, figurines, and lamps prove, she forged ever closer commercial relations. It was the alliance with Athens against Philip of Macedon's growing power that proved her undoing.

But Macedonians could build as well as destroy. In 334 Alexander founded in Asia Minor, thirty miles south of Ephesus, the model planned city of Priene (see map, Fig. 6.21), whose excavation (1895-98) by a German expedition under Theodor Wiegand was an early exemplar of precise, thorough, Prussian scientific method. The English had excavated the temple of Athena (on the far side of the model, Fig. 6.15) in 1869, and found in a specially cut niche in the footings of the base of the cult-statue a hoard of silver coins. This prompted the Turkish villagers to come in streams and virtually take the temple apart block by block. Excavation was imperative, for dilapidation was proceeding apace. But it took a year for Wiegand to get a *firman,* or permission to dig, from the Turkish authorities, and then the road from Söke had to be mended and an excavation house built. Even after the dig was under way, a twelve-ox team hauling a sample of the Athena temple entablature to Söke for shipment to Berlin bogged down and took two weeks for the nine-mile journey. Malaria, hurricanes, and earthquakes plagued excavators and excavation. Priene suffered six earthquakes in the four years the Germans were digging there; nearly 13,000 have occurred in the district since 500 B.C. For all that, Priene has its compensations: it is beautifully sited, on its four terraces in the lee of its acropolis, which looms twelve hundred feet above sea-level, reached by a dizzying flight of steps cut in the cliff. From the top and from the town, the view is south across the rich Meander valley, green with crops in the early spring, when the storks come in February, and anemones, asphodel, iris, and almond trees are in blossom.

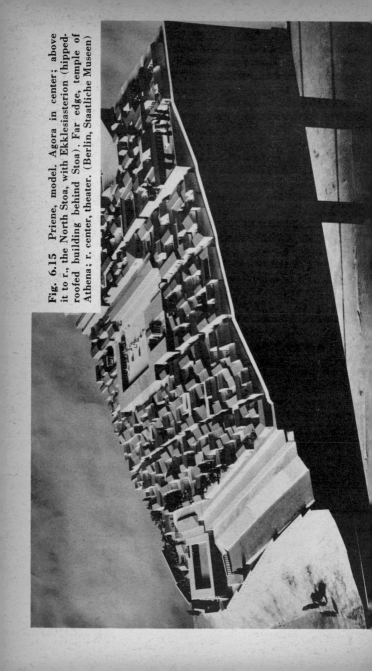

Fig. 6.15 Priene, model. Agora in center; above it to r., the North Stoa, with Ekklesiasterion (hipped-roofed building behind Stoa). Far edge, temple of Athena; r. center, theater. (Berlin, Staatliche Museen)

The excavated area of Priene is about the size of Pompeii, one sixth the area of Alexander's major foundations, Alexandria in Egypt. Behind its towered marble wall lived some 4000 inhabitants. Six streets running east and west, sixteen running north and south, make up its neat grid; about 1000 cubic yards of cliff had to be cut away to accommodate it. The plan centers on the Agora, two blocks wide, which takes up about a fifth of the total area, with buildings grouped around it like Greek house-rooms round a peristyle. In its center was an altar; east of it the Germans found twelve lettered blocks with put-holes in them; these must have been for the supports of a canopy or awning that shaded the town fathers upon state occasions. Shady porticoes, with shops or offices behind, surrounded the Agora on three sides; on the east was the sanctuary of Priene's second most important god, Zeus (the small temple in the center of the model). The north stoa, 377 feet long (it was extended eastward later) is the grandest. Its columns have holes for the pegs where once hung painted portraits. The Agora of Priene is full of monuments of personal or municipal vanity, a number of which show in the model. They survive to us as the inscribed bases—sometimes comfortable curved seats or exedrae—of statues in gilt bronze or marble. The inscriptions often specify that the likeness shall stand in the most conspicuous possible place. Honorific decrees authorizing the statues adorn all available wall space. But the architectural remains are scanty; the German model of this rich Agora is a triumph of archaeological inference from the most unlikely looking evidence.

Behind the Agora, and entered from the east end of the north stoa, is the Ekklesiasterion, or town-meeting place. Paradoxically, a fire preserved it: the roof fell in and covered everything, so that Christians never got at it. Its seats, for 640, are grouped around three sides of a square, with an altar in the middle. North of it was the theater, already described. The theater-quarter was the fashionable one: elegant private houses, with patterned stuccoed walls, furniture with lathe-turned bronze legs; hip-baths; and pleasant terracotta figurines reminiscent of the ones from Tanagra. One large dwelling, not in the theater quarter but by the west gate, the Germans called the Holy House, because in it was found a private chapel with offerings (including a marble statuette of Alexander), and an inscription bidding none to enter unless dressed in white. Probably an aristocratic family worshiped its ancestors here.

The Ionic temple of Athena is noteworthy for having no figured frieze, and because on the south anta or terminal pilaster of the pronaos was found the inscription, now in the British Museum, by which we know that Alexander dedicated this temple to Athena. The cult statue was a copy of Phidias' in the Parthenon in Athens. The masonry is careful, beautifully finished, restrained work; the proportions are harmoniously, even mathematically worked out: the cella door was sixteen by twenty-two Ionic feet; the statue base was eight feet high; column bases and interspaces each six feet, the pronaos thirty feet, the cella proper fifty, and the opisthodomos (room behind the cella, usually the temple treasury) twelve.

Altogether Priene makes a very pleasant impression, of an airy, sunny, clean little city surpassing all others of this century in the careful simplicity of its buildings in solid marble. As one approaches the Agora up the steep slope from the West Gate, noticing the fountain houses on the corners and the ⊐⊏ panels that once contained painted street signs, one can imagine the stuccoed houses with their red tile roofs, the Agora rich with bronze and marble, and buzzing with the inimitable noise of Greeks doing business. Priene, like Pompeii, is an ancient city that comes alive.

In 1899, following immediately upon his excavations at Priene, Wiegand transferred his activities ten miles south, to Miletus (map, Fig. 6.21), the birthplace of the fifth-century father of Greek city planning, Hippodamus; and the metropolis, and once, in the days of the Presocratic philosophers, the intellectual center of Ionian Asia Minor. Despite difficulties of climate (malarial), terrain (nowadays the main part of the ancient city is mostly under water), and land expropriation, Wiegand continued methodically season after season, laying bare block after block of the Hippodamian plan of Hippodamus' city. Hippodamus first laid down his grid either in 479 or in 466, when the city was rebuilt after the Persians destroyed it, but most of the public buildings Wiegand excavated are fourth century, Hellenistic, or Roman. Very recently, Mycenaean and Sub-Mycenaean remains have been found south of the Theater Bay, in the southwest quadrant of the city. Here too probably lay the oldest Agora, later transferred east and north, nearer the Lion Harbor, which was the commercial port; vessels lying in it could be protected from attack by closing off the mouth with chains. The North Agora is late fourth century; the South Agora (Fig. 6.16) could vie with any in the ancient world for size: it covered over 33,000 square yards, embracing sixteen city blocks, whereas Priene's occupied only two. The profits from its seventy-eight shops were used to build the gigantic temple of Apollo at Didyma, to be discussed later. There is also a convenient fifty-seat latrine. Other famous Milesian buildings, the Bouleuterion or council house, and the theater, seating 30,000, are of Hellenistic or Roman date. The importance of this city plan, like those of Priene and Olynthus, is that it expresses not regimentation but individuality; these cities were democracies; crooked, cramped streets suggest feudal conditions.

Fourth-century Ionia prospered, unafraid of the weak Persian kings; it used some of its profits to build sumptuous temples to the gods, or tombs for the rulers given credit for the prosperity. Two monuments, the Artemision at Ephesus and the Mausoleum at Halicarnassus, were reckoned (the

Fig. 6.16 Miletus, South Agora, model. Windowed, pilastered building, upper r. center, is Bouleuterion. (Berlin, Straatliche Museen)

criterion is chiefly size) among the Seven Wonders of the ancient world. (The others were the Pyramids of Gizeh, the Hanging Gardens of Babylon, the Temple of Zeus at Olympia, the Colossus of Rhodes, and the Pharos [lighthouse] at Alexandria. All the classical wonders are described in this book.)

Ephesus, thirty miles north of Priene (map, Fig. 6.21), was first excavated (1869–74), for the British Museum, at a cost of £16,000, by a British architect, John Turtle Wood. His account of his adventures is more picturesque than informative; and his methods, since continued funds depended on tangible results, more ruthless than scholarly; they included the use of gunpowder to blow apart a Byzantine church that stood in his way. His catalogue of woes is longer than Job's. At first he commuted to the dig from Smyrna, fifty miles away; when he moved to a chalet nearer his work, he was in constant danger of brigands. He broke his collarbone, was almost assassinated, a vessel laden with his loot was wrecked, his men went on strike, his deep excavations struck springs and left the temple pavement under standing water, mice ate the paper squeeze-impressions of his inscriptions, the saws he used to cut the marble (to reduce the weight of architectural blocks for transport) froze in the blocks. But he loved the picturesqueness; when officers of the British man-of-war detailed to carry his finds to London stayed with him, they hunted boar, played whist, and admired the black camel's-hair tents of the Arab workmen.

And he got his tangible results. He dug seventy-five trial pits the first year in his search for the temple, finally hitting upon its precinct wall by following up a road leading eastward from the Hellenistic city. He moved 132,221 cubic yards of earth, digging down twenty-five feet to uncover an area of 300 × 500 feet. His most rewarding find was a series of sculptured column-drums, from a double row at each end of the temple. It took fifteen men fifteen days to extract one. Several of these columns, the gift of kings (one is inscribed "dedicated by Croesus") were loaded onto a man-of-war to the sound of fifes. At the London end, it took twenty dray-horses to transport them to the British Museum.

In 1904–05 D. G. Hogarth, who had worked with Evans at Knossos, reopened Wood's dig, now overgrown with an impenetrable jungle, its reeds ten feet high. Though he installed a steam-pump and siphoned out 100,000 cubic meters of water, the site constantly refilled. Mornings had to be spent pumping; archaeological work could be done only in the afternoons, the men thigh-deep in liquid slime. Nevertheless Hogarth was able to distinguish five phases of the temple, of which the last, which he called E, is late fourth-century or Hellenistic. It was of the same colossal dimensions (180 × 377 feet, with sixty-foot columns) as its predecessor, D, which Hogarth called the "Croesus temple." The interior of the base of the cult-statue was filled with archaic objects: electrum (gold and silver alloy) coins, scarabs, earrings, *fibulae*, and the bones of innumerable small animals and birds. Other archaic finds came from around the base: bits of ivory inlay, a miniature ivory sphinx, studs and beads in crystal and onyx, figurines of hawks in glazed terracotta and electrum, a large statuette of Artemis (not, as later, many-breasted*), beads of tawny Baltic and (in greater quantity) red Sicilian amber, and a jar of nineteen electrum coins. They date the earliest temple, A, not earlier than 600-590, since one of them seems to bear the name of King Alyattes of Lydia, who reigned about 600. Hogarth failed to see the implications of the coin-hoard, and consequently dated all the temples too early; the correction was not made until 1951. Hogarth catalogued 3000 objects, all much earlier than the fourth century, but piously preserved by the fourth-century rebuilders. His most significant find was a silver plate inscribed with a record of the origin of Temple C, only one fourth the size of its successor. When he had finished, he filled everything in, and now only a stand of trees marks the temple over which the silversmiths of St. Paul's time rioted, crying, "Great is Diana of the Ephesians!"

Beginning in 1898, before Hogarth, and continuing at intervals to the present day, the site of the monumental city of Ephesus, as opposed to the Artemision, has been an Austrian dig. Most of what they have excavated is of Roman date (the Romans exalted Ephesus above Miletus), but the theater, with a capacity of 23,000, was probably begun at the very end of the fourth century, and the south gate of the Agora is contemporary with it.

Eleven miles south of Miletus, and connected with it by a Sacred Way, lined at the Didyma end with statues, lies the

---

* The Austrian F. Miltner wrote (1958) that the protuberances on the breast of the standard statues of Diana of the Ephesians represent not breasts but eggs! Either way, we have to do with a fertility symbol.

Fig. 6.17 Didyma, temple of Apollo, reconstruction drawing. (Knackfuss, 1941, Fig. Z.511)

temple of Apollo at Didyma (Fig. 6.21), which for size (163 × 341 feet, with sixty-foot columns), delicacy of detail, and the contribution it makes to 350 years of architectural history deserves to be (though it is not) ranked as one of the Seven Wonders of the World. It, like Miletus, is a German dig, begun in 1906 and continued, with interruptions, over a period of thirty-three years; if one man had worked alone, it would have taken him 178,800 days. Though all the expeditions's film negatives were burned and all the small finds destroyed or stolen during the Turkish-Greek troubles of 1916-22, the results, including over 600 inscriptions, have been exhaustively published. The work was rather one of clearing than of digging, since the blocks thrown down by an earthquake in 1493 encumbered the temple stylobate. One of them weighed over 100 tons. Many were built back into the walls by the excavators, to get them out of the way and to give some approximation of the grandeur of the temple when it was new (Fig. 6.17), in Alexander's time or slightly later. It replaced a temple destroyed about 479 in the Persian Wars: Alexander had propaganda reasons for building up what the Persians had knocked down. The bases of the front columns are varied in detail—palmettes, serpentines, meanders, panels with vegetable motifs, on twelve-sided plinths. Pairs of these match, on either side of the temple's central axis. The great central door, over eighteen feet wide, has a sill over five feet above the pavement. Obviously no one entered by it: it was rather a stage where the priest might appear or oracles be delivered. The entrances were lateral, through a pair of passages with barrel vaults, the earliest known in Greek lands; above these, stairs led to the temple roof. The striking feature of the temple was a sunken, probably unroofed, central court or adyton, a third as wide as it is long, approached by a monumental flight of steps. At its back, a small shrine or *naiskos* is oriented on a spring within its walls, which served some oracular purpose. The exterior steps on the temple's south side served as seats for the stadium adjoining. The labor involved in the building was colossal; the temple was still unfinished when the great earthquake of A.D. 17 struck it. In the environs, not yet excavated, must have been a complex of buildings like those at Olympia or Epidaurus.

A final example of monumental Ionic temple architecture of the fourth century is the Temple of Artemis at Sardis, the capital of Croesus' Lydia, forty-five miles up the Hermus valley east of Smyrna (Fig. 6.21). It was explored (1910-14) by the American H. C. Butler; excavations, in the hope of finding Croesus' palace, have been reopened by a joint Harvard-Cornell expedition, and are still under way. Butler's expedition was the most lavishly equipped of any up to his time: he had not only a light railway, but a locomotive, used to haul around the site a twenty-ton crane for raising large blocks. The great crane now lies abandoned near the temple, its rusted remains as impressive in their way as the temple itself. The workmen decorated the new engine with evergreens and flowers. Various parts of the site were interconnected by telephone, and the excavation house, Villa Omphale, was palatial, though it had been built in the record time of nine weeks. It had a tennis court, and a butler to serve cocktails; the excavators dressed for dinner.

The temple proved to be one of the largest in the Greek world. It measured 160 × 200 feet, and covered over 5000 square yards. Begun in Alexander's time (as mint-fresh tetradrachms of his testify, found in the base of the cult-statue), it, like Didyma, was never finished, for most of its sixty-five-foot Ionic columns (there were once seventy-eight in all) are unfluted. Butler found that trenches had been dug round the columns and filled with concrete, presumably as (vain) protection against earthquakes. Some of the columns are raised on pedestals left rough, but obviously intended to be carved like those of Ephesus. A capital from the temple at Sardis is in the Metropolitan Museum in New York.

It was not only the temples of fourth-century Asia Minor

that were colossal. When Mausolus, satrap of Caria, died in 353, his widow Artemisia decided to build for his body, on the heights behind his capital, Halicarnassus (Fig. 6.21), a huge tomb, which has given his name to all mausolea since. This Wonder of the World was explored in 1857 by C. T. Newton, and some of its sculptured frieze slabs, including four by the famous Scopas, were sent to the British Museum. Newton combined a keen eye for fragments on the ground with a good knowledge of ancient literature, including Vitruvius, who mentions the monument, and Pliny the Elder, who gives its dimensions. Using these clues, he narrowed down the possible location and then dug, using tunnels rather than trenches, for the ground in question belonged to many different owners, all recalcitrant and rapacious. He knew that he had had predecessors. Robbers in 1522, finding an opening like a cellar, had entered by candle-light to find themselves in a fine, large, square room, with marble half-columns and a frieze, which they first admired and then pulled to pieces to rebuild into a fort. A second chamber held a tomb. Postponing entry into it until next day, they were anticipated by yet other robbers (pirates, they called them). The first robbers on their return found nothing but strewn earth, fragments of cloth-of-gold, and spangles. Newton, in dismantling a wall made of column-drums, came upon a north-south cutting in the rock, with a pavement beyond it. Tunneling, he came to stairs, and a ten-ton block of green stone, which no doubt closed the tomb. Using Pliny's dimensions, he now found three of the four corners of the foundation, and at last knew which land to buy. He found masses of architectural and sculptural fragments and, along the east side, four slabs of a frieze of Greeks and Amazons, by Scopas: dramatic and pathetic, in his manner; vibrant with the antithesis of oblique parallel lines. The figures lunge or draw back, with one leg stretched out full length. The relief is deeply undercut, for it had to be seen from ninety feet below. Though there is some controversy about details of the restoration (Fig. 6.18), it is clear from ancient descriptions and from architectural fragments discovered by Newton, including pyramid steps hollowed out underneath and grooved to fit into each other, that the architect's aim was to persuade the viewer that a vast pyramid (80 × 100 feet) was supported by slim Ionic columns resting on a massive podium. (The pyramid was in fact supported by the cella walls.) Newton found a fragment of a colossal chariot wheel, seven feet seven inches in diameter, part of a quadriga or four-horse chariot group that crowned the pyramid. He found, too, the figures of Mausolus and Artemisia themselves, who were probably represented as riding in the chariot; they too are in the British Museum.

After the rather vulgar ostentation of these colossi, it is a relief to return to the comparative sanity of Lycurgan Athens. Though Lycurgus came to office in 338, the very year of Athens' crushing defeat by Philip of Macedon at Chaeronea, his faith in his city never wavered. But he backed his faith by legal precautions. During the period of his predominance, in 336 (the same year in which his fellow-citizens voted a gold crown to Demosthenes, despite the failure of his policy), was passed a decree against tyranny, found in the Agora in 1952, and now in the Agora Museum. The decree is in Lycurgus' doctrinaire spirit, and reflects the hysteria of the time by, in effect, abolishing due process and allowing each citizen to take the law into his own hands, for it empowers any Athenian to kill without fear of reprisal anyone whom he suspects of plotting against the democracy. The intent was apparently to prevent reactionaries in the high court of the

Fig. 6.18
Halicarnassus,
Mausoleum,
reconstruction
drawing.
(Krischen,
*Die griechische
Stadt*, Pl. 37, by
permission of
Gebrüder
Mann, Berlin)

Areopagus from supporting a pro-Macedonian dictatorship. The text is surmounted by a relief of Democracy crowning the Athenian People—as Athens had crowned Demosthenes. Some attempt was made in antiquity, whether by liberals, reactionaries, or connoisseurs of art is uncertain, to sever the relief from the text. The marks of the chisel are still visible. The mover of the decree, one Eukrates, died a martyr to the very tyranny he tried to circumvent: the pro-Macedonians executed him in 322, the year Demosthenes committed suicide, the year in which Athens' ancient political primacy ended forever.

But in Lycurgus' time Athens had not yet finally succumbed, and he proclaimed his belief in her future by his program of public works. Of his rebuilding the theater of Dionysus in stone we have already spoken. He also built, in a hollow by the Ilissus, 500 yards east of the Pisistratid Olympieium, a Panathenaic stadium that will be more appropriately discussed in the last chapter, in connection with its being restored in the second century A.D. by the millionaire Herodes Atticus. Lycurgus strengthened the city walls, and in a splendid if pathetic gesture built two stoas, promenades with shops in back, behind the assembly place on the Pnyx. His piety prompted him to build an altar between the stoas; the same piety moved him to add a portico to the Hall of the Mysteries at Eleusis, and probably to rebuild the temple of Apollo Patroos in the Athenian Agora, which had been purposely left in ruins after the sack of Athens in 479 as a reminder of Persian *Schrecklichkeit*. He also built the courtroom in the level beneath the north end of the Stoa of Attalus in the Agora, where the decree against tyranny was found. He was responsible, too, for the gymnasium in the Lyceum where Aristotle taught. His best-known building was the naval storehouse called the Arsenal, in Piraeus,* which is so clearly

* In July, 1959, workmen digging a sewer in Piraeus hit upon the arm of a bronze statue. This led to intensive exploration of the area, and more sensational finds: a whole set of bronze and marble statues, mostly of the fourth century, lying neatly together (Fig. 6.19) as though awaiting shipment, presumably to Rome. The warehouse was burnt, perhaps in the Sullan sack of 86 B.C., and the statues forgotten. They include an Artemis, a crested Athena, a Muse, and a large tragic mask, all in bronze, some with their marble-inset eyes in place. In the summer of 1961 two were being cleaned in Athens, two lay larger than life staring up from the floor of a room in the Piraeus

Fig. 6.19 Piraeus, bronze statues of Artemis and Athena, as found, 1959. Piraeus, Museum. (Vanderpool, 1960, Pl. 65.2)

Museum. When these finds are cleaned and properly displayed, they will make an impressive addition to the inventory of bronze statues of the classical age.

Fig. 6.20 Classical and post-classical sites in Greek lands, to illustrate Chs. 5-8, map.

described in a building inscription that it can be reconstructed (there is a model of it in the basement of the Piraeus Naval Museum at Pasha Limani), though not a single block of it survives. Used to store sails and tackle, it was 400 Attic feet long and 100 wide, divided into a long central hall and two side aisles supported by thirty-five Ionic columns. This divided the aisles into thirty-six rooms, closed off by wickets, on each side, each with a window, and each with an upper floor. The sails were stored in 134 cupboards below, the tackle above. Thus did Lycurgus, by the building of this impressive naval storehouse in a time of Athens' nadir, affirm her ancient supremacy on the sea.

Sanctuaries where the afflicted are healed by faith, theaters that are also assembly places, game sites where tyrants
proclaim their might and magnanimity, city plans that re-
affirm democratic individualism, colossal temples too expensive to finish, patriotism displayed after the tradition has
faded—all this is a part of the kaleidoscopic picture presented by archaeology of the Greek world in the fourth
century. It is customary to take 322, the date of the death
of Aristotle the philosopher and of Demosthenes the orator,
as the dividing line between the classical and the Hellenistic
Age, an age of monarchy and cosmopolitanism about which
archaeology has much to tell.

Fig. 6.21 Classical and post-classical sites in Greece and Asia Minor, to illustrate Chs. 5-8, map.

ADDENDUM
(all dates approximate)

B.C.
380 Epidaurus, Temple of Asclepius
     Olympia, Metroön
370 Mantinea; Messene earlier
368 Megalopolis, Thersilion & theater
360 Delphi, Temple of Apollo; Tholos earlier
     Nemea, Temple of Zeus
     Tegea, Temple of Athena Alea
356 Ephesus, Artemision E
353 Halicarnassus, Mausoleum (Scopas)
348 Olynthus destroyed
     Thasos, theater
338 Olympia, Leonidaion
     Athens, Theater of Dionysus; Stadium
334 Priene
     Olympia, Philippeion & Echo Stoa
     Hermes of Praxiteles
     Agias of Lysippus
330 Didyma, Temple of Apollo
     Eleusis, Prostoon
326 Athens, Stoas behind Pnyx; city walls
     Sardis, Temple of Artemis
300 Priene, theater

7 The Hellenistic Age
(322-146 B. C.)

For the years between the fall of Athens in 322 and Rome's destruction of Corinth in 146 B.C., excavation confirms the historical record: during these years Greece proper was in the doldrums. The wealth of building—palaces, new cities, grandiose works of engineering, splendid sanctuaries and stoas—was in the hands of the Hellenistic princes who succeeded Alexander: the Antigonids in Macedonia, the Ptolemies in Egypt, and the Attalids in Pergamum. (The Seleucids in Syria were great builders, colonizers, and city planners, too, but so far most of the archaeological evidence in Syria comes from Roman times.) At the sanctuaries—Ionian Claros, Lindos on Rhodes, Kos, Delos, the island of Thasos in the north Aegean—the gods competed with Mammon, and grandiosity was the hallmark of the age. Two of the Seven Wonders of the ancient world, the Pharos (lighthouse) at Alexandria and the Colossus of Rhodes, were built in Hellenistic times.

When in the spring of 1961 the Greek Archaeological Service celebrated the hundredth anniversary of excavation in Macedonia, the event they were commemorating was the excavation, by the Frenchman Leon Heuzey, of an axially planned building set in the wonderfully rich vale of Pieria, at Palatitsa, three hours south of Beroea, which in turn lies forty airline miles west of Salonika (Fig. 6.21). Heuzey discovered the site by the method that worked best before the days of air photography: incessant questioning of local inhabitants. On a plateau within the ancient city wall, which he had discovered in 1855, Heuzey noticed Doric and Ionic capitals built into the walls of a ruined church. Here he instructed his workmen, fifteen French sailors and forty Greeks and Bulgars, to dig a trial trench. Almost at once they struck footings. In the forty days before the sailors fell ill and the dig had to be abandoned, Heuzey uncovered half the building, enough to reveal its plan. A paved area led to a propylon between porticoes; on the left of the propylon he found a circular room with the footings of what he took to be a dais; beyond the propylon was a peristyle 150 Macedonian feet or 100 cubits wide; he did not dig back far enough to discover its length. Within the peristyle were traces of planting, flowerbeds or shrubs; around it, rooms were grouped, in at least two stories, for Heuzey found stairwells in two of the rooms, one on each side of the peristyle. The site was within eyeshot of Pella, the Macedonian capital. Heuzey concluded that what he had found was a summer palace, a Macedonian Fontainebleau; and he dated it, on the evidence of architectural technique, in the Periclean age. A Greek expedition under K. A. Rhomaios reopened the dig in 1953, and finished excavating the peristyle, which was found to be square, and with an epistyle furnished with triglyphs and metopes. Rhomaios discovered mosaic floors in the rooms at the back, or west side of the peristyle. The back wall was stuccoed to represent courses of stone. Rhomaios compared the circular room with the Philippeion at Olympia, and the architectural technique with the temple of Athena Alea at Tegea, and dated the building in the late fourth century. Perhaps its floors were once trodden by Philip II and Alexander. But archaeologists are a persistently unromantic breed, and many, noting the resemblance of the plan to the Leonidaion at Olympia and the pilgrims' hostel at Epidaurus, suppose the building to have been not a summer palace but a hotel.

Transcending Palatitsa in importance is Pella, where excavation has been going on since 1958. Pella's status as the ancient capital of Macedonia, the birthplace of Alexander the Great, has been emphasized by finds in the lower

Fig. 7.1   Pella, pebble mosaic of Dionysus riding on a panther, detail. Note how the lead strips emphasize the profile, eyebrow, and hair. (*AJA* 62 [1958] Pl. 84)

town. Roof tiles are stamped "Royal" or "Philip," some of
the streets are ten meters wide, the area is an impressive
three and a half square kilometers, and the private houses
are large, with rich bronze furnishings. But the most impressive finds have been the mosaic pavements of the late
fourth century B.C. One of the four courts and several of
the west rooms of a palatial structure that the Greek excavators call "Building 1" were floored with mosaics made of
natural pebbles, carefully matched and set, laid to bring
out the modeling of the figures. Profiles, eyes, ears, and toes
are outlined with thin strips of lead. One of the panels may
portray Alexander's trusted second-in-command, Craterus,
rescuing his young sovereign from the attack of a ferocious
lion. Other panels show Dionysus riding on a panther (detail,
Fig. 7.1), a griffin bringing down a stag, and a pair of centaurs. More mosaics were found in the late summer in
1961; all are on display in a temporary museum on the site.
All are masterpieces, ranking among the major discoveries
in Greece in recent years. Their effect must approximate
very closely that of monumental painting.

Alexander's most competent general was Ptolemy, who
took Egypt as his inheritance and made his capital at Alexandria (Fig. 6.20), that new foundation in a waste land by
the Canopic mouth of the Nile, between Lake Mareotis and
the sea, which was to become under the first three Ptolemies
the intellectual capital of the ancient world. From literature
we know much about the city, from archaeology tantalizingly
less, for Alexandria has been continuously inhabited since
its foundation, and the populous modern city of 1,150,000
lies over the ancient one. As late as 1866, when a plan of
the ancient city was made to the order of Napoleon III, it
was still possible to detect a part of the ancient grid (Fig.
7.2) of streets, and of the nine-and-a-half-mile circuit of
towered Ptolemaic walls, but now the Hellenistic city is almost entirely built over. The remains of a temple under the
modern bourse suggest that the present civic center was
also the ancient one.

The geographer Strabo describes the state of the palace
compound in 24 B.C. It lay southeast of the eastern harbor,
and occupied from a fourth to a third of the city's total
area. It took shape in the reign of Ptolemy II (285-246),
and included the mausoleum of Alexander, where the world
conqueror lay, according to legend, in diademed state, sur-

rounded by books and papyri in a sarcophagus of gold, replaced in the first century B.C. by one of glass. As recently as 1850 one Schilizzi pretended to have seen this marvel in its cage of glass in the crypt of a mosque by the Cairo railway station. Within the palace precinct was a botanical garden and zoo and, most important of all, the famous Library and Museum, "the birdcoop of the Muses," as an ancient satirist called it. It was a philanthropic foundation, like All Souls at Oxford or the Institute for Advanced Study at Princeton, where scholars subsidized by Ptolemy II lived, strolled in the shady peristyles, ate in the refectory, and read and wrote. Its collection of 700,000 scrolls, the cream of classical literature, was destroyed in a fire that broke out in the midst of rioting between Egyptian troops and Julius Caesar's occupation force in 47 B.C.

The palace was built of alabaster and polychrome marble (or marble veneer over brick); its furniture was inlaid with ivory, gold, and silver; its mosaics and rich rugs were famous. Of all this elegance all that archaeologists have been able to recover is a block of serpentine marble, a few syenite (Egyptian granite) columns, and Ionic and Corinthian column capitals of Hellenistic workmanship. These were found in the area indicated by Strabo as the palace site, on the waterfront near the present British consulate. Of the Library the only trace remaining is a block found in 1848, hollowed to contain three rolls of the works of Dioscorides, probably the epigrammatist; the botanist of the same name, author of a *materia medica* of which a number of handsome illustrated manuscripts exist, lived and wrote after the destruction of the Library. Of the Museum, nothing remains but a statue base inscribed with the name of a rhetorician, which probably once stood in its peristyle.

Of the city itself, too, literature has more to tell than archaeology, but the 1866 plan distinguishes, on uncertain evidence, eleven east-west streets and seven north-south ones. The main avenues, we are told, were 100 feet wide, and (as seldom in antiquity) lighted at night. From wall-paintings in tombs we know that the houses were high and towerlike. The city had a hippodrome, theaters, stadia, baths, gymnasia, temples of Greek and Egyptian gods, and a synagogue, for, in ancient as in modern times, Alexandria was a melting pot. It was famous for its multilevel vaulted reservoirs, 700 of which were still in use in 1866.

Alexandria's landscape, ancient temples, and public build-

Fig. 7.2 Alexandria, plan, made for Napoleon III in 1866. Ptolemaic palace was probably at east corner of Great Harbor (Grand Port); Library and Museum in Bruchium quarter. Pharos (lighthouse) at top of map. (Guide Bleu, Egypte, p. 41, by permission of Librairie Hachette, Paris)

ings reek of history and romance. On its beach were built the huts of the seventy rabbis who first translated the Old Testament from Hebrew into Greek, thus, as E. M. Forster drily remarks, enriching Greek literature with its earliest example of a book of revealed religion. West of Lake Hadra were found some granite columns of the Thesmophorion, where Antony and Cleopatra appeared as Osiris and Isis. An inscription bearing the name of Mark Antony was found in the area of the Caesareum, near the Ramleh railway station. In its precinct Cleopatra set up her obelisks in honor of Antony, the famous "Needles," one of which was set up on Victoria Embankment in London in 1877, the other in Central Park in New York in 1879. Near the east end of the main east-west street to Canopus was the gymnasium where Antony proclaimed Cleopatra Queen of Kings. When Pompey was murdered and decapitated by an Egyptian intriguer, on the beach at Alexandria in 48, the place where Caesar buried his head became a shrine or Heroön; its location is known, near the European cemetery. Another alleged memorial of Pompey, "Pompey's Pillar," near the Serapeum in the southwest quarter, is actually of the time of Diocletian (A.D. 284-305). Its eighty-eight-foot height was tempting to nineteenth-century travelers. In 1832 twenty-two people lunched on its top, "in a circle," and in 1843 an ascent was ingeniously made by flying over the Pillar a kite carrying a line and a hawser, which was then made fast on both sides, and people pulled up in a loop of rope to the top, where they drank Queen Victoria's health, eight at a time. More important archaeologically is the discovery, reported in 1942, of a mausoleum south of the Pillar so large as to be royal, probably the last resting place of the Ptolemies.

In the picturesque native village of Rosetta, east of Alexandria, a French officer discovered in 1799 the trilingual Rosetta Stone, now in the British Museum. When in 1822 Champollion guessed that the hieroglyphics enclosed in oval "cartouches" spelled a royal name, that of Ptolemy V Epiphanes (as he knew already from the Greek version of the honorific decree of 196/5 on the stone), Egyptian hieroglyphics had been deciphered, a landmark in the history of archaeology as important as Ventris' cracking of Linear B.

As often in archaeology, we know most about Alexandrians living from Alexandrians dead. A number of necropoleis has been excavated, a Greek one in the eastern quarter, Egyptian ones in the western and on the Pharos Island. At

Kom-el-Shugafa, near Pompey's Pillar, a three-level cata-
comb, discovered in 1900, filled with water; the results of
pumping it out and excavating it to the bottom were not
finally published till 1942. The striking thing about the
décor is the curious mixture of classical Greek and Egyp-
tain motifs. Hellenistic Greeks in Alexandria were far from
pure-bred, and a far cry from the nineteenth-century
ideal, which never actually existed, of classical Greeks, cool
and detached, seeing life steadily and seeing it whole. These
were Levantine types, clever at trade, intermarried with
natives. To the Matthew Arnold sort of classicist, they gave
Hellenistic Greek a bad name, from which it has hardly recovered until our own Hellenistic Age, in which E. M. Forster and Lawrence Durrell have felt and expressed the exotic
fascination of Alexandria.

Alexandria's most famous monument was of course its
lighthouse, the Pharos, the Wonder of the World, whose
name in Arabic, Manara, became the name of minarets on
mosques. Its white stone footings were discovered in 1898
in Fort Kait Bey, which guards the western arm of the
eastern harbor. To reconstruct its appearance in antiquity,
recourse must be had to Arabic descriptions made before an
earthquake felled it in A.D. 796, or before its complete
demolition in the thirteenth century. It rose over 400 feet
in the air from a terrace on the island cliffs. It was built in
three levels, the bottom one square and containing a reservoir and 300 stalls for beasts of burden, the middle one
octagonal, the top one round (Fig. 7.3). A ramp and circular
stair mounted to the light; they wound about a central shaft
in which fuel could be raised, probably by a hydraulic lift.
The light itself was reflected from a curved metal mirror,
which made it visible from twenty miles at sea. Apparently
the mirror could also be used as a burning glass to set
enemy ships on fire. It took twenty years to build, and was
probably finished under Ptolemy II Philadelphus, about 280.
Its towering height and ingenious mechanisms made it a
symbol of the might of the Ptolemies and the engineering
skill of the Hellenistic Age.

Ptolemaic influence at its height extended widely over the
Aegean basin.* Part of the archaeological evidence for it

* An interesting out-of-the-way example of it turned up at Thera,
which became a main Ptolemaic base for control of the Aegean. Here
Hiller found dozens of inscriptions set up by a pious Hellenistic
soldier who had fought for Philadelphus in the Arabian desert, and

Fig. 7.3 Alexandria, Pharos, reconstruction drawing. (Thiersch, *Pharos*, front., by permission of B. G. Teubner Verlag, Leipzig)

has been found on the remote, lovely, and inaccessible island of Samothrace (Fig. 6.21) in the north Aegean, where since 1863 French, Austrian, and American investigators have been at work on the sanctuary of the Samothracian gods, which profited richly from Ptolemy II's benefactions. The sanctuary was the Delos of the north Aegean, second only to Eleusis as a center for initiation into mysteries. Its soil has yielded a bilingual inscription in Greek and Latin reading, "Let no uninitiate enter here." The cult buildings stand picturesquely in a ravine shaded by plane trees. Interest in them was first aroused by the French discovery there (1863), in over 100 fragments, of the famous Victory of Samothrace (Fig. 7.4) now in the Louvre. Austrian excavations in 1873, 1875, and 1891 barely scratched the surface. Definitive results were first obtained by a series of

then served as admiral on the Thera station. His name was Artemidorus of Perge, and he enriched the island with a rock-cut Altar of Harmony, an eagle for Zeus, a lion for Apollo, a dolphin for Poseidon, and a splendid medallion of himself. He gives an excellent idea of the half-educated upper crust of the great world that now centered on Alexandria.

New York University campaigns begun in 1939 under the late Karl Lehmann († 1960), interrupted by World War II, and continued under his successors. Among other things, they investigated the actual findspot of the Victory, a fountain house where the statue had stood on a prow above and

Fig. 7.4 Nike of Samothrace. (Paris, Louvre)

behind a water basin amid the natural rocks in an architectural frame. They actually found more fragments of the statue: the ring finger of the right hand, and parts of the prow. Professor Lehmann's phenomenal memory enabled him to identify still more fragments in the storeroom of the Vienna Museum, where they had lain since the Austrian expeditions of the nineteenth century: all are now on display beside the statue in the Louvre. More important, he found pottery in the fountain house which at last firmly dates the statue, until 1952 a controversial point. The pottery is of the early second century; the statue, its drapery windswept and swirling like storm-tossed waves, was a dedication of the Rhodians (a fragmentary inscription with the name of a Rhodian sculptor was found with the statue) for a victory of about 190 over Antiochus III of Syria.

Excavation revealed that though the sanctuary was at the height of its prosperity during Ptolemy II's reign, the site had been occupied since the sixth century B.C. Though the ancient town southeast of the sacred precinct remains unexcavated, the builders of the government tourist pavilion in 1957 hit upon the town cemetery, which had been in uninterrupted use for 700 years from the sixth century B.C. Cremation burials were the rule until the fourth century, when inhumation began. The excavators noted that the Samothracians were generally short in stature and had bad teeth. One of the finds, from a grave of the third century B.C., was a terracotta model of an air-inflated ball, with polygonal sections and lacing, very like a modern basketball.

From the sixth century, too, date the earliest Hieron, or shrine of the Samothracian gods (see plan, Fig. 7.5), and a stoa east of it where votive gifts were displayed. In the fifth century the Anaktoron or Hall of Mysteries was built; the excavators found in it the put-holes for seats as in a theater, from which the initiation ceremonies could be viewed. Initiation involved a confession of sins and a religious trial, which very few passed. The challenge made successful candidacy all the more attractive, especially, in later times, to the Roman aristocracy. Yet slaves, too, were eligible, and the symbol of initiation was a simple iron finger-ring.

In the fourth century Philip and Olympias, the parents of Alexander the Great, met here and fell in love. To this century belong an archaistic frieze of dancing-girls from the temenos-propylon found in 1950, and an altar east of the Hieron.

Fig. 7.5 Samothrace, plan. A, Anaktoron; B, Sacristy;
C, Arsinoeion; D, Temenos; E, Hieron; F, Hall of Votive
Gifts; G, Altar Court; H, Theater; I, fountain with Nike;
J, Stoa; K, Propylon; L, "Ruinenviereck." (Lehmann, 1960,
back, by permission of J. J. Augustin, Inc., Locust Valley,
N. Y.)

In the third century the sanctuary was in its prime: Arsinoe, wife of King Lysimachus of Thrace (she later married Ptolemy II), dedicated (289-281 B.C.) to the Great Gods the Arsinoeion (see plan), over twenty meters in diameter, the largest round building known in classical architecture till Hadrian's Pantheon in Rome, built over 400 years later. Ptolemy built, too, the impressive western propylon. Evidence for the ruler-cult that the Ptolemies took over as a political expedient from the Pharaohs of Egypt was a colossal statue of Ptolemy II as Dionysus-Osiris, which once stood just east of the Hieron. The Hieron itself in its Hellenistic phase is dated about 250, late in Ptolemy II's reign; to excavate it, Lehmann's workmen had to move over 500 fallen blocks. Its uniquely early domed apse exerted its influence later on Roman buildings. The two hearths in the nave are an archaic feature; the *bothros* (sacrificial pit) in the apse reminds us that the Samothracian gods were deities of the underworld. The ceremonies were witnessed by the community of initiates seated behind parapets on marble benches in the lateral aisles. Finds of lamps prove that there were night services; finds of crockery, that the service included a cult meal. When the theater was built in 225 B.C., Samothrace had all the buildings it needed to make it one of the great Panhellenic shrines.

After two seasons, World War II interrupted the American excavations at Samothrace. When Lehmann returned in 1948, he found that the Bulgarians who had occupied the island had wantonly destroyed and damaged the ruins, the finds, and his equipment. They had pulled down what was left of the Arsinoeion, scrambled the carefully sorted pottery, and stolen his tents, the building material for the projected museum, and the rails of his light railway. The latter were subsequently recovered in Alexandroupolis, the nearest mainland town, and a Greek collaborator who had robbed stone from the Anaktoron was caught and tried. Samothrace had suffered what was neither its first nor probably its last destruction. Carefully kept excavation notebooks made it possible to re-sort the pottery; the museum has been built; but Bulgarian wantonness has inevitably delayed the final reports. It is poor consolation that Samothrace was not the only archaeological site to suffer war damage.

Important inscriptional evidence for Ptolemaic influence

has turned up also at Claros, between Colophon and Ephesus, where Louis Robert has been excavating since 1950. As often happens in the history of archaeology, he was attracted there on a search for inscriptions. He found many, mostly lists of visiting delegations from all over Asia Minor and Crete. But the search led to the discovery of something even more important and interesting. This time it was an early Hellenistic oracular shrine of Apollo, nearly as great in area as the temple at Delphi, with complicated and fascinating underground arrangements. Its general location had been known since 1907, but World War I interrupted the dig, and it was not until Robert found under four meters of silt some fallen Doric columns from the temple that a more precise idea of how the oracle worked could be obtained.

Robert found that from the temple porch a steep and initially winding stair gave access to a labyrinthine corridor, which changed direction at right angles seven times in thirty meters, to arrive at the first of two underground rooms with vaults too low to permit standing erect. The rooms were below water level, and full of fallen marble. They had to be pumped out and cleared before investigation could proceed. The necessary equipment was borrowed from a French company working in the harbor of Izmir (Smyrna).

One of the encumbrances was the colossal arm of the cult statue of Apollo. The arm was over ten feet long: the statue must then have been over five times life size. Later the sandaled foot was found. It bore on the buckle the figure of a sphinx, the symbol of the oracle. Other colossal fragments, this time of female statues, showed that Apollo had been flanked by his mother Leto and his sister Artemis. The trio appears on Roman imperial coins of Colophon.

The cleared front room of the underground oracular shrine proved to be equipped with benches where privileged consultants might await the oracle's response. The wait might be long, for the priests, as we know from inscriptions, retained the services of a functionary called the *thespiode,* whose job it was to put the god's answer into verse. At the back of the waiting room was a postern, through which Apollo's prophet used to go alone, at night, into the mystery of the dark, low, stifling inner chamber, where he drew his inspiration from a secret well. Robert found the well. It still held water, and, undeterred by the ancient report (of Pliny the Elder) that it was dangerous to drink, he tried it. It proved perfectly potable.

The colossal size of the cult statue, the long lists of visitors, who must have paid handsomely for the responses they sought, symbolize the tastelessness, the credulity, the commercializing of religion that archaeology has found to be increasingly characteristic of Greek culture in Hellenistic and Roman times. For monumentality not quite so tasteless we must travel north from Claros to Pergamum, capital of the Attalid dynasty.

Among the greatest rivals of the Ptolemies in politics and in philanthropic support of scholarship and the arts were the Attalids of Pergamum, a small kingdom in northwest Asia Minor (Fig. 6.21). The Attalid dynasty had risen to power through the defeat by its founder, Eumenes I (263-241 B.C.), of a wave of marauding Gauls who swept over mainland Greece and northern Asia Minor in the mid-third century. Defeated, they settled down on the central Anatolian plateau; their descendants were the Galatians to whom St. Paul wrote. Pergamum was at the height of its power and prestige in the first half of the second century B.C.; in 133 the last of the Attalids bequeathed his kingdom to Rome.

The modern rediscoverer of Pergamum was the German architect Carl Humann. Prevented by tuberculosis from finishing his studies in Berlin, he came in 1861 to the dry climate of Samos, where he helped to dig the Heraion. As a traveling surveyor, he first visited Pergamum in 1864, and prevented the Turks from breaking up for the limekiln the marble sculpture of the Attalid kings. He became chief road-engineer for the western Ottoman Empire, and in 1868 set up his headquarters in Pergamum, where he ruled like a Pasha over a population of 2000 workmen, 1000 oxen, and 500 camels, horses, and mules. Here he began a collection of antiquities, which he showed in 1871 to Curtius and Adler, the future excavators of Olympia. They encouraged him to send some of his finds to Berlin. Thus began, as a museum dig to recover *objets d'art,* an excavation that was to develop over a span of ninety years into a scientific exploration of a whole city, and to be responsible for making the whole of Turkey-in-Asia into a German archaeological domain.

On a chilly day in December, 1871, Humann extracted from the exceedingly tough mortar of a Byzantine wall on the Acropolis of ancient Pergamum a marble slab with the figure of a giant in relief, which he recognized as a masterpiece, and sketched with frost-stiffened fingers. He got the slab down from the Acropolis on a sledge and shipped it to

Berlin, where it evoked wide comment. Humann knew that it came from a frieze, but he thought it was the frieze of the nearby temple of Athena. However, in 1872 a scholar in Berlin happened upon a passage in Ampelius, an obscure late-Roman author of a book *On the Wonders of the World,* mentioning as one of the wonders an Altar of Giants at Pergamum. It was obviously a slab from this frieze that Humann had found. It proved to be the first of a series of ninety-four, plus some 2000 fragments, which archaeological ingenuity pieced together and set in order in a frieze 400 feet long, the second most extensive in all Greek art—only the Parthenon frieze exceeds it. Around it were built in 1901 the collections of the Pergamon Museum in Berlin. During World War II the slabs were first hidden in a bunker under the Reichsbank, then in an anti-aircraft tower in the Tiergarten, but the Russians discovered them and carried them off. They became a ponderous plaything in the propaganda war over Berlin. Since the Pergamon Museum is in the Russian zone, the captors of the frieze sent it back (1958), and it is now reinstalled, available once more for admiration and study as the most extensive and characteristic example of Hellenistic art, massive, bursting, explosive, a far cry from the repose which for Winckelmann in the eighteenth century had been the hallmark of classical art.

Humann knew that the heavy slabs built into the Byzantine wall could not have come from far away: one ten-ton piece took twenty men half a day to get down from the Acropolis. Exploring near the wall, he soon exposed the ground plan of the altar, a rectangular grid of foundation blocks. But it was not until almost the last stroke of the pick in cleaning the altar that its first architectural member was found in place: it proved to be a step on the west side. Here architecture and sculpture interlock: one of the frieze-slabs had a stepped bottom profile, along which a giant's serpent leg wound its way. Another giant supports his knee and hand on a step, so that it is clear that the altar had, enclosing the stair, two projecting wings, sculptured on their inner faces. All three outer walls of the altar were sculptured. The twenty-eight steps led through a double Ionic colonnade to a rectangular court enclosing the altar proper. Round this court ran a smaller frieze illustrating—an innovation—the story of Telephus, the mythical ancestor of the Attalid dynasty. The tale bears some resemblance to that of Moses in the bulrushes, or Romulus and Remus. The subjects on the thirty-five slabs found include Telephus' parents, Heracles and Augê (Heracles, who appears also on the Great Frieze, provides a link between the two compositions); the child Telephus being exposed on a hillside to die, in accordance with an oracle; mother and child being put into a sort of ark; and the landing in Mysia, whose king, Teuthras, rescues them.

It remained to determine the order of the slabs of the Great Frieze. Its cornice blocks bore key letters in three series, to help the workmen assemble the slabs in proper order on each of the three outer faces of the altar. Besides, the figures on some of the slabs were labeled, their names inscribed on the stone. The arrangement thus determined could be double-checked by observing mason's marks, and the put-holes for clamps and dowels, as Dinsmoor was to do later at Bassae. In addition, there were joins between slabs, which were cut in varying widths, the principle being not to cut through torsos. (An incidental inference from this is that the frieze must have been carved from an over-all cartoon, though over a dozen hands have been detected in its execution.) The juxtaposition at one corner was established by noting a sophisticated, even a humorous touch: Ares and Aphrodite, who were once caught in a compromising position by Aphrodite's husband Hephaestus, are portrayed fighting, rather shamefacedly, back to back. This detail has been used to argue that the altar was conceived not as a religious dedication but as a courtly monument, too learned for ordinary mortals. But the allusion would not have escaped any reader of Homer, who tells the story, and Homer was everybody's poet.

The key letters begin on a slab that portrays Zeus impaling with his thunderbolt the giant Porphyrion, who had bright inlaid eyes. This strikes the leitmotif of the whole composition: as Zeus, the symbol of civilization, defeats the giant, symbol of barbarism, so had the civilized Eumenes defeated the barbaric Gauls. But the altar belongs not to the time of the third-century Gallic invasion, but to the embellishment of the whole Acropolis after Eumenes II's victory over King Prusias of Bithynia at Magnesia in 190 B.C. So the symbolism is plural, and the frieze projects, in a thoroughly Greek way, historical events into a mythological world.

The Porphyrion slab had adorned the altar's east face. As one entered the precinct through a gate on the south-

Fig. 7.6 Pergamum, Great Altar, Biter Group from east face. The contorted features, writhing snakes, weapon raised to strike in upper right corner typify violence of this sculpture. (Berlin, Staatliche Museen)

east, the eye was attracted to the figures of Zeus and Athena on this same face, which is therefore established as the main one in the composition. Athena has the giant Alcyoneus by the hair to pull him off the ground, but his outstretched left foot still touches the strength-giving breast of his mother, Earth. From this face, too, come the "Biter Group" illustrated here (Fig. 7.6) as typical of the violence of the whole composition. Chariots and teams frame Zeus and Athena, as on the Parthenon west pediment. This is not the only tribute to Phidias by the Pergamene sculptor. On the altar's south face are represented the gods of light; on the north face, the gods of darkness; just so, the Parthenon east pediment is framed by the horses of the sun in one corner of the gable and of the moon in the other. Sea-gods line the altar's left stair wall (the side nearest the Aegean), Dionysus and his mountain band the right. Thus the great central battle on the east face is enclosed between day and night, mountain and sea.

Humann, besides being a skilled engineer, was something of a pirate, combining energy and ingenuity with ruthlessness. He spent 1300 working days dismantling the Byzantine wall, 700 on tracing the plan of the altar, 600 on transporting and loading the slabs. For this purpose he built a serpentine road that wound round the Acropolis; when the excavation was finished he cut away a stretch of the road to discourage dilapidators. He had made the Turks build their bridges of wood to teach them the necessity for maintenance, but he found himself hoist with his own petard when the cameldrivers used the wood from the bridges for their campfires, thus cutting his precious slabs off from the port. He got them there at last, but lighters could not come close enough to shore for direct loading, so, until he could build a new jetty, he slid the slabs onto the lighters on railway rails. Thus he loaded his treasure on a German gunboat, and quickly transshipped it to a Lloyd Triestino freighter before the Turks should realize he was violating his firman. He had little use for either Greeks or Turks, referring to the former as "half-educated sons of Hellas," or "Bulgarian lumps who want only to dicker," and remarking on the latter that the frieze fragments in the Constantinople Museum could be extracted by the judicious use of backsheesh. Lest the Turks should discover the beauty of the slabs, he left the Byzantine mortar on them, or left them lying face down (thus postponing his own discovery of the key slab with Zeus and the thunderbolt). His compatriots appreciated all this more than the Greeks and Turks: when he visited Berlin in 1880 he was received like a victorious general. In 1884 the Turks forbade all further export of antiquities.

Aesthetic judgments on the frieze vary, but, even granting that Hellenistic art is not absolutely of the first rank, the judgment of a distinguished English critic, Sir Bernard

Ashmole, that the frieze is a creaking pageant, seems unduly harsh. The sculptor's powers of invention are well-nigh inexhaustible, the drama he unfolds is immense and cosmic. He is a master at representing violent movement; his rendering of drapery, with its pronounced ridges and valleys, has been well described as "loud." Perhaps we can best epitomize the equivocal position of the Pergamum frieze in art criticism by noting that it appealed strongly to Roman taste, and that the notorious Laocoön in the Vatican is deeply influenced by it.

The frieze is by no means the only thing that Pergamum has yielded up to the archaeologist's spade. The excavation of the altar precinct was only the beginning; it led to the exploration of the whole city; first, in the nineteenth century,

Fig. 7.7 Pergamum, Acropolis, model. From top to bottom, arsenal, palace, temple and precinct of Trajan, Library (the two-storied building), with temple of Athena in front and theater below, left; Great Altar (left of center), and Upper Agora. (Berlin, Staatliche Museen)

the Upper Agora (see model, Fig. 7.7) and temple of Athena.
The latter's orientation, together with that of the precinct
entrance, determined that of the Great Altar, which was so
placed that the line of the temple's northwest side, pro-
longed, would just touch its northwest corner. From a round
building near the temple came the famous sculpture of the
dying Gaul, a copy of which is in the Capitoline Museum
in Rome. Enclosing the temple was a two-storied stoa, containing, appropriately enough in the precinct of the goddess
of wisdom, a library, the second largest in the Hellenistic
world. (The word "parchment" is derived from the name
"Pergamum.") Antony made a present of this library to
Cleopatra.

Also on the Acropolis were excavated the Trajaneum, of
Hadrianic date (A.D. 117-138), on the topmost point. Here,
too, is the spectacular theater, of about 170 B.C., one of
Pergamum's five, with steeply sloping tiers of seats. The
theater terrace has five floors of rooms below it, and on top
a temple of Dionysus transformed in the early third century
A.D. into a temple of the Roman Emperor Caracalla. The
Acropolis boasts no less than five palaces, with mosaic floors
in black-and-white triangles with green and red banded or
floral surrounds, and walls painted in yellow, blue, rose, and
red, with dados imitating marble; meanders and egg-and-
dart moldings painted to look three-dimensional; and wall
paintings of swags of fruit and flowers, and birds, as in the
Villa of Livia at Prima Porta near Rome. In an area once
known as the "Queen's Garden" excavation in 1927 unearthed a complex whose thick walls and heavy floors proclaimed it an arsenal, built probably about 200 B.C. against
the threat of Philip V of Macedon. Its warehouses could
hold a year's supply of grain for 1000 men. Most interesting
of all was the discovery here of 894 stone catapult-balls, in
seven calibers, ranging in weight from a mina (14.3 lbs.)
to three talents (167.2 lbs.).

Between 1900 and 1914, the Germans excavated the middle and lower cities, and found a massive triple-terraced
gymnasium, dated by an inscription 147/6, whose amenities
included an odeum, or covered theater, seating 1000; sanctuaries of Demeter and Hera, the former with impressive buttressed walls. East of the latter they excavated two-storied
private houses of Roman times, unpublished since 1913,
with frescoes and mosaics. Since World War II the building
of a new road to the Acropolis, to replace the one deliberately

cut away by Humann, disclosed a residential quarter of Hellenistic and Roman date, the houses crowded together on a forty-five-degree slope. Unfortunately no archaeologist was present when the road was built, so that the pottery found has no context. But the molded ware called *terra sigillata*, which used to be considered of Roman date, has had to be pushed back into Hellenistic times as a result of discoveries at Pergamum, and so has the encrusted stucco interior decoration called Pompeian First Style.

Since 1927 activity has concentrated on the lower town. Modern Bergama, a city of 25,000 (about the size of ancient Pergamum) overlies the Roman city; its streets and alleys follow the ancient ones, as digging of trenches for water mains has proved. The most interesting recent excavation (since 1951) has centered in the Asklepieion, founded in Hellenistic times (with Sub-Mycenaean or Protogeometric sherds from lower habitation levels) but at its height in the second century A.D., when Galen the physician taught and practiced here, and the rhetorician Aelius Aristides lectured in its theater. The theater has been reconstructed, and is used for performances of ancient Greek plays and modern

Fig. 7.8 Pergamum, Asklepieion, model, from southwest. Across back, from left to right, library, propylon, temple of Asclepius, and Pump Room, where patients slept. (*SPHS Arch. Rpts.*, 1960, P. 33)

Turkish folk dances. It lies on the northwest side of a large peristyle (see model, Fig. 7.8). Bordering the east side are a library, Asclepius' temple, modeled on the Pantheon in Rome and therefore to be dated after A.D. 125; and a round building with six apses, the dormitory where, as at Epidaurus, the faithful were healed in their sleep. (The sanctuary was founded, as an inscription records, by a Pergamene who had been cured at Epidaurus.) Mud-packs assisted faith in the healing, and neither, apparently, was always entirely successful, for the body of a woman with arthritis, found in the sanctuary, bears evidence of having been buried in a hurry, before the other patients should discover that the god was fallible. From the dormitory building an underground passage leads to a well near the middle of the enclosure, and a vaulted corridor leads westward to an elegant latrine, with thirty-five marble seats and handsome Corinthian columns.

During World War II Pergamum suffered vandalism, though not to the same extent as Samothrace: 525 heaps of ancient architectural members, piled in the peristyled enclosure, were stolen and put to some practical use; they might have been used in further reconstruction of the sanctuary.

Despite the wealth of finds, which makes Pergamum the best-documented of Hellenistic sites as well as one of the most interesting, 40 per cent of the work remains to be done, and fascinating discoveries are to be expected from the excavation of the Sacred Way that approaches the Asklepieion from the east, where lies, for example, the largest of Pergamum's five theaters, with a Hellenistic level dated by stamped amphora handles to 180-100 B.C.

The Attalids were not content to adorn only their own city. Attalus II (159-138) had been educated in Athens, and in gratitude he built on the east side of the Athenian Agora the stoa that bears his name. Attalus' brother, Eumenes II (197-159) had already set the example by building a stoa on the south slope of the Athenian Acropolis, between the theater of Dionysus and the spot where later the Odeum of Herodes Atticus was to stand. Both served practical purposes: promenade, shopping center, grandstand—the Panathenaic procession passed the Stoa of Attalus on its way to the Parthenon. The Middle Stoa, at right angles to the Stoa of Attalus (see plan, Fig. 7.9), half promenade, half mar-

Fig. 7.9   Athens, Hellenistic Agora, plan. (Agora Excavations)

ket, like the Stoa of Philip V at Delos (to be described later) was probably the gift of Attalus' brother-in-law and fellow-student in Athens, King Ariarathes V of Cappadocia

(162-130). What the excavators call South Stoa II belongs to the same period. It served, with the Middle and East Stoas, to separate off a smaller area from the main square, perhaps for a market, though the excavators found no shops, booths, stalls, weights, or measures in it.

The Stoa of Attalus has been completely rebuilt, and now houses the Agora Museum, storerooms, workrooms, and offices. A description of the Agora excavations as a whole is best postponed to the chapter on the Greek world under Roman sway, since the Agora reached its peak of development under Augustus, but this is the place to describe the Stoa and its reconstruction.

Its dimensions (382 feet long, 64 feet broad) and plan (two-storied double colonnade, with twenty-one shops behind on each floor) had been known since Greek excavations of 1859-62. It was then that the discovery of epistyle fragments bearing King Attalus' name put the identification of the building beyond doubt. Much of the remains had been shielded by the so-called "Valerian Wall" which was built right through the ruins of the building after its woodwork had been burned in the Herulian sack of A.D. 267. Under the north end were found several Mycenaean chamber tombs, and a room in use in the fifth and fourth centuries was part of a law court, an inference from some jurors' ballots found in it. These are bronze disks with an axle through the middle, pierced for conviction, solid for acquittal. If the juror held the disk by the axle between thumb and forefinger, he could drop his ballot into the urn without anyone's knowing how he had voted. These ballots had apparently fallen by accident at the time the room was abandoned. A gutter-block that had settled out of position proved to conceal a well that yielded sixty-five five-gallon containers of sherds datable 520-480 B.C., obviously from a retail potter's shop, since many of the vases were of the same type or even by the same hand. The Hellenistic shops served a variety of purposes: several have been restored for museum exhibits, with shelving modeled on the ancient, whose position was revealed by cuttings in the walls. One shop yielded surgical instruments. At the north end the oldest visible arch in the history of Greek architecture masks the end of a barrel-vault supporting the stairs.

The story of the reconstruction of the Stoa provides one of the most interesting examples in the history of archaeology of scientific inference at work. The guiding spirit was

Homer A. Thompson, Director of the Agora Excavations, acutely and ingeniously assisted by John Travlos, the Agora architect. From surviving ancient blocks they knew the materials needed: blue Hymettus marble for the steps, gray Piraeus limestone for the walls, white Pentelic marble for the façade, columns, and interior trim, clay from the clay-pits of Attica for the roof tiles. Material from the same places was used when the reconstruction began in 1953. The drums for the columns were delivered from the quarry roughly squared; the corners were then chamfered, and with careful hand work, by sixty marble-workers, using toothed and straight-edged chisels little changed since antiquity, the marble began slowly to assume cylindrical shape. The restorers knew from surviving capitals that the outer columns were Doric on the ground floor, double Ionic above, with a balustrade for safety closing the intercolumniations. Only the outer row of columns was fluted, since fluting depends for its effect on being struck by the sun. The inner row was Ionic on the ground floor, palmleaf above, the latter capital being one much favored by Pergamene architects. The columns of the bottom outer row, since each consisted of three drums, were best fluted *in situ,* the bottom drum being left unfluted to avoid damage from foot traffic. Teams of four men worked seventy-six man-days to flute the first column, at a cost of $300. (The Erechtheum building-accounts show that in 407/6 teams of five to seven men worked 350 man-days per column, at 350 drachmas per man, but those were taller columns, fully fluted, and of harder stone.) The original floors had been a rough mosaic of marble chips (*lithostroton*); the reconstruction uses the same material which, polished, is called *terrazzo.* The ancient beams were restored, for protection against fire, in reinforced concrete, reveted with laminated wood (imported, but so must the wood have been to deforested Attica in Hellenistic times.) The position and size of the beams were determined from sockets in the ancient stonework. Reinforced concrete piers were inserted in the heart of the ancient walls, but enough ancient blocks were bonded with the modern to show the evidence on which the reconstruction was based.

In September, 1956, the finished Stoa (Fig. 7.10) was dedicated by the Patriarch of Athens and All Greece, in the presence of King Paul and Queen Frederica, and 1500 invited guests, for all of whom the building successfully discharged its original function of keeping crowds of people

Fig. 7.10 Athens, Stoa of Attalus, reconstructed, photo taken before dedication, 1956. (Agora Excavations)

cool on a hot day. Again as in Attalus' time it serves as a
screen between market and city. Since it sits low, it does
not compete with the buildings on the Acropolis or the
Hephaistaion, and, as the loving hand-work weathers, it
serves better and better to allow modern visitors a unique
opportunity to appreciate the scale and spatial effect of a
splendid piece of Hellenistic civic architecture. And ten shops
thrown together on the ground floor house the Agora Museum, whose displayed finds, from Neolithic to Turkish, span
5000 years of Athenian history. In the lower portico, statues
and inscriptions are set up near where they were found,
showing to advantage in a raking light. In the basement and
upper story a large bulk of material (over 68,000 inventoried items, plus over 94,000 coins, in June, 1961), un-
suitable for public display, is made accessible to scholars,
and a model of the Agora enables visitors (47,000 the first
year, 150,000 the second, the numbers growing annually)
to orient themselves from a point of vantage. Thus a phil-
hellenic gesture of a Hellenistic philanthropist from the east
has been repeated in our time by philanthropists from the
west: the new world redressing the balance of the old.

The remaining Hellenistic monuments to be described in
this chapter all happen to be on islands, five in the Aegean
and one on Sicily (see maps, Figs. 6.20 and 6.21). This is
more coincidental than important, except insofar as it illustrates once more the comparative poverty and obscurity
of mainland Greece in the Hellenistic Age. The more significant common feature of all six is that though they all
have something to do with religion, they have, in one way
or another, more to do with commerce: the Hellenistic Age
is an age of God and Mammon.

Delos, holy city and mart of trade, vastly expanded in
extent and scale since archaic days, reached the height of
its prosperity in the Hellenistic Age. The French excavators,
who, it may be remembered, have been working here since
1872, subsidized by a rain of gold from the philanthropic
Duc de Loubat, found that Hellenistic Delos "masked and
stifled" the rest. To the Hellenistic Age, when pilgrimages—
or tourism—were especially fostered, belonged "a Marble
Stair-cafe, moft of whofe steps have been taken away, and
carry'd to Mycone to make Window-cafes of" which a
French traveler saw on Mt. Cynthus in 1729 (English translation of 1741). Delos remained, during the first three quar-

ters of the nineteenth century, a vast ruin-covered expanse with a few courses of wall rising here and there above the rest. Now, thanks to the French excavators, it is, with its Hellenistic temples, theater, stoas, gymnasia, stadium, palaestra, houses, port, quays, moles, warehouses, and dockside taverns, the most varied—as well as the most ravaged—site in Greek lands, the Pompeii and the Ostia of the Aegean world. The staff of the American School of Classical Studies in Athens regards it, and rightly, as the ideal site on which to introduce students to the fascination and complexity of archaeology. The French used it as a training ground for the young fellows of their School in Athens, who were to become their most distinguished archaeologists. Oblivious to boredom, an austere and Spartan standard of living, and bouts of fever, they would stay on the island for five and a half months at a time, supervising gangs of 160 to 200 workmen, measuring, drawing plans and reconstructions, restoring, cataloging, deciphering inscriptions. These last they found especially valuable. During the period of Delian "independence" (314-166), and even more in the following years, when Delos was an Athenian colony, the dated temple-accounts are detailed enough to make possible an architectural history of the Hellenistic city. Expenditures recorded for varnishing wood or replacing roof tiles tell us when a temple was restored; lists of over thirty buildings, arranged by regions, make the epigraphic evidence as useful as Pausanias. The records of nineteen sacred houses and estates survive, including those of farms on the island of Rheneia, westward across a narrow channel: the farmhouses were provided with towers for lookouts and defense against pirates. All combine to show how rich and powerful the temple bureaucracy was.

Delos, nominally independent, came successively under the influence of the Ptolemies, the Antigonids of Macedon, and the Attalids, who vied with each other to adorn the temples, monumentalize their setting, and provide amenities. Thus Ptolemy I built about 308 a sanctuary of Asclepius at the south end of the island, and beautified the temple of Apollo; Ptolemies and Antigonids both contributed, over a period of sixty years from about 300, to the building of a theater (see plan, Fig. 7.11) modeled on the one in Athens. Sheltered from the prevailing north wind, it has seats for 4000 to 5000, a stage eleven feet high; the proscenium had slots for inserting painted scenery. An inscription records that King Antigonus

Fig. 7.11 Delos, plan. The Lion Terrace (TL) lies below Sacred Lake (Etang); H₂, temple of Apollo; left of H₄, Stoa of Antigonus; 51-55-56, Stoa of Philip; 59, Hypostyle Hall. Theater and theater quarter in lower right quadrant; sanctuaries of foreign

gods to r. of center; Mt. Cynthus in upper r. quadrant. (Vallois, Documents [1953], folding plan at back, by permission of Ecole Française, Athens)

Gonatas of Macedon (283-239), to celebrate a victory over the Egyptian fleet off the island of Kos in 246, built north of the temple of Apollo a vast double stoa, some 400 feet long, with projecting wings, modeled on Philip II's at Megalopolis and the Stoa of Zeus in the Agora in Athens. Philip V of Macedon (211-179) built early in his reign another stoa southwest of the temple, also identified by its dedicatory inscription. It is the largest roofed building in the sanctuary; it was intended to compete in grandeur with a rival building of Attalus I of Pergamum (241-197). The Attalids finished, though the Ptolemies or the Antigonids began, a south stoa that combined in a typically Delian way the customs house and a chapel to Hera of the Harbor.

Foreign trade attracted foreign gods, whose sanctuaries clustered on the slopes of Mt. Cynthus, above the theater. The Samothracian gods were there, and from Egypt came Serapis, Isis, and Anubis, who cured the sick and saved sailors; from Syria Hadad and Atargatis. From their temple come lead figurines, bringing down curses on the person of the dedicant's choice. The heads are hammered away and iron nails are driven through the bodies. Thence, too, comes a pair of bronze ears, to help Atargatis listen to the prayers of the faithful. Among the foreign interlopers old Greek heroes still had a place, like Castor and Pollux, before whose shrine runners bearing torches ran races under the stars.

The whole island, marsh, plain, hill, and shore, was crammed with sanctuaries, and the sacred precincts swarmed with pilgrims, tourists, and souvenir-sellers. The pilgrims would disembark, singing, pass along the processional way and the Lion Terrace to Apollo's temple, and whip themselves around the venerable Altar of Horns. The air was full of chanting, the smoke of sacrifice, the smell of incense, the beat of the sacred choral dance, in which the daughters of the first families of Delos and Athens took part. Apollo's temple was full of dedications and relics: crowns high on the walls, cups on shelves below, more dedications on tripods and tables, minor or discarded offerings in chests. Among relics* the credulous could admire Eriphyle's necklace, Aga-

---

* The cult of relics in antiquity is a fascinating subject. The temple of Apollo in Sicyon, west of Corinth, boasted Agamemnon's sword and shield, Odysseus' cloak and breastplate, a sample of Penelope's weaving, the kettle Pelias was boiled in, the Argonauts' oars, the hide of Marsyas (the satyr who was flayed alive for daring to compete with Apollo in a musical contest), and Athena's ballot cast to acquit Orestes on the charge of matricide.

memnon's tiller, the jewels and ivory daggers of Darius' generals, and the helmet of Leonidas, the Spartan hero of Thermopylae (for Delos, like Delphi, played both sides).

Delos the holy city flourished as a mart of trade. An index of its prosperity, provided by inscriptions, is soaring house-rents. A rich merchant would buy a block of houses, knock down walls, enlarge the peristyle, and build colonnades. The result is such a palatial residence as the House of the Masks (discovered in 1939), whose nineteen rooms include four with mosaics (from one of which the house is named), latrines, terracotta baths sunk in the floors, slave quarters (Delos was a mart where 10,000 slaves might change hands in a day), and a porter's lodge. Delian houses are better preserved than the temples, because their walls were built of less valuable and tempting materials, and so less subject to stone-robbing. The mosaics are famous, as in the House of the Dionysus, where the god is portrayed riding on a particularly ferocious panther; and the House of the Dolphin, where the French have done a particularly fine job of restoration. The houses were sometimes oriental in their ostentation, their peristyle columns reveted with plaques of gilt bronze.

Delian streets were winding and steep, often with steps, but paved, and lighted at night by lamps in niches on each side of the doors of the principal houses. These were often owned by South Italians, who began to come to Delos as early as 250 B.C., to engage in marine insurance, or the prof-itable grain trade. They and other foreigners founded gilds and cult associations, often splendidly housed, like the Poseidoniasts of Beirut. The Italians built toward the end of the second century an Agora of their own, north of the Stoa of Antigonus. It is the most spacious on the island, covering nearly 7800 square yards; it is surrounded by offices, like the Piazzale delle Corporazioni at Ostia. There is no physical connection between the warehouses where the grain was stored and the city proper, for goods reaching Delos were usually in transit, not intended for home consumption. The commodities stored in the warehouses were bought, sold, and speculated in in the Delian Stock Market, the Hypostyle Hall, northwest of the temple of Apollo, a huge building—only Philip's Stoa is bigger—covering some 2000 square yards, with a roof supported, a little shakily, by a forest of columns. The excavators date it about 208.

Visitors to Delos, businessmen or pilgrims, were housed in a hostel on the slopes of Mt. Cynthus, and fed in the quayside restaurants. They and the permanent residents formed a motley crowd, speaking every language of the Near East, and of every profession: inscriptions and shop signs mention grain-, oil-, and wine-dealers, fullers, millers, flute-makers, sculptors, contractors, architects, stonemasons, potters, jewelers, blacksmiths, workers in bronze and lead, carpenters, mosaic-makers, and painters. All worshiped the gods and made money. Some time not long before 166 the Athenians expelled the Delians to Achaea and replaced them with their own colonists. Of these, 20,000 out of 35,000 were massacred by King Mithridates of Bithynia in 88, and the survivors became victims of the pirate Athenodorus in 69. By Pausanias' time the only inhabitants of Delos were the guards of the ruins; when the Athenians tried to put the island up for sale, they could not find a single bidder, not even for one drachma. It was left for Christian writers to rejoice in the death-throes of Apollo in the solitude of his deserted island.

When the Athenians made Delos a free port in 166, it spelled the ruin of what had become one of the most prosperous centers of the Hellenistic world, the city of Rhodes. Rhodes is inevitably associated with that wonder of the world, the bronze Colossus, which guarded but did not span the harbor. If it had, the straddle of its legs would have had to be 400 yards! Archaeologists know from literary evidence that it was built between 304 and 292, broken off at the knees by an earthquake in 227/6, and finally demolished by the Arabs in A.D. 653. But they may also have some three-dimensional evidence. The most likely location for it is Fort St. Nicholas, at the end of the picturesque mole, dotted with windmills, which separates the Mandraki from the commercial harbor. The mole is ancient, and a great deal of ancient material is built into the tower of the fort, notably a doorsill, Hellenistic work, with a curved profile that would fit a base fifty-five feet in diameter, the right size to fit the Colossus, which was seventy cubits (something over 100 feet) high. Limestone blocks lying in the sea by the mole may come from the fill of the Colossus. If present plans to re-erect the Colossus materialize, archaeologists can use a Byzantine author, Philo, for details of how the statue was constructed. For scaffolding, the contractor used a 135-foot tower built by King Demetrius of Macedon, whose unsuccessful siege of Rhodes earned him the sarcastic epithet Poliorcetes, "Sacker-of-Cities." This tower the Rhodians had toppled and captured. The bronze was poured stage by stage (Fig. 7.12), the bronze skin held by dowels to an inner armature of iron, and the hollow core filled with blocks of stone, perhaps the very ones that now lie by the mole. The whole was braced with earth and scaffolding; when the bronze had set, its surface was polished and the scaffolding taken away.

Since World War II, archaeologists have learned something more about the city plan of Hellenistic Rhodes. Air photography, the tragedy of air bombardment, and the necessity of building bomb-shelters have provided the evidence; J. D. Kondis, Greek Ephor of Antiquities for Rhodes, and John Bradford* have interpreted it. The fifth-century city planner Hippodamus of Miletus is said to have laid down the grid, but the present evidence—pottery, amphora stamps, profiles of moldings, lamps, fragments of mosaic—does not antedate the fourth century, and the great bulk of it is Hellenistic. It shows that Hellenistic Rhodes was of immense size, five or six times that of the medieval town of the Knights. But the medieval main thoroughfare, the Street of the Knights, overlies a Hellenistic predecessor, and the Palace of the Grand Master is built over an important ancient building. As long ago as 1936, when the Italians controlled the Dodecanese, the Italian archaeological plan of the city recorded thirty-four classical finds within the medieval walls. But the westward suburbs, rising steeply to the Acropolis, Mt. Smith, (named for the English admiral who watched the movements of Napoleon's fleet from it in 1802) provide better evidence for the grid, and for ancient buildings. On the Acropolis are two temples, a stadium, a theater, and a gymnasium, excavated by the Italians but never published. The stadium occupied two blocks of the grid; lines of ancient drains underlie the modern street leading to it. The more northerly temple, dedicated to Athena, lay on a terrace like that of the gymnasium on the Acropolis of Pergamum and, as we shall see, the Asklepieion of Kos.

In the north Aegean, two and a half hours southeast of the Thracian port of Kavala, the French have been excavating on the lush and beautiful, hilly, pine-scented island of Thasos, thickly wooded with conifers, ilex, gnarled old olives, and chestnuts. Since World War II they have concentrated

* For Bradford's work in air photography, see *The Mute Stones Speak*, pp. 1-7 and Index.

Fig. 7.12 Rhodes, Colossus, sketch showing method of construction: armature, scaffolding, blocks within. (Gabriel, 1932, p. 337)

their efforts on the Agora. Its most impressive building, the northwest stoa (see plan, Fig. 7.13) they date on the evidence of its proportions to about 300. It is remarkable in having no interior colonnade; huge beams from the forests of Macedonia made it possible for the builders to span wide spaces without intermediate support. The stoa with projecting wings on the northeast side of the Agora, which probably slightly antedates the Hellenistic Age, illustrates the common language of Greek architecture: it has parallels in the Stoa of Zeus in Athens, of Philip at Megalopolis, of Artemis at Brauron in Attica, of Antigonus at Delos, of Athena Lindia on Rhodes (to be described later), at Mantinea and in another building, not mentioned in this book, at Calauria near Epidaurus (where Demosthenes committed suicide). An inscription from the Agora honors a Thasian named Theogenes who won 1300 times at Olympia! The agora, monumentalized as it is by the stoas that surround it, is typical of Hellenistic market squares or precincts, like the Commercial Agora at Miletus, the Delian sanctuary of Apollo after the building of Philip V's stoa, or the Attalid phase of the Agora in Athens.

The town of Thasos was girt by a wall with twelve towers and nine gates, nearly two and a half miles in perimeter. It rises steeply to the Acropolis, which is crowned with temples, and commands a sweeping view as far as Samothrace, fifty miles to the east. The town had its theater, odeum, and the usual complement of temples, some of which go back to archaic times. Its central interest lies in its being steeped in history. It was founded in the seventh century from the island of Paros; an archaic inscription found in the Agora memorializes a friend of the Parian satiric poet Archilochus. Polygnotus the artist was a Thasian. Thucydides the historian, as admiral of the Athenian fleet, operated in these waters in 425/4, and was exiled for defending Thasos (in whose mines his enemies said he had an interest) when his orders were to protect Amphipolis. Hippocrates the physician of Kos spent three years here beginning about 410, and recorded some observations made on the island. The body of Cassius, he of the lean and hungry look, was brought here after the battle of Philippi in 42. It is these associations that make the stones of Thasos speak.

Proceeding chronologically, we next make a great leap in space westward to Morgantina, in central Sicily near Piazza Armerina, where a Princeton expedition under Eric Sjöqvist

Fig. 7.13   Thasos, Agora, plan, actual state. Northwest Stoa
at left. (Martin, 1959, Plan A, by permission of Ecole Française,
Athens)

and Richard Stilwell has since 1955 been excavating a major
city, its location unrecorded in literature. It proves to be
Hellenistic and earlier, with an early grid plan. Paolo Orsi,
the great Sicilian archaeologist, discovered it in 1912. What
he hit upon, the Princeton expedition excavated completely:
two splendid monumental flights of steps meeting at an ob-
tuse angle (Fig. 7.14), which probably served as what the Ro-

Fig. 7.14 Morgantina, Agora steps. (Author)

mans would have called a *comitium,* or town-meeting place.
A Princeton geological survey shows its builder's clear technical insight: the steps and their retaining wall were carefully
planned to stabilize gliding banks of clay in the subsoil. A
nearby house with a mosaic of Ganymede, cupbearer to the
gods, is dated by coins somewhere between 260 and 211, and
the Agora steps must have been built close to the earlier date.
A stoa with shops in the Agora was left unfinished, probably
when the Romans overran Sicily in 212. A long thin building,
five times as long as it was wide, reminded the excavators of
the descriptions of the arsenal in Piraeus; it was probably a
warehouse. In the southwest corner of the Agora a building
emerged so crammed with lamps, that the excavators call it the
"Lamp Factory." Another Agora find was an offertory box
containing bronze coins of the third and second century.
Beyond the Agora an early altar was overlaid, in what we
have discovered to be typical fashion, with a meat market.
In May, 1961, an inscription revealed that Morgantina had a
theater as early as the fourth century; it has been dug, and
proves, uniquely, to be native Sicel instead of Greek in its
décor. The city wall (late fourth century) was over four and
a half miles around; its gates and posterns were sited in
relation to springs. Finds outside the wall include houses
and burials, some of the latter rock-cut, which go back to

archaic and even Neolithic times (in Italy, twelfth century B.C.), as determined by the latest techniques of pollen- and carbon 14-analysis.

Of all the sites selected for treatment in this chapter, perhaps the handsomest is the sanctuary of Athena Lindia on the Acropolis of Lindos, thirty-four miles southeast of the city of Rhodes. The temple was set on the edge of a sheer cliff high above the blue Aegean, and the golden patina of the limestone columns of its propylon and stoa makes a brave effect against the equally deep blue of the incomparable Greek sky. A Danish expedition under Kinch and Blinkenberg excavated here (1902-14), and another Dane, Einar Dyggve, studied the architecture further in 1952. He found that the temple's off-center position (see model, Fig. 7.15) was dictated by the presence directly beneath it in the face of the cliff of a sacred grotto, still venerated, though the Panagia—the Virgin Mary—has supplanted the maiden goddess Athena. The temple was finished about 330, its propylon about 300, and the stoa with its projecting wings (now seen to be typical of Hellenistic architecture) toward the end of the third century. Discreet restoration has made the Stoa particularly effective. The terraced treatment, the monumental staircases, the axial symmetry, the supporting of the terrace in front of the stoa on transverse barrel vaults have parallels, as we shall see, in the Asklepieion near Kos, and both had their effect upon Roman architecture, especially the splendidly terraced Sanctuary of Fortune at Praeneste,* while the barrel vaults reappear in the Coliseum. Distinguished Romans knew Rhodes well: Scipio the Younger studied here under the Stoic philosopher Panaetius, who came from Lindos and held religious office here in 149, as an inscription found by the Danes records. Caesar, Brutus, Cassius, and Cicero all studied here, and Sulla (who probably sponsored the sanctuary at Praeneste) and Pompey were visitors.

One of the most interesting finds from Lindos is the Temple Chronicle, discovered in 1904 in re-use, fortunately face down, in the pavement of an early Christian church on the west slope of the Acropolis, northwest of the cult theater. It is now in the Ny Carlsberg Museum in Copenhagen. It records gifts to the goddess by mythological and historical characters: King Cadmus of Thebes, King Minos of Crete, Telephus of

* See *The Mute Stones Speak*, 124-153.

Fig. 7.15 Lindos, Acropolis from east, model.
Note vaulted substructure, stoa with.

Mysia (the mythical ancestor, it will be recalled, of the Pergamene kings), Heracles, Menelaus, Helen (a breast-shaped cup); Cleobulus of Lindos, one of the Seven Wise Men of Greece (a large masonry tumulus fifteen minutes away to the east is allegedly his tomb, but the workmanship looks fourth-century); Phalaris the cruel Sicilian tyrant; King Amasis of Egypt, King Artaphernes of Persia, Alexander, Ptolemy I, King Pyrrhus of Epirus, Hiero tyrant of Syracuse, Philip V of Macedon. The chronicle also records miraculous apparitions of the goddess in time of Rhodian peril, as in the sieges by Darius and Demetrius Poliorcetes. Lindos was the center of a famous school of sculptors: Chares, who built the Colossus of Rhodes, was a native son; the name of Pythokritos, the sculptor of the Victory of Samothrace, is recorded here, and, cut in the rock beside the steep stair leading to the Acropolis, is a handsome ship that was a statue-base, like the Victory's prow; the Danes date it about 170; it supported, appropriately, the figure of a priest of the sea god Poseidon. If the Danes are right in believing that they have also found the names of the sculptors of the Laocoön, they were born between 80 and 75, and that sculpture must be of the late first century B.C., but this is a controversial matter.

The last Hellenistic complex to be discussed is close in spirit and plan to the Acropolis of Lindos: it is the triple-terraced Sanctuary of Asclepius, about two miles southwest of the island city of Kos. The first scientific visit to the site, then known locally as "Hippocrates' Castle," was made in 1891 by the Englishman W. R. Paton, in search of inscriptions. He found and published 450; Rudolf Herzog, a young instructor at Tübingen, following after him, found 575 more. They made it clear that the site was an Asklepieion. (That one existed in the suburbs of Kos was known from a vignette in verse, one of the *Mimes* of Herondas, who flourished about 275; it describes the crush of visitors to the shrine and the feeding of the sacred snake.) Herzog, convinced that the complex would rival Epidaurus, determined to excavate it, with his own modest means. He hit almost at once upon the stylobate of the crowning temple (see reconstruction drawing, Fig. 7.16); on the third day he turned up an inscription to the goddess Hygieia (Health); on the eighth, one mentioning Asclepius. His finds roused great excitement in the town and great greed among the local landowners, who asked exorbitant prices for the land on which the sanctuary stood. But the

Fig. 7.16 Kos, Asklepieion, reconstruction drawing. (Kerenyi, *Der göttliche Arzt*, Fig. 30, by permission of CIBA, Basle)

Turkish government, which then ruled Kos, expropriated the land, and the proprietors ended with less than Herzog would have been willing to pay them in the first place. Herzog was on excellent terms both with the Turkish bureaucrats, who gave him official status, thus saving him the price of a firman, and his Greek and Turkish workmen, who dug in amity side by side, and whom he saved from having all their wages taken in taxes. The German Archaeological Institute finally gave him a modest subsidy, renewable only on condition that he keep up prompt preliminary reports, and that each campaign should yield tangible finds. Even so, he ran the dig on a shoestring, doing his own cooking, and doing without a light railway. Working under drenching rains and suffering bouts of malaria, he nevertheless by December, 1902, could report the excavation of three temples, an altar, an exedra, and a monumental stair. The dig lasted from 1898 to 1907, progress being slowed by the necessity of Herzog's lecturing at Tübingen each winter. What finally emerged is indicated in the reconstruction drawing: a sanctuary on three terraces, set in a sacred grove of cypresses, with a Doric temple at the top built entirely of white island marble, and surrounded on three sides by a U-shaped portico, all dated by Herzog about 160, and all, though built on a shelf of mountain and not at the top, commanding a splendid view of the sea and the peninsula beyond where Cnidus and Halicarnassus lay. The middle terrace contained older buildings: an altar like the Great Altar at Pergamum, facing a temple dated about 280; behind the temple an Ionic building, which perhaps housed the priests; behind the altar a stoa or *leschê*, perhaps built about 205, for the display of votive offerings, as at Samothrace. The lowest terrace, whose U-shaped stoa faced the one two terraces above, is the earliest in date (360-250), and contained the rooms where the patients slept. It is supported on vaults as at Lindos. Though the total effect is axially symmetrical, the terraces are not all on one axis but slightly skewed, as at Pergamum. Indeed the monumentality, the sense of the theatrical, the central altar, all show that the complex in its latest phases was under strong Pergamene influence.

In 1933 an earthquake destroyed most of the city of Kos. The Italians, who then controlled the island, seized the opportunity to excavate the ancient city, where Hippocrates had lived and worked; credulous tourists may still admire the spreading plane tree under which he allegedly held his consultations. What the Italians found was a planned Hellenistic city, with a circuit wall, stadium, main cross-streets, the *cardo* paved and the *decumanus* lined with porticoes. The houses are of the type familiar from Delos, and they, too, yielded mosaics. Lower levels go back in unbroken sequence to Mycenaean times. The Italians also excavated below the bottom terrace of the sanctuary and did a great deal of restoration throughout. They found Roman baths (where faith was aided by water containing salts of sulphur and iron) and an inscription honoring the Emperor Nero as the New Asclepius.

Such, in selection, is the picture archaeology draws for us of the Hellenistic Age, an age of cosmopolitanism in society, monarchy in politics, eclecticism and commercialism in religion, monumentality in architecture, and strong theatricality in sculpture. Classical restraint, if it ever existed, is in this age conspicuous by its absence. As periodically in Greek cultural history, influence from the east is strong: it is symbolized by the translation of the Hebrew Old Testament into Greek at Alexandria, and by the temples of exotic foreign gods on Delos. In this age, too, the heavy hand of Rome is first felt in Greece, with the influx of Italian businessmen into Delian countinghouses. In 196 the Roman general Flamininus proclaimed the freedom of Greece in the stadium at the Isthmian games near Corinth, but fifty years later Corinth lay in ruins, wrought by Roman hands. Hellenistic monumentality is the work of kings: the Pharos at Alexandria, the Acropolis of Pergamum, the Stoa of Attalus in Athens. Only the Colossus of Rhodes is a work of a Greek city-state on the old model: the prosperous Rhodian burghers proudly refused a subsidy for the purpose from Ptolemy I. Of commercialism in religion we have presented abundant evidence: its best symbol is perhaps the meat market built over the altar at Morgantina. Axial symmetry enters the picture at Lindos and Kos. The sculpture of the Pergamene altar is unforgettably theatrical. All these tendencies were intensified and extended in the next phase of Greek archaeological history, the last to be treated in this book, the era in which captive Greece took captive her fierce conqueror, and Romans built Greek buildings in a Greek world under Roman sway.

Addendum

(All dates approximate)

B.C.

360-250	Kos, bottom terrace
after 338	Palatitsa, summer palace, Pella, mosaics
330	Thasos, Agora, N.E. Stoa; Lindos, Temple of Athena
308	Delos, Asklepieion
304-292	Rhodes, Colossus
300	Lindos, propylon; Thasos, Agora, N.W. Stoa
300 ff.	Delos, theater
289-81	Samothrace, Arsinolion
Early Hel-lenistic	Claros, oracle of Apollo
280	Alexandria, Pharos; Kos, Temple B (on middle terrace)
270-263	Pergamum, Temple of Demeter
260	Morgantina, agora
250	Samothrace, Hellenistic Hieron
246	Delos, Stoa of Antigonus
225	Samothrace, theater
220	Delos, Stoa of Philip V
208	Delos, Hypostyle Hall
205	Kos, leschê
200	Lindos, stoa; Pergamum, arsenal
180	Pergamum, Great Altar
170	Pergamum, upper theater
160	Kos, Asklepieion; Pergamum, Library; Athens, Stoa of Attalus & Middle Stoa
150	Athens, South Stoa II

8 The Greek World under Roman Sway

(146 B. C.—A. D. 267)

To read the archaeological record of the Greek world under Roman sway we shall have to range far and wide, from Dura-Europus on the Euphrates to the parts of Libya round about Cyrene (see map, Fig. 6.20). We shall visit sites where we have been before, such as Delos, Athens, Cyrene, and Ephesus, and see to what extent the Romans, creatively imitating Greek architecture and sculpture, overlaid Greek glory with Roman grandeur, at the expense of a Roman emperor or an Athenian millionaire. We shall visit new and exotic places to see to what extent native architects and sculptors understood, misinterpreted, or transformed the Greek tradition: on a mountaintop metamorphosed into a tomb at the very back of Turkey, in baroque temples in Lebanon, in monumental cities on oases in the Syrian desert, in Jordan, and in Mesopotamia. We shall see Corinth and Ephesus as St. Paul saw them, and after. Everywhere we shall see Greek forms monumentalized, exaggerated, made massive; provincialized, orientalized, barbarized. To those for whom everything after Pericles is decadence, all this makes a picture from which to avert the eyes, but the point is that this is the unvarnished archaeological record of what happened to Greek art and architecture in the Roman Em-

pire: intentions were nearly always good, results sometimes
striking and almost invariably stupendous. If classical Greek
rationality and simplicity of line seem to be missing, that
may mean not that the new forms are un-Greek, but that
the sources of Greco-Roman flamboyance, latent in earlier
Greek art forms, have been ignored or unnoticed by those
espousing an untenable thesis: that Greeks were always cool,
detached, and restrained, in their lives, in their art, and in
their architecture. The archaeological excavations reported
here should help to break the stereotype forever.

For the century following the Roman destruction of Corinth in 146 B.C., the Greek archaeological record is singu-
larly sparse, sparser than for any period since the "Dark
Ages." The inference is that Greece during these years was
undergoing a depression. Only on Delos is any building
activity noticeable. There an Athenian, Theophrastus,
built in 126 northwest of Apollo's temple (see plan, Fig. 7.11)
an Agora of ambitious proportions: it covered over 7000

**Fig. 8.1   Athens, Roman Market-place (left),
and Tower of the Winds (Horologion), plan.
(Travlos, *op. cit.*, p. 99, Fig. 55, lower half)**

square yards. North of it, on the seaward side of the Lion Terrace, the Posidoniasts, a guild of Syrian shipowners and traders from Beirut, built in 112 the previously mentioned large peristyle house as their headquarters; typically, it included four chapels, three to their native triad of gods, and one to the goddess Roma. After the pirate raid of 69 the Roman legate Triarius built out of secondhand architectural blocks an emergency wall—too little and too late—around the sacred precinct and the residential quarter near the theater.

Athens showed perverse genius in always choosing the wrong side in Rome's civil wars. Sulla sacked Athens in 86, and cut down the trees in Plato's Academy and Aristotle's Lyceum, outside the walls, to make his siege-engines. But about the middle of the century there is evidence of revival, in the Lesser Propylaea at Eleusis, built by Cicero's contemporary Appius Claudius Pulcher in the 40's, and in the building, perhaps as early as 50, of the octagonal Tower of the Winds (Fig. 8.1), which in Turkish Athens travelers used to visit to watch the whirling dervishes. Each face of the tower bears a sculptured allegorical representation of a wind, and a sundial. There was an interior waterclock, perhaps worked by some sort of clockwork mechanism like the modern ones in Munich and Venice. The building was apparently accessible at all hours of the day and night; at any rate there is no evidence that its doors were lockable from the outside. It adjoined the Roman Agora, planned by Julius Caesar in 44, an area still partly encumbered by modern buildings and a Turkish mosque. Its marble pavement survives in part, and an inscription dates its west Propylaea, the Gate of Athena Archegetis, to 10 B.C. By this time Augustus was in power in Rome, and disposed, in view of the propaganda value of exploiting Athens' glorious past, to forgive her for having taken Antony's side against him. He allowed to be built on the Acropolis, just east of the Parthenon, a small round temple of Rome and Augustus, on the model of the shrine of Vesta in the Roman Forum. Its ruins seem an effrontery, but a puny one, beside the splendor of the great temple adjoining it.

Augustus' lieutenant Agrippa built in the center of the Greek Agora an Odeum, the last major building to grace the area. The account of how it was excavated and identified will provide at long last an opportunity to describe in some detail the Agora excavations as a whole, which were

for nearly thirty years (1931-40, 1946 to date) the major
American archaeological enterprise in Greek lands. Here the
archaeologist's threefold duty, to dig, to preserve, and to
publish, has been carried out scientifically, efficiently, and
promptly, under two directors, T. Leslie Shear (†1945),
and Homer A. Thompson, with lavish support from John
D. Rockefeller, Jr., Ward Canaday, and other American philanthropists. To have laid bare 5000 years of the history of
the working center of a major city-state of mainland Greece
has been well worth the time, money, and energy expended.
The statistics are impressive: 365 houses equitably expropriated, between 4000 and 5000 people resettled, sixteen acres
excavated, over 246,000 tons of earth removed (to fill in
malarial marshes along the Sacred Way to Eleusis); the
68,000 objects (exclusive of 94,000 coins) catalogued so

Fig. 8.2   Athens, Agora, excavation notebooks
and catalog card, illustrating method. The
black-figured amphora, center left, is completely
recorded: pottery inventory number, findspot,
date of finding, complete description, references
to publications, and photograph. (Agora Excavations)

efficiently, thanks to the inventory's presiding genius, Miss Lucy Talcott, that any object can be made instantly available to scholars. The collection is so rich in pottery that when *Paris-Match* asked Miss Talcott for a picture of how Themistocles' dinner-table might have looked, she was able to provide every item of crockery without difficulty. The catalogue derives from the contents of carefully kept excavation notebooks, transferred to cards (Fig. 8.2). There are different-colored cards, with photograph attached, for each category: sculpture, pottery, 16,000 stamped and datable amphora handles (much of this from over 100 closed deposits from wells, especially valuable for dating); nearly 7000 new inscriptions; 5400 lamps, and over 1200 ostraka. Each card bears a tab indicating whether the catalogued object is Greek, Roman, or Byzantine.

The work of conservation included general tidying up, and landscaping. The plans of the stoa of Zeus and the temple of Apollo Patroös, on the west side (lower center to right center of the model, Fig. 8.3), for example, were outlined with ancient blocks and filled in with excavated field stone, while the original crumbly poros walls were buried. The Hephaisteion east pediment sculptures were cleaned by swathing them in wet burlap, and chipping away the softened deposit with a light steel chisel, judiciously used. The result was to reveal once more the lovely Parian marble, the delicate modeling, and even the color: blue background, red drapery, green rocks. Landscaping, planned by the landscape architect Ralph Griswold, defines areas, takes account of the dry climate (with the assistance of a special irrigation system), and is faithful to the ancient flora, so that the Agora and environs are now green and blooming with oak and laurel (the first trees planted by the King and Queen of Greece), pomegranate, myrtle, oleander, pine, cypress, and olive.

Hundreds of dedicated workers cooperated on the job. Each sector, meticulously divided into one-meter squares, was supervised by an archaeologist, seasoned or in training. Each kept a field notebook, assigning a serial number to each object found, recording its dimensions, and supplying a drawing or photograph. Each group of objects found in a given square was given a wooden tag bearing date, number, and findspot. The tag remained with the group until each object was washed, catalogued, and painted with its own inventory number.

Fig. 8.3 Athens, Agora in Roman times, model, from northwest. Odeum of Agrippa in center; to its left, Stoa of Attalus and Library of Pantainos; behind it, Middle Stoa; in front of it, temple of Ares and Altar of Pity. Near center of r. edge, Hephaisteion; below it, from north to south, Stoa of Zeus, temple of Apollo Patroos, Metroon, Bouleuterion, Tholos. (Agora Excavations)

A chemical branch analyzed finds, identifying, for example, resin from the island of Chios in the bottom of a wine jar, tin plate on copper, the varying content of bronze in coins, for arranging them in sequences; and beeswax in marble ceiling coffers painted by the encaustic process, where wax is the binder for the pigment. This branch cleaned coins electrolytically, finishing the job, to avoid abrasion, with a dental polishing-machine and a felt brush. Bronze coins thinly plated with silver proved to come from a crisis-year, 339, the year before Philip II of Macedon defeated the Athenians at Chaeronea.

Miss Alison Frantz, some of whose exquisite pictures embellish this book, was in charge of photography, and John Travlos' alchemy of skill, feeling for architecture, and patience produced the plans. Foremen and workmen—up to 300 in a given season—who had learned their craft at Corinth, Delphi, or Mycenae, contributed their skills; the personalities of some of them, as Professor Thompson writes, "made Aristophanes credible." World War II interrupted the work for six seasons (1940-45). The staff carefully packed important finds and records for the duration; duplicate catalogue-cards, photographs, and microfilm of the field notebooks were sent to America for safekeeping. The excavated area reverted to use as a garden or pasture, and loyal foremen performed miracles of maintenance under conditions that did not allow them the use of a single board or nail.

It should not be thought that all this efficiency was inhuman. The excavation reports often record the pathetic, the homely commonplace, or the amusing: the kitchen struck by catastrophe, containing the remains of a small donkey and a purse of thirty-four coins; the dog buried with a large beef bone close to his nose; the stillborn babies, between a hundred and two hundred of them, lovingly buried in the sanctuary of Aphrodite Urania under the north slope of the Acropolis; the two superimposed pots, the upper one with a large hole in the front and one in the bottom, which remained puzzling till the pot-mender set his baby in the upper one and made it plain that it was a child's "potty"; the ashes from ancient workmen's lunch-fires, the remains of broken jars for their drinking water, and the plain little dishes from which they ate their mid-day beans and olives.

Agora finds from earlier centuries have been recorded in earlier chapters. Of Roman buildings the most impressive is Agrippa's Odeum, which rose majestic in the Agora's very center (see plan, Fig. 8.4), over the old Orchestra. John Travlos and Homer Thompson, using the techniques of archaeological inference with consummate skill, have since 1934 succeeded in winning back the design of this great building from a few scattered blocks. Its corner emerged in 1934; the 1935 campaign produced the outline of an orchestra and some marble benches which proved that the building was a theater; the earth scooped out for the orchestra had been used to support the cavea seats. Tiles, some marble, some terracotta, showed that the structure had been roofed, and was therefore an Odeum. When the Herulians, a marauding Teutonic tribe, sacked Athens in A.D. 267 the building was set on fire, which sealed in some readable blocks; more were found in the Valerian Wall.

The core of the building was the auditorium, lobby, and dressing-rooms. The auditorium once had seats for 1000, in eighteen rows of seats with comfortable scooped tops; the foundation walls of the core are very heavy, suggesting (see model, Fig. 8.5) an upper story, for which three series of large columns are available. Surrounding the core on three sides was a balcony, once used, like the second story of the Stoa of Attalus, for viewing the Panathenaic procession. Its entrance was narrow, like a wicket-gate, which justifies the inference that admission was charged. The basement under the balcony could have stored theater properties, but it seems to have been very little used. The terracotta roof tiles are stamped; there are five series, the earliest from a factory which was in production in the time of Augustus. This confirms the attribution of the building to Agrippa, who is recorded in literary sources as having visited Athens about 15 B.C. and donated the Odeum about that date. The auditorium span is extraordinarily wide (over seventy-seven feet); therefore it must have been bridged by a self-supported timber truss, a method recommended by the architect Vitruvius, who was Agrippa's contemporary. The core proved to have been enclosed on three sides by a thin wall reinforced with Corinthian pilasters; on the south, not visible in the model, was an open colonnade of heavy Corinthian columns, the Romans' favorite order (because it was most ornate). The technique of the capitals resembles that of the Tower of the Winds, which helps to confirm the dating. The orchestra pavement was five layers thick: a bottom course of fist-sized stones, then mortar, more stones, more mortar, and finally slabs of different-colored marble:

Fig. 8.4   Athens, Agora in Roman times, plan. (Agora Excavations)

Fig. 8.5 Athens, Odeum of Agrippa, model. (Agora Excavations)

white, gray-blue, green, purple, and pink. This is the method of paving recommended by Vitruvius. Pausanias mentions in the Odeum a statue of Dionysus "worth seeing": Professor Thompson found fragments of it. It must have been a colossus, for one "flake" of it was a full burden for four workmen. More pieces were found in the Valerian Wall in 1959. Since all were unweathered, the statue must have stood under the shelter of the north porch, where most of the fragments were found.

Agrippa's gift was timely, for the Periclean Odeum, on the Acropolis south slope by the theater of Dionysus, was sadly out of date. Too many of its seats were behind columns, and it had been used for the grain dole, as a cavalry barracks, and as a haunt of lounging philosophers. The new site was appropriate: the ancient Orchestra had been here, and a large and lofty building axial at the back of a colonnaded square was a Hellenistic idea very much to Roman taste: we may compare the temple of Zeus by the Agora at Priene, the North Agora at Miletus, and, in Italy, the Fora of Caesar and of Augustus in Rome and the temple of Hercules Victor at Tivoli.

In 1937 the Americans excavated, at right angles to the Odeum and northwest of it, a temple (in the center of the model, Fig. 8.3), known from Pausanias to have been dedicated to Ares, god of war. Its technique was a puzzle: it was fifth-century, by the same architect as the Hephaisteion, but it stood on a podium in Roman fashion. The solution to the problem was finally published in 1959, worked out from three key Greek letters, in a style typical of the Augustan period, cut in each of 230 blocks. In the third place in each set of three key letters, only four different symbols occurred: the monogram for AR, D, E, and O. Once these were interpreted as meaning *Aristera* (left), *Dexia* (right), *Eisodos* (entrance), and *Opisteros* (back), it was clear that they represented the four sides of the temple, and that the Romans had dismantled it stone by stone, transported the blocks from their original (undetermined) site, and reconstructed the temple in the Agora, where its new location defined the west side of a more or less symmetrical square. The other key letters stood, one for the course in which the block fell, the other for its position in the course. The altar, too, was reassembled in front of the temple, on its axis, and on the axis of the Odeum north porch (see plan, Fig. 8.4). North of the altar a marble block with an iron ring inset with an eye-pin was the hitching-post for fastening animals to be sacrificed. The motive for all this reassembling, reminiscent of tales of American millionaires dismantling Scottish castles stone by stone for reconstruction in California, seems to have been propagandistic: Augustus' grandson Lucius Caesar was adulated as the New Ares; the fifth-century temple in its new location had the double advantage of high antiquity and a prominent site.

The years from Tiberius to Trajan (14-98 *) were lean ones for building in the Agora. The first clue to a structure of note from just after this period turned up south of the Stoa of Attalus in 1933, in the form of a notice carved on stone, whose austerity would delight any librarian's heart: "NO BOOKS CIRCULATE. OPEN FROM SIX A.M. TO TWELVE NOON." Another inscription, of about 100, found in the Valerian Wall, records the donors of the library, one Ti. Flavius Pantainos, his son, and his daughter. The library rooms were grouped about a peristyle; there were porticoes facing the Panathenaic Way and the Stoa of Attalus. The rooms opening behind these porticoes were not connected with the library and could be rented separately as shops, thus providing endowment revenue for the library. Two of them served as a sculptor's studio, as was revealed

---

* Henceforth all dates are A.D. unless otherwise indicated.

by the discovery in them of marble chips, emery dust, and some sculptures "of mediocre quality." As long ago as 1869 the library's chief and very appropriate *objets d'art* had been found: two female figures in armor, personifying, as an inscribed base found in 1953 disclosed, the *Iliad* and the *Odyssey*.

The Romans and their satellites built massively in the Greek style all over the world they now controlled. One of the most impressive and remote of these complexes, discovered by a German engineer in 1881, was not scientifically excavated until 1953-56, by a joint German-American expedition, in spite of severe extremes of climate, danger of landslides, and shortage of workmen. It all began when the German engineer noticed that the top of the 7000-foot eagle-haunted peak of Nemrud Dagh, in the inaccessible Antitaurus mountain range in southeast Turkey, was manmade, an enormous artificial tumulus 160 feet high and 480 feet in diameter. The next year Otto Puchstein (who was to work on the temple of Zeus at Agrigento) visited it from Alexandretta, a grueling nineteen-day journey on stubborn horses wearing highly uncomfortable pack-saddles. The following year he revisited it with Carl Humann, the excavator of Pergamum, this time with a large caravan of horses and mules, to carry excavation gear, architects' instruments, and four hundredweight of plaster to take casts of the colossal sculpture he had found there. His description of the site is particularly vivid; like a mountain on top of a mountain, surrounded by snow-covered peaks whose rugged lower slopes were twisted into fantastic shapes, like the sea in a hurricane, while in the eastern distance gleamed the upper waters of the Euphrates. Heads, each taller than a man, fallen from colossal statues, lay scattered about in confusion. By night, bears prowled round the camp. Footing was difficult on the sliding gravel of the tumulus: *"Scharf schnitten die Steine in das Schuhleder,"* wrote Humann alliteratively.

But the complicated work of cast-making proceeded apace. One cast, of a lion, was made in 170 pieces; all the casts, packed in hay, filled twenty-eight cases on the caravan's return journey.

An inscription early revealed the nature and date of this complex: it was a tomb, built in his lifetime by the self-deified King Antiochus I (69-34 B.C.) of Commagene, a

Roman puppet-state on the upper Euphrates. Antiochus, having submitted to Pompey (64 B.C.) got a part of Mesopotamia as a reward; Antony deposed him (38 B.C.) for helping Rome's enemies, the Parthians. On three sides, terraces hewn in the living rock flanked his tumulus (see plan, Fig. 8.6). They were approached from below by a winding

Fig. 8.6 Nemrud Dagh, Hierothesion of Antiochus I of Commagene, plan. Colossal statues of Antiochus and his gods are flanked on ends by lions and eagles. Along north side of East Terrace, Antiochus' Persian ancestors; on south, his Greek ancestors, and their deifications. On east, a stepped altar. The West Terrace (at left) has a related arrangement. (Courtesy Teresa Goell, 1962)

processional way, and connected by paths running on top of the retaining wall of the tumulus. On each terrace, backed against the tumulus, were limestone colossi, twenty-three to twenty-five feet high, of Antiochus enthroned among his tutelary gods, half-Greek, half-Persian. Antiochus' tiara (Fig. 8.7) is typical of the artistic style of this extraordinary place: on it are represented a striding lion against a background of pomegranate blossoms and fruits; his diadem shows a procession of lions, highly orientalized. The colossi of the east terrace face a court; lining its sides are life-sized relief portraits of Antiochus' ancestors, Greek and Persian, and portraits of himself greeted by his gods; on the backs are genealogies and dedications, in Greek. Facing the colossi is a stepped altar; on their bases are engraved inscriptions, of which the American expedition took latex squeezes: they provide for the celebration and maintenance of Antiochus' cult. One is a horoscope, supplying an exact date for the dedication of the complex: July 7, 62 B.C.

Tunneling to find the tomb proved unsuccessful, but did reveal the sloping stepped revetment of the tumulus, a ramp, and the tunnels of previous searchers. At Eski Kale, nearby, however, excavators found the burial-place, unfortunately already plundered, of Antiochus' father Mithridates Kallinikos. A vaulted entrance led to a stair hewn in the solid rock down to a chamber so far within the mountain—over 500 feet—that there must have been some artificial means of supplying air to the workmen.

At Nemrud Dagh, architecture, sculpture, and inscriptions all interlock, to symbolize the fusion of Persian, Hellenistic, and Anatolian traditions in this puppet kingdom under Roman sway.

Of the kingdoms founded by Alexander's generals, Seleucid Syria has left little archaeological evidence from Hellenistic times, but finds from the Roman period are abundant and impressive, especially at Baalbek and Palmyra.

Baalbek, ancient Heliopolis, the City of the Sun, lies 3850 feet above sea level, between the Lebanon and the Antilebanon, fifty-one miles east of Beirut, on the caravan route between Damascus and Emesa. Its archaeological interest lies in the incredibly baroque massiveness of its complex of temples, to Jupiter, Bacchus, and Venus (Fig. 8.8), inspired by Greek forms, paid for with Roman money, built by Syrian architects for Syrians to worship in. The site was

Fig. 8.7   Nemrud Dagh, Colossal head of Antiochus I of Commagene (NDA, p. 5, Fig. 2, by permission of the excavator, Miss Theresa Goell)

1 Northwest Tower   2 Hospital   3 Northwestern   4 Basin
5 Northeast Tower   6 Temple of Jupiter Heliopolitanus   7 Temple-stair   8 Altar   9 Basilica   10 Court of the Altar
11 Hexagonal Court   12 Propylaea   13 Moat and Fortification   14 Copper Gate   15 Arabian Tunnel   16 Southeast
Tower   17 West-Tower   18 Old Gate   19 Moat   20 Mosque
21 Temple of Bacchus   22 Donjon   23 South Gate   24 Khan   25 Southwest Tower   26 South Gate

Fig. 8.8 Baalbek, plan. (Robinson, 1946, fac. p. 7, by permission of J. J. Augustin, Inc., Locust Valley, N. Y.)

first visited in modern times by a German, Martin Baumgarten, in 1508. Some of its columns were taken (1550-56) to build the Soliman mosque in Istanbul. Fifty-five columns of the temple of Jupiter were standing in 1618, thirty years later only nine; earthquakes and stone-robbing accounted for the rest. An earthquake in 1759 must have wrought havoc, for it lasted twenty-seven days and nights. In 1668 the Frenchman Desmonceaux was in Baalbek, looking for statues for the collection of Louis XIV's minister Colbert, who was a humanist as well as a financier. The ubiquitous Englishmen Stuart and Revett were there in 1751; the French poet Lamartine shipped a camel-load of sculpture fragments from Baalbek in 1833, but they appear to have been lost in transit. In 1860 the sculptor Rénan headed an archaeological mission thither. Richard Burton, the English author, as Consul-General in Damascus, studied the site for his *Encyclopaedia Britannica* article of 1870. But the inspiration for modern scientific work there arose from a state visit by Kaiser Wilhelm II in 1898. Koldewey and Puchstein dug there (1899-1904); their architect spent five solid years on the site (escaping epidemics of cholera and plague but not dysentery). Publication was not finished till 1925, but the job is not yet done, for the residential quarter remains unexcavated.

The temple of Jupiter (Syrian Baal) stands on a terrace 880 feet long and 400 feet wide, built up artificially with enormous blocks, one of which, sixty-three feet long, fourteen feet high, and eleven feet thick, weighs 1650 tons, and contains enough stone to build a house sixty feet square and forty feet high with foot-thick walls. One still larger, still in the quarry, would have taken 40,000 men to move. Baal was the chief god of the Syrians, as Jupiter was of the Romans. This colossal temple had a double propagandistic value. It symbolized the might of Rome while it flattered Syrian self-importance. The date of the temple is controversial, naturally, since so enormous a structure could, like the temple at Didyma, never really be finished, and must have been worked on over a period of several centuries. But the massiveness is Roman, and the earliest possible date for a Roman temple at Baalbek is about 10, when Augustus planted a colony there. But there must have been a temple here in Seleucid times, and one distinguished archaeologist dates the gigantic podium blocks late in that period. A safe if unsatisfactorily vague solution is that the whole complex as we have it dates, in its final form, from the times of the Antonine and Severan emperors (138-217).

The approach to the temple of Jupiter is through tower-flanked Propylaea, 165 feet wide and thirty-eight feet deep. The towers (one restored by the French in 1933), thirty feet square and 100 feet high (as tall as an eight-story building), are faced with two stories of engaged pilasters. Between them ran a row of twelve tall, polished, unfluted columns with gilded Corinthian capitals; over the middle six was a pediment with a raking cornice, over the middle two, a relieving arch, the latter a hallmark of the second century A.D. in architecture. The portico had gilded bronze niches with a shell-ornament in their half-domes. The Propylaea typifies the mixture of influences in the whole plan: the towers are Egyptian (compare the Egyptian temple on the Barberini mosaic in Praeneste), the colonnade Greco-Roman, the décor oriental.

Behind the Propylaea is a hexagonal court with a double colonnade and exedrae (rectangular recesses for sitting). A hexagonal plan allows for four triangular corner rooms; in these the priests of Baal may have lived. From the hexagonal court a triple entrance leads into the enormous Altar Court (120-200). It is 340 feet square. Eighty-four columns, polished and unfluted like those of the Propylaea, formed the peristyle. On either side of the central altar were basins for ritual washing. They were rectangular, with semicircular niches in their outer faces. The altar itself rose in four stepped stories to a height of fifty-eight feet, a third as tall as the Statue of Liberty. In the walls of the court are twelve niches (one for each of the twelve Olympian gods) alternately semicircular and rectangular, as in the Pantheon in Rome, and the total effect is like one of the Imperial Fora there; one wonders if the architect was not the famous Syrian Apollodorus of Damascus, who worked for Trajan, or one of his school.

From the Altar Court sixteen steps led up to the temple, which had originally ten Corinthian columns across the front and nineteen along the sides, counting the corner columns twice. They enclosed a 160 × 290-foot cella, over five times the size of the Parthenon's. Six hundred-ton columns remained standing. The golden patina of their stone, sandstone or granite, makes a striking effect at sunset. They are sixty-five feet high and carry a sixteen-foot entablature, every inch of which is decorated: first a fascia and a frieze of fantastic fauna and flora, then dentils, egg-and-dart, corbels and rosettes, a meander, and finally the cornice, repeating the acanthus motif of the column-capitals.

The temple of Bacchus, adjoining Jupiter's, is the best-preserved and most richly decorated Greco-Roman ruin in all Lebanon and Syria. It must have been standing in 130, for it bears an inscription in honor of Hadrian, who visited Baalbek in that year. The inscription is in Greek, whereas most Baalbek inscriptions are in Latin: another symbol of the combination of influences at work. It stands in Roman fashion, like its neighbor, on a high podium, with a crypt within. The podium steps are used for dramatic performances (in 1961 by the Comédie Française), opera, and ballet, and at night a tableau of sound and light, "The Wrath of the Gods," is played out with the temple as background. The taste of this widespread enterprise, which is bad on the Athenian Acropolis, dubious in the Roman Forum, perhaps appropriate at Versailles, is unquestionably suited to Baalbek's baroque extravagance (see model, Fig. 8.9). Nineteen of the temple's forty-six columns (of the Composite order, combining Corinthian acanthus with Ionic volutes) are standing. Though they are eight feet shorter than those of the temple of Jupiter, the temple itself, with its 75×87-foot cella, is bigger than the Parthenon. (Whether it is *better* is quite another question.) The cella portal is uniquely rich in its décor, though inspired by the quieter motifs of the door from the Erechtheum north porch in Athens. Like it, it has its lintel supported by consoles, but here the under side of the lintel bears a great spread eagle in relief. The Germans in 1902 replaced the enormous central lintel block, in danger of falling, by ingeniously raising a tower of bricks under it. The jambs are carved with bacchantes (appropriate to a temple of Bacchus), satyrs, genii, birds, lizards, and other small animals, amidst clusters of grapes, nuts, and garlands, all reminiscent of the Altar of Peace in Rome, though there again the taste is far quieter. The bacchante motif is repeated in a frieze just above eye level on the cella's outer front wall. The peripteros ceiling is coffered with six-pointed stars (Semitic influence?), with heads in relief in their centers. The stone entablature decoration is almost incredibly lavish: it has eighteen elements, Greek, Roman, and oriental in their various origins: strigils (parallel concave grooves, simulating the marks of the workman's thumbs in the days when temple décor was rendered

Fig. 8.9 Baalbek, model, in Museo della civiltà romana, Rome. Lower left, temple of Venus; left center, temple of Bacchus; lower right, propylon, hexagonal court, altar court, and temple of Jupiter. (Fototeca)

in clay), egg-and-dart, bead-and-reel, palmettes, an alternation of projecting bull's and lion's heads, a Lesbian cyma (quarter-round molding), a console, a meander, and a crowning cornice in which, repeating motifs below, palmettes alternate with lion's heads. The outer face of the cella wall is theatrically enriched with pilasters partly concealed by fluted Corinthian half-columns; stairs in the pilasters lead to the roof. The pediment has doors and windows, which would have made possible some effects of religious pageantry, possibly even more spectacular than *Son et Lumière*. The inner cella wall has arches below, niches containing Victories above. In a deeply recessed, vaulted, coffered *aedicula* (shrine) with a shell half-dome, at the back of the cella, stood the cult-statue, flanked by sculptured animals, and wearing a curious oriental paneled garment, bearing representations of the planets. Pilasters framed the aedicula; they were framed in turn by pairs of polychrome marble columns, enclosing two stories of statues in their own subsidiary aediculas. Over all was a relieving arch and a pediment with acroteria (roof-ornaments). No briefer or less detailed description can possibly convey the bizarre profusion of the carved décor that the architect has lavished upon his temple. To compare it with the archaic temples of Dreros, Perachora, or Thermon is to revise radically one's views of what progress means.

Compared with this staggering magnificence, the neighboring temple of Venus, extravagant as it is, seems a mere afterthought. In its final form it dates from about 245. It is a round building on an apsidal podium approached by steps, and with two rows of four columns. Four columns support the peristyle; their stylobate, in elevation, is scalloped out in niches, as is the outer cella wall, which supports a stone dome. Within the cella is a ring of twelve columns. The whole effect anticipates and in profuseness outdoes a garden-house of the Renaissance.

Halfway between the Mediterranean and the Euphrates (its very location a symbol), 150 miles northeast of Damascus, 1300 feet above sea level, is the oasis of Palmyra, the City of Palms. It lies on an age-old caravan route: ancient Chinese silks were found there, and the caravan road is the *decumanus*, one of the grandest avenues in all Syria, 1240 yards long, once bordered by 375 columns of rose-white limestone each as tall as a five-story building, of which about 150 are

Fig. 8.10 Palmyra, monumental street. Note consoles on columns. (Author)

still standing (Fig. 8.10) clear-cut against the gray-gold background of the desert. Germans dug it, first in 1902, again in 1917, on a wartime mission for the protection of monuments; the results were published in 1932 by the German Archaeological Institute in Istanbul. While Syria was a French protectorate, French archaeologists did some work of conservation, and cleared away a squalid Arab village from the precinct of the main temple (not without resistance: a Bedouin shot a French architect), but no French publication of the site has yet appeared.

The approach to Palmyra is through a necropolis of exotic, thoroughly un-Greek tower-tombs, rising out of a smoking film of windblown sand. As inscription dates an early phase of its main temple (see plan, Fig. 8.11), to Bel, in 32, but there is a later phase, also dated by an inscription, in 70, when its gigantic 650-foot peristyle court was built, and the temple was equipped with a curious off-center side entrance: in 174 a Propylaea and towers were added. Though the temple has been described as the grandest monument in all Syria, the total effect is barbaric. It was the holy place of an

Aramaic population with Roman names, who used Greek architectural forms without understanding them, perhaps as a tribute to the Macedonian origin of the old Seleucid kings. One recent historian of archaeology has said, perhaps partly with tongue in cheek, "The true admirer of classical architecture cannot be expected to describe the temple of Bel, so cruelly does it debase his favorite forms." Debased they may be, but this is what happened to Greek architecture, and it is salutary for the classicist who admires nothing after Pericles to recognize that from beginning to end, from Minoan times to the present, the reciprocal relations of the Aegean world to the Near East are an established, if to him unpalatable, fact.

The next area in date is probably the Agora; in it were found two inscriptions of 76 and 81, but the architectural style is Severan (*ca.* 200). An exotic touch is provided by an inscriptional reference to caravans, so that this market square might better be called a caravanserai. A temple in the Agora's west corner was used for religious banquets; to these admission was charged, for the excavators found some of the tickets. The Corinthian temple east of the Agora, because it is differently oriented from neighboring complexes, is differently dated, in about 100. The neighboring complexes are the theater and the monumental main street with its four-way gate, which the excavators date between 120 and 150. The theater was probably also used for town-meetings.

Palmyra was the financial capital of the eastern world in the mid-second century. An inscription of 137 reveals the nature of her trade. It mentions slaves, dates, pine-cones, purple (antiquity's most expensive luxury cloth), oil, salt fish, skins (camel-skins are duty-free), grain, and wine. The customs officials were not connoisseurs: bronze statues pay duty as bronze, not as works of art. Rich merchants advertised their own philanthropy by putting statues of themselves on consoles on the columns they donated for Palmyra's splendid main street. The city was laid out on a grid plan; arches mark the junction of the main with the principal cross-streets. The most impressive of these are the tetrapylon, a quadruple arch near the Agora and theater, and the tripylon near the Corinthian temple, the latter a marvel of illusionary architecture, its purpose being to mask the avenue's change in direction to approach the temple of Bel. Palmyrene houses were balconied, and of the Olynthus type. Near the crossing of the main streets (*cardo* and *decumanus*) lies the so-called "Camp of Diocletian," actually older than the

Legend:

□ Tomb Tower   ▷ Funeral Temple
● Tomb House   □ Peristyle

1 Temple of Bēl: a High portico and Propylaea   b Cella   c Sacrificial altar   d Sacrificial basin   e Ramp   f Surrounding fortress wall
2 Southwest Necropolis   3 Valley of Tomb: a Tomb of Elāhbēl   b Tomb of Atenatan   c Tomb-house   d Archaic tombs   e Tomb of Yarhai or private building
j Tomb-house   g Tomb of Jamblic   h Tomb of Aailani and Zebida
i Subterranean cellar   j Ancient surrounding fortress wall   k Aqueduct
4 Southeast Necropolis   5 Museum   6 a b c Great Colonnade   7 Temple
8 Baths of Diocletian   9 Theater   10 Senate   11 Transverse Colonnade
12 Column of Honor   13 Temple or Market   14 Agora   15 Tetrapyle
16 Inscription of Zenobia   17 Transverse Colonnade   18 Funeral Temple
19 Tomb-houses   20 Tomb-house   21 Camp of Diocletian   22 Public or private building   23 Peristyle House   24 Peristyle House   25 Rhodian Peristyle House   26 House to the East of the Temple   27 Jewish House   28 Christian Basilica   29 Christian Basilica   30 Omayyad wall
31 Temple of Bēlshamin   32 Spring of the Harem   33 Column of Honor
34 Building with great court   35 Bastion of Justinian   36 Modern village

Fig. 3.11 Athens, Ceramicus, Geometric vases. Note typical hatched meanders, upper right. Ceramicus, Museum. (Karo, op. cit., Pl. 10)

Emperor; it was in use as early as 148. It is a Roman *praetorium*, or military headquarters, in plan not unlike the Hadrianic firemen's barracks at Ostia, with its shrine for the worship of Roman Emperors centered at the back. Palmyra in her prime defied the Roman Empire, but Aurelian humbled her. In 272 her Queen Zenobia walked in gold chains in Aurelian's triumph, and perhaps pined in elegant exile in Hadrian's Villa at Tivoli.

Another Seleucid foundation bearing the Greco-Roman stamp is the rectangular-gridded city of Gerasa, eighty-five miles northeast of Jerusalem and twenty-six miles north of the Jordanian capital Amman. A Yale expedition dug it (1928-34), removing the fallen columns that encumbered its streets, recovering the plan (Fig. 8.12) of its north and south theaters, until then choked with vegetable gardens. The south theater, built before 83, had a capacity of 3000, and had numbered seats; the north theater is eighty years younger. The Yale archaeologists drew the ground plans of twenty temples. One of them, the temple of Artemis, covered, with its precinct, over 35,000 square yards, and was buried seven feet deep. Its columns, restored to the light of day, were weathered to a rich bronze color. Its podium was designed hollow, to provide chambers or water reservoirs. The excavators deciphered 150 inscriptions, besides inventorying thousands of coins and small finds. They traced Gerasa's two-mile circuit wall, with its 101 towers. The wall enclosed 210 acres, nearly three times the area of Roman Ostia. An inscription by the northwest gate reveals that the walls were finished before 75. Gerasa's nerve-center, the crossing of the *cardo* and the *decumanus*, was marked by an elliptical colonnaded caravanserai. The whole presents yet another picture of the adaptation of Greco-Roman civic amenities to the needs of a desert culture.

At these Syrian sites, the Romans built on and monumentalized Hellenistic Greek foundations. They did so also in a North African city, Cyrene, whose lower levels, as we have seen, go back to archaic times. Cyrene fell to the Romans under Ptolemy VII's will in 96 B.C. "The parts of Libya about Cyrene" became a Roman province in 74 B.C., which under Augustus was combined with Crete. Domitian (81-96) monumentalized the Agora (see plan, Fig. 4.17). Italian archaeologists in 1956, in 1200 man-days, re-erected the Caryatids in the stoa east of the Agora: thirteen herms, alternately

Fig. 8.12 Gerasa, plan. Note north and south theaters, and huge precinct (upper left quadrant) of Temple of Artemis. (Kraeling, 1938, Plan 1)

of Hermes and Heracles, flanking wide windows and supporting a heavy Doric entablature. They spent 1500 man-days
on the north side of the Agora, and excavated the east side
of the Trajanic Caesareum. At the sanctuary of Apollo they
studied the theater, and found the great baths in the Apollo
precinct to be Hadrianic. Romans, they discovered, re-erected
the colossal temple of Zeus, after an earthquake had felled it
in 185. Here again the Greco-Roman décor is a thin veneer
over a native culture, one curious evidence of which is a
series of peculiar statues from the huge necropolis. They are
of women or goddesses; some have no bottom half, some have
no faces, some have the face half-veiled. In 1959 the Italians
published the catalogue of sculpture from Cyrene, containing
the impressive total of 483 items, most of them in the Greco-
Roman tradition, but few as good as the Aphrodite.

The associations of Cyrene with the *Acts of the Apostles*
make a convenient point of transition back to mainland
Greece: to Corinth, where in the Agora (Fig. 8.13) the
Americans have excavated the very bema or rostrum from
which in 51 St. Paul addressed the Corinthians. For many
visitors Corinth's chief interest will center in its associations
with St. Paul, who lived here for eighteen months (51-52),
plying his trade of tentmaker, his preaching tolerated under
the non-interference policy of the Roman governor, Gallio,
who "cared for none of these things." Discussion of Corinth
has perhaps been too long postponed, for its origins go back
to Neolithic times, and it flourished in the archaic period,
the evidence being the archaic temple of Apollo (550-525
B.C.), "a squat surly building with no nonsense about it," and
the handsome pottery. But the Romans destroyed the old city
in 146 B.C., and most of what the American excavators
have found dates from the years in and after Corinth's re-
foundation by Julius Caesar as a Roman colony in 44 B.C.
Corinth is one of the earliest American digs in Greece; excavation began in 1896, and is still continuing, as a
training-ground for young archaeologists. The final publication (incomplete) has reached sixteen volumes, several of
them in multiple parts.

Of Corinth's pre-Roman remains the most impressive and
best-known is of course the archaic temple. Just south of it
the Americans discovered mute evidence of the savagery of
the Roman destruction of 146 B.C.: ash, burned wood, fire-
damaged rooftiles, sling-bullets, spearheads, stone catapult-

Fig. 8.13 Corinth, central area, plan. Three rectangular exedrae should be added at back of Julian Basilica. (Broneer, 1947, Plan 1)

balls of five different calibers. The area was the object of particularly ferocious Roman wrath because it was Corinth's arsenal. Above it, two to three feet of earth and gravel, with a few coins of neighboring Sicyon (to which the Romans gave charge of the ruined city) and some orderly piles of debris summarize Corinthian history during a century of eclipse.

Northwest of the Agora the Americans excavated the theater, which proved to be originally of the fifth century B.C., with seats for 18,000. It suffered several revisions in Roman times. Nero had a special Imperial box built in it, from which in 67 he reaffirmed the liberation of Greece, first proclaimed by Flamininus at the Isthmian Games in 196 B.C. (The text of Nero's proclamation was discovered in 1888 inscribed on a stone slab in the Boeotian town of Acraephnium. It is now in the museum in Thebes.) It was in 67 that Nero tried (and failed) to dig a canal through the isthmus of Corinth, using 5000 captives sent to him by Vespasian from the war in Palestine. About 135 the theater was rebuilt in marble, and between 211 and 217 its orchestra was remodeled for water ballets (by ballerinas like those represented in the later mosaics from Piazza Armerina*), and gladiatorial contests. An inscription records the familiar story of the gladiator Androcles, spared in a beast-fight by a lion from whose paw he had once extracted a thorn. Connected with the theater by a peristyle court is the 3000-seat odeum, of about A.D. 175, of which only an unrecognizable piece of rubble masonry was above ground when excavation started. The court, if not the odeum itself, is one of the many benefactions of the Athenian millionaire Herodes Atticus, some of whose other gifts of buildings, in Athens and elsewhere, will be described in a later section of this chapter.

Corinth's Agora slopes upward from north to south. Just southwest of the main basilica (see plan) the Romans overlooked (because it had been built over before 146 B.C.) a Greek oracular shrine of the fourth century B.C., which presents interesting evidence of the manipulation of human credulity. It centers on a small circular altar with a retaining wall beside it, faced with triglyphs and metopes. The altar was served by an underground channel for pouring libations. Parallel to this channel runs a tunnel just big enough for a man, the entrance to which was through one of the metopes, cleverly made into a secret door. Behind this was another door, with a lock, and beside the wall was an inscription forbidding trespass, on the pretext that the spot was sacred. Protected by all these precautions, a priest could slip through the secret doors into the tunnel and crawl to the altar end, where his sepulchral voice could utter oracles through a hole in the pavement to the assembled faithful.

* See *The Mute Stones Speak,* p. 324 and Fig. 13.1.

Early in the colonial period (about 44 B.C.) the Romans remodeled the South Stoa, a two-storied fourth-century building with thirty-three shops on the ground floor, each thoughtfully equipped with a well in the center for cooling wine. A vast quantity of drinking cups was found in the wells, together with fragments of marble bar-tops, and roof tiles and architectural terracottas thrown there at the time of the Roman sack; enough were found to make possible the reconstruction of the cornice, displayed, together with some Roman mosaic floors, under an adjoining shed roof. The upper story contained guest rooms, which may not have been exactly havens of rest, in view of the taverns below. The excavators think that these rooms were planned to house the delegates to sessions of the Panhellenic League convened at Corinth by Philip II of Macedon in 338.

Some 500 yards north of the civic center was a fourth-century B.C. sanctuary of Asclepius, remodeled under Marcus Aurelius, with dormitory, dining-rooms, and a sacred fountain; a number of terracotta dedications from here, by grateful patients, is on display in the museum west of the Agora. There are fourth-century B.C. walls on Acrocorinth, a steep climb of over an hour south of the city, and a temple of Aphrodite, where 1000 temple-prostitutes plied their trade: it was naturally a favorite haunt of sailors. But most of the ruins are seventeenth-century, and the classicist climbs Acrocorinth chiefly for the magnificent view, from Mt. Cyllene on the west to Cape Sunium on the east. While the classical remains were being excavated, one archaeologist climbed Acrocorinth fifty-six times in one season.

The Agora, larger than the Forum in Rome, was the glory of Roman Corinth. Beside its monumental approach, the colonnaded Lechaion Street, the Romans when they refounded Corinth as a colony built a basilica on the canonical plan, with a nave and two side aisles, not unlike the Basilica Julia in the Forum at Rome. It was the legal and commercial center of the colony; in the second century it was enlarged and equipped with a monumental two-storied false front, the Captives' Façade, adorned with colossal figures of barbarians, standing on bases carved with representations of Roman victories. Beside them is the monumental entrance to the Agora, through a triumphal arch built in Augustan times. Only its foundations remain, but Pausanias says it was surmounted by the chariots of Apollo and his son Phaethon, in gilt bronze.

The excavators date between 25 and 50, on the evidence of coins, the central shops axially arranged on either side of the Bema. They marked the dividing line between the upper and the lower Agora, which the Romans treated as two terraces. In the lower (north) Agora the dig revealed four levels. The lowest, just over the Hellenistic pavement, was gravel. A level of clay and sand above this is the pavement trodden by the first Roman colonists. A level of thin cement followed; by the end of the first century it had been covered by marble slabs bedded in cement and stones.

At the west end of the row of central shops was a shrine of Dionysus, at the east end a circular monument surmounted by a column; it may have belonged to a hero-cult. In front of it a curved retaining wall must have supported a tribunal for the judges of foot races, for beneath it, at an early Hellenistic level, the excavators found two sets of stadium starting-blocks, one fifth-century, the other—differently oriented—Hellenistic. Apparently at Corinth, as at the Isthmian sanctuary, the burial place of a hero determined the starting-point of races in his honor.

The line of the Hellenistic starting-blocks runs under the steps of the Julian Basilica, bounding the Agora on the east. It is named from portraits of the Julian family found in its cryptoporticus in 1914 and 1915. In 1948 the excavation of three rectangular exedras in its back wall proved that it was the exact twin of the South Basilica, squeezed in behind the South Stoa. On the evidence of coins, both were built in Claudius' reign, about 40. A statue of Lucius Caesar, Augustus' grandson, from the South Basilica, bears the pointing-marks used by sculptors making an exact copy; the original turned up in the other basilica. Handsome inscriptions, treated as part of the décor, adorned the interior walls.

The monumental entrance to the South Basilica was added in Antonine times (mid-second century). The evidence is from lamps, which at Corinth were first accurately classified by Broneer, in a book published in 1930, to help archaeologists in dating. His method was to analyze with the greatest precision the shapes, profiles, spouts, and molded decoration of over 1400 Corinthian lamps, some of which, having been found in dated contexts, provided firm benchmarks. He distinguished thirty-four types, best presented in a tabular view:

Type	No. of Examples	Date
I-III	58	sixth century B.C. or earlier
IV-VII	69	fifth and fourth centuries B.C.
VIII-XVIII	185	Hellenistic
XIX	60	early Roman
XX-XXIII	84	Augustan
XXIV-XXVI	76	A.D. 50-100
XXVII-XXX	903	second to fourth century A.D.
XXXI-XXXIV	66	Christian

It was to Type XXVII that the lamps found in the porch of the South Basilica belonged. Fifty-seven per cent of all the lamps studied were in use between the years 100 and 400; this is evidence that Corinth survived the Herulian sack of 267. The South Basilica is across the road from the apsidal Council Chamber; the Julian Basilica adjoins the Southeast Building, which housed the archives. This suggests that both buildings served administrative purposes, but the possibility of commercial use cannot be excluded, since they closely resemble in plan the Eumachia in the Forum of Pompeii, which was a cloth-market.

In 79—the same year as the eruption of Vesuvius that destroyed Pompeii—Corinth suffered from an earthquake, after which the northwest shops were rebuilt. Thereafter the excavators have found little evidence of building activity, except in the theater, until 161, when the fountain Pirene, east of the Propylaea, underwent the grandest of its many transformations, this time at the expense of Herodes Atticus, in honor of his wife Regilla, as an inscribed statue-base discloses. Pirene always has water, even in the depths of summer, a rare thing in Greece; an underground reservoir with a 400-cubic-yard capacity feeds six draw-basins, one of which has on its side wall some Roman paintings of local fish. According to legend, Pirene first bubbled up where Bellerophon's winged horse Pegasus stamped his foot; in consequence, Pegasus appears as Corinth's device on her silver coins. Many generations of Corinthians delighted in adorning Pirene with various styles of marble façades; unpublished excavation notes by B. H. Hill distinguish nine phases. Herodes further enriched it by adding to the north, around an open pool, a cloverleaf of three semicircular covered exedras, each with three niches for statues of members of his family.

Two hundred yards west of Pirene is the Fountain of Glaukê, of similar plan. Its origins are very old, as old as Greek mythology: it is named for the princess Jason married, who is said to have flung herself into it, vainly seeking relief from the poisoned robe which was Medea's wedding present to her. The adjoining Roman temple (C on the plan) may have been dedicated to Hera Akraia, on the spot where Medea's children vainly sought refuge from the avenging fury of the citizens of Corinth.

The Romans defined the Agora's west end with six small temples, of which the central pair, Poseidon's (185) and Heracles' (191) belong to the reign of the Emperor Commodus, who fancied himself as the reincarnation of the hero of the twelve labors. These were Roman temples, on high podia. Corinth had become a Roman city, seat of the governor of the Roman province of Achaea. Of its major published inscriptions, 226 are in Latin. But 331 are Greek; the great archaic Greek temple looms over all, so that what the American archaeologists have excavated is a Roman provincial capital, whose main square combines the functional and the aesthetic in a balanced and orderly way, which is Roman, but not with rigid symmetry, which would have been very un-Greek.

Another historic Greek city that prospered under Roman sway was Ephesus, which the Romans elevated to be the capital of the province of Asia. Its excavators calculate that at its peak it reached a population of 500,000. Austrian archaeologists, in part subsidized with Rockefeller money, excavated its Roman phase under Josef Keil (1926-35), and again, from 1954 until his death in 1959, under F. Miltner, who boasted that his was the most modern dig in Anatolia. A Latin inscription (with "IMPERATOR" misspelled "IMBERATOR") dated the Agora west gate (see plan, Fig. 8.14) in 4/3 B.C. The theater was remodeled under Claudius (41-54) and Trajan (98-117). About 54 the monumental "Marble Street" took a form which the Austrians have revealed to perfection: lined with monuments on both sides, it gives a splendid idea of what Ephesus was like in its prime. Nero gave the city a stadium: the excavators found built into a later pavement its balustrade, with a crude representation of the prizes offered. Later the stadium was

Fig. 8.14 Ephesus, plan. Road in upper r. corner leads eastward to Artemision, 200 yards away. Vedius' gymnasium, upper r.; Celsus' library, center, just south of Agora; Verulanius' portico, east of Harbor Baths (Thermen). (Keil, *Führer*⁴, fac. p. 110)

Planskizze
der lysimachischen Stadt.

lysimachische Stadtmauer
byzantinische   "
Aqu. = Aquädukt

0   100   500   1000m

remodeled for gladiatorial shows (except at Dura, there are no amphitheaters in the East). In the Agora Miltner found the shops of the silversmiths who cried "Great is Diana of the Ephesians!" Domitian (81-96) permitted a temple to himself, on a terrace, where the excavators found the colossal head and arm (Fig. 8.15) of his cult-statue. The pseudo-philosopher Apollonius of Tyana persuaded the Ephesians to pull it down in the second century. In Domitian's reign, too, a strip 650 yards long and 270 yards wide, from the theater to the harbor, was lined with gymnasia, and a set of baths with three colossal windows facing the harbor, each over thirty-three feet square. Miltner is eloquent about the exotic goods that were landed at Ephesus harbor: cloth and spices from Syria and Palestine, cedar of Lebanon, golden grain from Egypt and south Russia, shimmering marble from the Greek islands, copper from Cyprus, silver from Spain, tin from Britain, and slaves skilled at cookery or at making love.

An inscription dates the Library of Celsus in 106; in it the Austrians found the lead-lined sarcophagus of its donor. Another public-spirited citizen, with a Roman name, Verulanius, donated (124-127) a huge portico between the theater and the harbor. From the age of the Antonine emperors (138-161) date the Vedius Gymnasium, donated by another public-spirited citizen with a Roman name, and the odeum, for 1400, donated by his wife. The Vedius Gymnasium baths, covering 260 × 455 feet, compare in scale, plan, elegance, and sophistication with the huge later baths of Caracalla and Diocletian in Rome. The dressing-rooms had lockers under the seats and hooks for clothes. Statues of river-gods poured water from urns into the plunge-bath. In the basement were at least fourteen furnace-rooms, needed to heat over 10,000 square yards of floor space. The floors were so hot that bathers in the *caldarium* (steamroom had to wear wooden clogs. The huge west windows took advantage of solar heat, as in the Forum Baths at Ostia. Though archaeologists have occasionally found Greek-designed baths on purely Greek sites, for example, at Olympia, none compare in grandeur with the Roman baths of Ephesus.

A few decades after Vedius donated his baths, Ephesus was enriched, under the Severan Emperors, with a temple of Serapis opposite the Agora. The Austrians were able to reconstruct it on paper. Its columns weigh twenty-seven tons each; their capitals are the height of a man. Miltner

brings it to life with his description of the exotic rites practiced here in torchlight, to the rattle of the *sistrum*.

On the hills overlooking the civic center were the houses, some with peristyle, private baths, and private chapels. All this grandeur fell before the Goths in 263. The story of the city's revival, of the "House of the Virgin," of the Council held here in 431, of the Austrian reconstruction of the sixth-century church of St. John, is fascinating, but falls outside the scope of this book.

While Corinth and Ephesus flourished as provincial capitals, Athens went on placidly as a quiet university town. Her most impressive memorial from Trajan's reign is the Philopappos Monument, on the Hill of the Muses, southwest of the Acropolis. Balanos restored it in the 'thirties, and the Italians studied it just before World War II. The Athenians built it—it is a tomb—about 116, to honor a prince of Commagene, a descendant of the builder of the tomb on Nemrud Dagh, C. Julius Antiochus Philopappos, who was at once a Syrian prince, a Roman dignitary, and an Athenian citizen, archon, and benefactor, a typical cosmopolitan of the Greek world under Roman sway. His tomb (Fig. 8.16, an old print) is a semicircular exedra of Pentelic marble, built to face the Parthenon; the best view of the Acropolis is from here. It has three niches for the statue of Philopappos flanked by his ancestors. Symbolic of the fusion of cultures are two inscriptions, one giving his public career in Latin, the other his princely titles in Greek.

Soon after the dedication of the Philopappos monument, Athens received (124/5) an Imperial visitor, the Emperor Hadrian, whose advent was to usher in a Renaissance. The Athenians compared him to their mythical King Theseus, who first united Attica under Athenian rule, but as a builder he is in the line of such historical figures as Pisistratus, Pericles, and Lycurgus. He delighted to embellish Athens, and she delighted to honor him. He was initiated into the Mysteries at Eleusis, presided over the dramatic competition in the theater of Dionysus (which he adorned with statues and new marble thrones for priests and dignitaries), was elected archon—chief magistrate—and had a tribe named after him. In return he built a new stretch of circuit wall, adding 25 per cent to the city's area. One of its gates survives, with a pair of metrical inscriptions, on one side calling Athens Theseus' city; on the other, Hadrian's. Just southeast

Fig. 8.16 Athens, Philopappos Monument, before restoration. (DAI, Athens)

of this gate rises Hadrian's most monumental gift to his favorite city: the huge precinct (half a mile around) and gigantic temple (173 × 359 feet) of Olympian Zeus. Begun by Pisistratus in the sixth century B.C. (some of his column-drums were found in 1949 in the city wall nearby), rebuilt

Fig. 8.17 Athens, Olympieion, floodlit at night, from southeast. (Émile Séraf)

by King Antiochus Epiphanes of Syria about 174 B.C. (some of the surviving columns may be his), and assuming its final form under Hadrian about 130, it has one of the longest building-histories in the annals of architecture. The Hadrianic temple had 104 huge Corinthian columns, of which fifteen are still standing (Fig. 8.17). One, felled by a hurricane in 1852, was measured as it lay: it was sixty feet long, the height of a five-story building. Some of the missing ones went to the limekilns: the mortar of a mosque in a corner of Hadrian's Library came from the columns of Hadrian's temple.

Hadrian's Library, north of the Roman Agora, dates from his third visit to Athens in 131/2. It was not conclusively identified till 1919, when an English architect, M. A. Sisson, triumphing over the complications of a site encumbered by modern streets, houses, shops, a military barracks and prison, and a mosque, published the definitive study (Fig. 8.18). Stuart and Revett had thought it was the Painted Porch and later writers had called it merely a stoa. Sisson's method exploited literary sources, observation on the spot, and comparisons with similar buildings. Pausanias mentions 100 columns of Phrygian marble; Sisson was able to count exactly that number of bases in the peristyle: twenty-two each front and back, and twenty-eight each on the sides. The central room on the east has two stories of recesses, compensated for by buttresses on the outside. The recesses are too shallow for statues, but just deep enough to shelve scrolls in their containers; Sisson remembered a parallel in the Library ("Sala dei Filosofi") of Hadrian's Villa near Tivoli. Behind the recesses is an air space, a provision against damp like that found in the Library of Celsus at Ephesus and in those of Trajan in Rome, of about the same date. There is one deeper, arched, central recess for a statue of Athena, who as goddess of wisdom, should preside over libraries. Sisson calculated that the four eastern rooms, fitted with two stories of shelves round the walls and in the middle, would hold 200,000 rolls. The building technique proves the edifice to be of Hadrianic date: the free-standing pedestaled columns and the architrave with only two fascias instead of three are identical with those on Hadrian's arch near the Olympieum, and the wall-blocks with their carefully finished edges are like those of the Olympieum's precinct wall. The flanking rooms may have housed public archives, but they are very grand for so humdrum a function: more probably

Fig. 8.18 Athens, Library of Hadrian, plan. Note 100 columned peristyle, book recesses in central room on east (at top in plan), and flanking rooms, probably for lectures. (Sisson, 1929, Pl. 21, by permission of the British School at Rome)

Fig. 8.19 Athens, Stadium of Herodes Atticus, as restored for Olympics of 1896. Herms and other remains in curve are ancient.

they were used for lectures or poets' recitations. (In that case, Sisson's calculations based on central shelving for scrolls will have to be reduced.) Centrally located, with an imposing façade, enclosed for security and quiet in blank walls with but a single entrance, furnished with stoa, garden, and exedras, it must have been a cool and agreeable retreat for scholars: one wonders whether the Alexandrian Library was not like this on a larger scale.

The Library does not exhaust the list of Hadrian's benefactions. He built a gymnasium (site as yet undiscovered), and rebuilt the Pompeion in the Ceramicus. A bridge of his building was found in 1950 on the Sacred Way to Eleusis, and, like Pisistratus, he built an aqueduct. It is still in use, having been reconditioned along with its reservoir.

When Hadrian ascended the throne in 117, a tongue-tied seventeen-year-old student of rhetoric named Herodes Atticus was sent to greet him in camp on the Danube. The boy was to grow up to be not only tutor to the Emperor Marcus Aurelius, but also one of the greatest rhetoricians (Aelius Aristides was his pupil), and the wealthiest, most philanthropic, and most cordially hated man of his time. The wealth was inherited, his father having discovered a treasure. The hatred was inherited, too: it came about through a provision of his father's will, which left five *minae* (about $100) apiece to each Athenian citizen, *after* the citizen's debts to Atticus *père* had been paid. Of course the upshot was that most Athenians found themselves in debt to the estate, and they were perverse and human enough to argue that Herodes' buildings, in consequence, were built with *their* money.

The earliest of Herodes' sumptuous gifts to his city was a complete remodeling of the Panathenaic Stadium, in emulation of Pisistratus the founder of the games and Lycurgus the earlier builder. It was promised in 139/40, finished in 143/4, the year Herodes held the consulship in Rome. Herodes used Pentelic marble: the project was so huge that it temporarily exhausted the Pentelic quarries. A modern millionaire, Averoff, using the studies of archaeologists as basis, restored the stadium yet again (Fig. 8.19) for the revived Olympics in 1896. Its capacity was 50,000, the size of the average modern football stadium. Certain features resemble the Coliseum at Rome: a tunnel at the south end, possibly for wild beasts, and a grille to protect the spectators from them. From the north there was a monumental approach by a bridge across the Ilissus. The propylon had side rooms with mosaic floors: these were probably the athletes' dressing-rooms. Herms (marble pillars surmounted by a bust) marked the turns on the track, and a Doric colonnade over thirty feet deep (missing in the modern reconstruction) crowned the whole structure. On the hill to the west Herodes built a temple to Fortune (*Tychê,* the presiding genius of the Roman, as she had been of the Hellenistic Age), a goddess to whom he owed much. The eastern hill may have held his tomb, though there is a rival claimant in the Athenian suburb of Cephissia, and also the

Fig. 8.20   Olympia, exedra of Herodes Atticus, reconstruction drawing. Most of the statues shown are now in the Olympia Museum. (*Olymp. Forsch.* I, Pl. 36)

possibility that he was buried on his estate near Marathon, whose entrance is inscribed "Gate of Eternal Harmony." This Herodes never achieved: his life was troubled not only by the unpopularity he inherited, but also by a lawsuit on a charge of having connived at his wife's death (159/60), and by a charge of having bribed the Athenian archons (174). He was disappointed also in his son, who was said to have been so stupid that the only way he could learn his letters was to have twenty-four slaves, bearing sandwich-boards inscribed with the letters of the Greek alphabet, parade constantly in order before him.

Perhaps Herodes' mania for building was a compensation for his unhappy personal life. In 147 he undertook to provide marble seats for 7000 in the stadium at Delphi. At Olympia in 153/4 he built his exedra (Fig. 8.20) to mask the end of an aqueduct. The exedra was of brick faced with marble. Its niches held twenty-four statues, utterly medi-ocre in technique: they are relegated to a side room in the Olympia Museum. Nine are of members of the imperial family, fifteen of members of his own. Rising over 100 feet high, the exedra was taller than any other building in the Altis except the temple of Zeus. In tastelessness it is hard to match: perhaps the best parallel is the colossal marble monument in Rome to Victor Emmanuel II, nicknamed "the typewriter," which also uses classical motifs in a well-meaning but moribund and derivative way. Herodes' bene-factions to Corinth, possible (the odeum), and certain (Pi-rene remodeled) we have already mentioned. He also built an aqueduct for the city of Alexandria Troas in northwest Asia Minor.

Herodes' final gift to Athens was his roofed theater or odeum, built in 161 for 5000 people on the south slope of the Acropolis at the west end of the Stoa of Eumenes. Vari-ously identified until the nineteenth century as the theater of Dionysus, the Areopagus, and the School of the Peripa-tetic Philosophers, it was excavated and finally identified by Greek archaeologists in 1848, and explored again in 1857-58. Reconstructed since World War II on a sound archaeological basis (Fig. 8.21) it is now used for summer performances of ancient Greek drama and for symphony concerts. Roman in materials—brick and *opus incertum* (fist-sized stones set irregularly in cement)—it is Greek in being built into the hillside instead of on man-made foun-dations. The entrances were barrel-vaulted in the Roman

Fig. 8.21 Athens, Odeum of Herodes Atticus. Note barrel-vaulted entrance, architectural backdrop and checkerboard paving of orchestra. (Greek National Tourist Bureau)

way; buttresses braced the walls against the strain of the cedarwood roof; the front of the stage building (*scaenae frons*) was an architectural backdrop three stories high. The orchestra is paved in a checkerboard pattern with white and with green Carystus marble (*cippollino*, "onion-stone").

An odeum was traditionally for musical performances. Herodes was more interested in the function of his odeum as a lecture-hall, for, under imperial appointment, he was as it were Regius Professor of Rhetoric in the University of Athens. When Agrippa's odeum in the Agora was remodeled about 150, there is no evidence that Herodes paid the bill, but he almost certainly lectured in its auditorium, now reduced to a capacity of 500, more appropriate for university lectures than its former size. Pairs of seated statues of philosophers, one pair for each school (Stoic, Academic, Peripatetic, and Epicurean), now adorned the new stair, and the new north porch would have made a fine place for Peripatetic tutorials. To the north façade of this phase belong the giant and the two colossal tritons (derived from the Parthenon west pediment) still *in situ*.

Fig. 8.22 Piraeus, Museum. Marble plaque found in harbor in 1931, showing Theseus and an Amazon on the Acropolis (note Ionic columns of Erechtheum North Porch, upper left), and probably derived from Phidias' rendering of the shield of Athena. (DAI, Athens)

To the last half of the second century belongs a set of marble plaques, now in the Piraeus Museum, which were discovered bedded in harbor mud during dredging operations in 1931. They bear traces of fire that presumably sank a marble-laden ship bound for Rome. Like other sculpture of that period, they are classicistic, imitating the style of the mid-fifth century B.C.; that they are not originals is proved by their heavy moldings, which could not possibly be fifth century; they were left rough for finishing when set in place in Rome. The plaques portray several subjects, each in several copies. The most interesting (Fig. 8.22) shows an Amazon of heroic size, jumping from a cliff rather than fall into the hands of a boyish Greek who pursues her. In the background is a wall, with four Ionic capitals peeping over it. When photographs of the finds were published, in bad half-tone, in the press, this wall provided one clue to the sharp eye of Hans Schrader: he saw that it was the north wall of the Athenian Acropolis; the four columns represent the north porch of the Erechtheum. He also noticed that the composition of the figures was better suited to a round than to a rectangular original, and triumphantly concluded, knowing that Theseus and the Amazons had been a subject on the shield of Phidias' statue of Athena, that the Piraeus finds imitated a Phidian original. The technique, he argued, resembles that of the Parthenon metopes but not that of the pediment or most of the frieze, which would therefore not be Phidian. Thus he turned a chance find into a controversy of great significance in the history of art.

All the buildings in the Agora and many others in Corinth and elsewhere in Greece were burnt in the Herulian sack of 267. With the details of Athens' archaeological history after that date this book, which has traced it for 1500 years, is not concerned; suffice it to say that the odeum in the Agora came into use again about 400, and served educational purposes until Justinian closed the university in 529. The discovery of an olive-press on the west side of the Agora shows what it then became: here was an untidy farmhouse on the edge of a straggling village.

For a final example of archaeological discovery illuminating the Greek world under Roman sway, we travel to the Roman frontier-post of Dura-Europus on the Euphrates 150 miles east of Palmyra. A British sapper digging trenches there in 1920 discovered the site; he reported his discovery to the Baghdad authorities while the great American Orientalist J. H. Breasted was in town. Breasted brought the discovery to the attention of the learned world, and the French under Franz Cumont began digging in 1922-23, the workmen being members of the Foreign Legion. Excavation was resumed (1928-37) by a Yale expedition headed by the great economic historian of the Hellenistic and Roman worlds, M. I. Rostovtzeff. What he found was a grid-planned city (Fig. 8.23), a curious mixture of Greek, Semitic, Anatolian, and Parthian influences, going back, he discovered, to 300 B.C., and with a Roman overlay. He called it a Greco-Macedonian islet in a Semitic sea. The dry desert climate preserved wood, textiles, leather, and paper there, so that for scientific interest the finds, in quantity, quality, variety, and state of preservation, rival and sometimes exceed those of Pompeii and Delos.

The excavators worked under trying conditions. In the 'twenties the journey to Dura from Beirut took four days and three nights, with the desert as the only road. (Dura was on the ancient caravan route from Antioch to Seleucia-

FORTIFICATIONS

1. Citadel and its palace.
2. Main gate.
3. Subsidiary gate on the desert front.
4. South gate.
4a. Brick wall of the Roman Military Camp.

TEMPLES

5. Temple of Artemis-Nanaia.
6. Zeus Megistos.
7. Atargatis.
8. Azzanathcona.
9. Bel (?) NW. corner.
10. Zeus Kyrios.
11. Aphlad.
12. Gaddé.
13. Zeus Theos.
14. Adonis.
15. Tyche.
16. Military chapel.
17. Christian church.
18. Synagogue.

PUBLIC BUILDINGS

19. Acropolis Strategion.
20. Agora.
21. Sukhs.
22. Khan.
23. Baths.

MILITARY BUILDINGS

24. Praetorium.
25. House of a Higher Officer.
26. Palace of the dux.
27. Mithraeum.
28. Dolicheneum.
29. Amphitheatre.
30. Barracks.

PRIVATE HOUSES

31. House of Lysias.
31. House of the Scribes.

Note. The excavated buildings are shown in plan. The excavated streets are shown with solid outlines. The excavated streets are shown with dotted lines.

Fig. 8.23 Dura-Europus, plan. (Rostovtzeff, 1938, Fig. 6, by permission of the Clarendon Press, Oxford) on-the-Tigris.) Digging conditions were unsatisfactory: not only were the Bedouin poor workmen, but the job was dirty, dusty, hot, and tiring. Sandstorms were frequent; the clack of water-wheels and the cry of fox and jackal got on the nerves. The first camp was in the citadel (1 on the plan), whose arches made a dining-room and study, while its roofless towers served for kitchen and storage. There might have been hunting, for food and for diversion—there was wild boar in the tamarisk thickets, and partridge, pigeon, gazelle, and rabbit—but the French, in fear of native uprisings, confiscated all guns. The Euphrates flowed directly below the citadel (a sheer drop: part of the citadel had fallen into the river), but the path to the river was four miles long, the current was too swift for swimming, and the water unsafe for drinking. Under these conditions the patience and devotion of the Yale archaeologists, season after season, was the more remarkable and praiseworthy, and the results, as so often, made the hardships worth while.

The most interesting outcome of the Dura campaigns was to document what happened to a Greco-Macedonian town under oriental and Roman influences. Founded as a fortress-city, Dura-Europus became a caravan town, with unique oriental sukhs or bazaars, like no other Hellenistic or Roman city. The hyphenated name of the place is symbolic: Dura is Babylonian; the original Europus was a town of Macedonia, birthplace of Seleucus I, the founder of the Syrian dynasty. Very little of the Hellenistic city survives, but the walls follow the original line; the grid plan and perhaps the colonnaded main street go back to 300 B.C. The Hellenistic Agora, however (20 on the plan) was overlaid with later buildings. The ruling aristocracy tried to keep its Macedonian stock and nomenclature pure, but it was a losing battle, though Greek remained the official language. The Macedonian colonists began as landowners, but became merchants, took Levantine business partners and wives, and became Levantine themselves. The excavators found the diary of a typical businessman of Dura: he was land-agent, money-lender, merchant, and old-clothes dealer, and his partners were Iranian and Semitic. In one family the father had a Greek name, while his wife's was Semitic, and the children's Greek, Iranian, and Semitic. Palmyrene and, later, Latin occur beside Greek in inscriptions; one *graffito* is significant: it is Latin, but written in Greek letters; it records the number of hams to be served to the Roman *dux ripae* (Officer-in-

Command, Euphrates). The houses begin as Macedonian peristyle types, as at Olynthus; they evolve into Babylonian ones, with stables for camels (the evidence is the mangers, set higher than they would be for horses), separate courts for men and women, and flat roofs for sleeping. The wall decoration becomes more and more like an oriental carpet: even Nemrud Dagh is more Greek (though at Dura the more palatial the house, the stronger the Greek influence). The oriental décor is Parthian in inspiration, for the Parthians took Dura in 141 B.C., and, though their policy was non-interference with the city's political, social, economic, cultural, or religious life, the excavators found no Greek buildings datable after 50 B.C., and no civic edifices such as would have served a Greek city-state. The temple of Artemis (5 on the plan) became the center of civilian worship, with a small *bouleutêrion;* the temple-court served as Agora or Forum. Dura became an oriental city: its only public buildings were palaces and temples (and later, under Rome, barracks). The temples are un-Greek: they stand in courts surrounded by chambers with an altar in the middle, but there is no central temple building that a Greek would recognize. The temple of Atargatis (in its second phase, dated by the Yale archaeologists in 31/2) had a small theater with reserved seats for women only. The town's aristocracy with its Greek blood came to worship Palmyrene gods, Zeus appears in Iranian dress, and other gods in Roman uniform.

An earthquake struck Dura in 160 or 161; the citizens must have felt they had suffered another when under the Severan dynasty the Romans took over and made the city into a mere garrison-town, existing to feed and house Roman soldiers. Roman officers had little or no contact with civilians, though the petty officers probably made an occupation force's usual informal arrangements. The whole northwest quarter became a Roman armed camp, set off by a brick wall (4A), its private houses made over into barracks. It had an amphitheater (29) for the gladiatorial shows that Roman soldiers loved, a Mithraeum (27) for their favorite worship, a praetorium (dated 211), with propylon, court, and sanctuary for the legion's standards. The Roman army's religious calendar, the *Feriale Duranum,* records oriental gods beside the deified Roman imperial family. Among the townsfolk Judaism and Christianity flourished. The evidence is a synagogue (17) of about 190, discovered by chance under a ramp near the main gate (2), and a Christian church near-

Fig. 8.24 Dura-Europus, font and west wall of Christian church, reconstructed. (New Haven, Yale Gallery of Fine Arts)

by (18), made over in about 232 from a private house. It is most unusual in having wall-paintings of living people, as well as such standbys of Christian art as the Good Shepherd and the three Marys at the tomb of Christ. The synagogue is restored in the Damascus Museum, the church (Fig. 8.24) in Yale's Museum of Fine Arts. Paradoxically and significantly, Christian art at Dura is much more Greek than the rest of Dura's décor, for the Christian influence came to Dura from Greek Antioch or Alexandria.

As the third century wore on, Rome, racked by domestic anarchy, grew progressively less able to protect the caravan routes, which in consequence bypassed Dura, and the town began to decline. In 256 Sapur I, King of the new Persian Sassenid dynasty, struck, and Dura fell. The excavators found the mute and tragic evidence in a tunnel under the wall: some twenty Roman skeletons, armed, with money in their belts; opposite them, a single Sassanian, with a sword.

Here ends our selective survey of the Greek world under Roman sway. Its wide range, from Cyrene to Dura, has told everywhere the same story, one of a mixture of influences, Greek, Roman, and native. Greek architectural forms are usually the inspiration (as at Nemrud Dagh, Augustan Athens, Roman Corinth, and Christian Dura); the massiveness and the money are usually Roman (Baalbek, Hadrianic Athens), but Herodes Atticus was a Greek patron of architects in a tradition that goes back to the tyrants of archaic times. Against this architectural background native life went on, taking its own way, but influenced and pervaded, as the world has been ever since, by the culture that we have traced from its Neolithic beginning through Bronze Age richness, Iron Age decline, archaic lyrical strength, Periclean prime, fourth-century status quo, and Hellenistic baroque revival. This complicated, important, and fascinating story the archaeologists' spade and pen have revealed: our world owes them a great debt for so eloquently making the Greek stones speak.

Addendum

(All dates approximate)

B.C.

126	Delos, Agora of Theophrastus
112	Delos, House of Poseidoniasts
after 69	Delos, Triarius' Wall
62	Nemrud Dagh, Antiochus I's tomb
50	Athens, Tower of the Winds
44	Corinth, Basilica; South Stoa (phase)
	Eleusis, Lesser Propylaea
	Athens, Roman Agora
after 31	Athens, Temple of Rome and Augustus
	Athens, Temple of Ares, reconstruction
	Corinth, Propylaea arch
15	Athens, Odeum of Agrippa
10	Athens, Gate of Athena Archegetis
4/3	Ephesus, Agora, west gate

A.D.

10	Baalbek, Temple of Jupiter (phase)
25-50	Corinth, central shops
31/2	Dura, Temple of Atargatis, Phase II
32	Palmyra, Temple of Bel, Phase I
40	Corinth, twin basilicas
41-54	Ephesus, theater (phase)
54	Ephesus, Marble Street; stadium
67	Corinth, theater (phase)
70	Palmyra, Temple of Bel, court
before 75	Gerasa, walls
76 ff.	Palmyra, Agora
81-96	Ephesus, Temple of Domitian; Harbor Baths
before 83	Gerasa, South Theater
98-117	Ephesus, theater (phase)
	Cyrene, Caesareum
100	Palmyra, Corinthian temple
	Athens, Library of Pantainos
106	Ephesus, Library of Celsus
116	Athens, Philopappos monument
120-150	Palmyra, theater; tetrapylon
120-200	Baalbek, Temple of Jupiter, Altar Court
124-127	Ephesus, Portico of Verulanius

before	
130	Baalbek, Temple of Bacchus
130	Athens, Olympieum, Hadrian's Wall, Gate, Library, etc.
135	Corinth, theater, marble phase
138-161	Ephesus, Vedius Gymnasium, Baths, & Odeum
143/4	Athens, Stadium of Herodes Atticus
147	Delphi, stadium, marble seats
148	Palmyra, "Camp of Diocletian"
150	Athens, Agora Odeum, Phase II
150-200	Piraeus, marble plaques
153/4	Olympia, Exedra of Herodes Atticus
161 ff.	Athens, Odeum of Herodes Atticus
161	Corinth, Pirene, Herodes Atticus phase
163	Gerasa, North Theater
174	Palmyra, Temple of Bel, Propylaea, towers
175	Corinth, Odeum
185	Corinth, Temple of Poseidon
after 185	Cyrene, Temple of Zeus, rebuilding
190	Dura, synagogue
191	Corinth, Temple of Heracles
192	Ephesus, Serapeum
211	Dura, Praetorium
211-217	Corinth, theater remodeled into arena
232	Dura, Christian church
245	Baalbek, Temple of Venus
256	Dura falls to Sassanians
263	Ephesus destroyed by Goths
267	Athens, Herulian sack
272	Palmyra destroyed by Valerian

Abbreviations

AA: Archäologischer Anzeiger
AbhBay: Abhandlungen der philosophisch-philologischen Klasse der königlich Bayerischen Akademie der Wissenschaften
AJA: American Journal of Archaeology
AM: Mitteilungen des Deutschen Archäologischen Instituts, Athenische Abteilung
AntJ: Antiquaries' Journal
APB: Agora Picture Books
Arch: Archaeology
ArchEph: Archaiologike Ephemeris
ASAtene: Annuario della R. Scuola Archeologica di Atene
ASCS: American School of Classical Studies
BASOR: Bulletin of the American Schools of Oriental Research
BCH: Bulletin de correspondance hellénique
BdA: Bolletino d'Arte
BMMA: Bulletin of the Metropolitan Museum of Art, New York
BSA: British School at Athens, Annual
BSR: British School of Archaeology at Rome, Papers
BSRAA: Bulletin de la Société r. d'archéologie d'Alexandrie
CAH: Cambridge Ancient History
CJ: Classical Journal
DAI: Deutsches Archäologisches Institut
Delt: Archaiologikon Deltion
EI: Enciclopedia italiana
Erg: To Ergon tes Archaiologikes Hetaireias
EtCret: Études crétoises
FA: Fasti Archaeologici
FdD: Fouilles de Delphes
Hdbh: Handbuch
Hesp: Hesperia
HSCP: Harvard Studies in Classical Philology
ILN: Illustrated London News
JHS: Journal of Hellenic Studies
JNES: Journal of Near Eastern Studies
MMS: Metropolitan Museum Studies
NDA: Neue deutsche Ausgrabungen, Berlin 1959
OpusArch: Opuscula Archaeologica
Prakt: Praktika tes en Athenais Archaiologikes Hetairias
ProcPS: Proceedings of the Prehistoric Society
ProcPhilSoc: Proceedings of the American Philosophical Society
RA: Revue archéologique
RE: Pauly-Wissowa, Real-Encyclopädie der klassischen Altertumswissenschaft
SkrLund: Skrifter utgivna av Vetenskaps-Societeten i Lund
SPHS: Society for the Promotion of Hellenic Studies

Books and Articles Consulted

CHAPTER 1: *The Aegean in Prehistory*

T. D. Atkinson *et al.,* "Excavations at Phylakopi in Melos," *SPHS Suppl. Papers* 4 (London 1904)

L. Bernabò Brea, "A Bronze Age House at Poliochni (Lemnos)," *ProcPS* 21 (1955) 144-155; *id. ILN* 231 (1957), 197-199. A new 3-vol. work by B. B. on Poliochni is forthcoming.

C. W. Blegen, "Preclassical Greece," U. of Penn. Bicentennial Conference, *Studies in the Arts and Architecture* (Philadelphia 1941) 1-4

———— *et al., Troy* I (Princeton 1950)

H. Bulle, "Orchomenos I," *AbhBay* 24 (1907)

J. L. Caskey, "The Early Helladic Period in the Argolid," *Hesp* 29 (1960) 285-303

P. Dikaios, *A Guide to the Cyprus Museum* (Nicosia 1947)

W. Dörpfeld, *Troia und Ilion* (Berlin 1902)

S. Dow, "The Greeks in the Bronze Age," (*Rapports du XIe Congrès International des Sciences Historiques* 2 (Göteborg 1960) 1-34

Sir Arthur Evans, *The Palace of Minos* I-IV (Oxford 1921-36)

Joan Evans, *Time and Chance* (London 1943)

H. Goldman, *Excavations at Eutresis in Boeotia* (Cambridge, Mass. 1931)

N. G. L. Hammond, *A History of Greece to 322* B.C. (Oxford 1959)

E. Kunze, "Orchomenos II-III," *AbhBay* n.F. 5 (1931); 8 (1934)

W. Lamb, *Excavations at Thermi in Lesbos* (Cambridge 1936)

D. Levi, "Attività della Scuola archeologica italiana di Atene nel anno 1951," *BdA* ser. 4, 37 (1952) 320-348

F. Matz, "Die Agäis," *Hdbh der Archäologie* VI, ii (Munich 1954) 180-308

————, *Kreta, Mykene, Troia* (Stuttgart 1956) 1-41

K. Müller, *Tiryns: die Ergebnisse der Ausgrabungen,* III (Augsburg 1930); IV (Munich 1938)

D. L. Page, *History and the Homeric Iliad* (Berkeley 1959)

J. D. S. Pendlebury, *The Archaeology of Crete* (London 1939)

————, *A Handbook to the Palace of Minos at Knossos* (London 1954)

F. Schachermeyr, *Die ältesten Kulturen Griechenlands* (Stuttgart 1955)

——, "Prähistorische Kulturen Greichenlands," *RE* (1954) Sp. 1350-1548

Chr. Tsountas, *Hai prohistorikai akropoleis Diminiou kai Sesklou* (Athens 1908)

——, "Kykladika," *ArchEph* 1898, 138-212; *ib.* 1899, 73-134

CHAPTER 2: *"Mycenae, Rich in Gold"*

Works already cited: Atkinson, Bulle, Dow, Evans, Levi, Müller, Page, Pendlebury, Schachermeyr

C. W. Blegen, "Excavations at Pylos," *AJA* 43 (1939) 557-576; 57 (1953) 59-64; 58 (1954) 27-32; 59 (1955) 31-37; 60 (1956) 95-101; 61 (1957) 129-135; 62 (1958) 175-191; 63 (1959) 121-137; 64 (1960) 153-164; 65 (1961) 152-163; 66 (1962) 145-152

—— *et al., Troy IV* (Princeton 1958)

J. Chadwick, *The Decipherment of Linear B* (Cambridge 1958)

F. Chapouthier *et al.*, "Fouilles executées à Mallia," *EtCret* 1 (Paris 1928); 2 (1930); 4 (1936); 6 (1942); 7 (1945); 9 (1953)

R. M. Dawkins, J. P. Droop, "Excavations at Phylakopi in Melos 1911," *BSA* 17 (1911) 1-22

W. B. Dinsmoor, *The Architecture of Ancient Greece*[3] (London 1950)

H. D. Ephron, "Hygieia Tharso and Iaon: The Phaistos Disk," *HSCP* 66 (1962) 1-91

A. Furumark, "Linear A und die altkretische Sprache" (Berlin 1956) Mimeographed lecture to Arch. Gesellschaft.

G. Glotz, *The Aegean Civilization* (London 1925)

J. W. Graham, *The Cretan Palaces* (Princeton 1962)

H. B. Hawes *et al., Gournia* (Philadelphia 1908)

J. Hazzidakis, "Les villas minoennes de Tylissos," *EtCret* 3 (Paris 1934)

A. W. Lawrence, *Greek Architecture* (Harmondsworth 1957) 1-82

O. Montelius, *La Grèce préclassique* I (Stockholm 1924) 134-148 (Gla)

G. E. Mylonas, *Ancient Mycenae* (Princeton 1957)

——, *Eleusis and the Eleusinian Mysteries* (Princeton 1961)

L. Pernier, L. Banti, *Il palazzo minoico di Festòs*, 2 vols. (Rome 1935, 1951)

——, ——, *Guida degli scavi italiani in Creta* (Rome 1947) 28-38 (H. Triada)

A. W. Persson, "The Royal Tombs at Dendra," *SkrLund* 15 (1931)

——, "New Tombs at Dendra," *ib.* 34 (1942)

D. S. Robertson. *A Handbook of Greek and Roman Architecture*[2] (Cambridge 1954)

K. Scholes, "The Cyclades in the Later Bronze Age: A Synopsis," *BSA* 51 (1956) 9-40

B. Schwartz, "The Phaistos Disk, *JNES* 18 (1959) 105-112, 222-228

M. Ventris, J. Chadwick, "Evidence for Greek Dialect in the Mycenaean Archives," *JHS* 73 (1953) 84-103

———, ———, *Documents in Mycenaean Greek* (Cambridge 1956)

T. B. L. Webster, *From Mycenae to Homer* (London 1958)

CHAPTER 3: *Mycenaean Athens,* etc.

J. L. Angel, "Skeletal Material from Attica," *Hesp* 14 (1945) 279-363

J. Boardman, *The Cretan Collection in Oxford* (Oxford 1961), esp. Ch. V

O. Broneer, "A Mycenaean Fountain on the Athenian Acropolis," *Hesp* 8 (1939) 317-429

———, "Athens in the Late Bronze Age," *Antiquity* 30 (1956) 9-18

D. Burr, "A Geometric House," *Hesp* 2 (1933) 542-640

E. Buschor, "Heraion von Samos: frühe Bauten," *AM* 55 (1930) 1-99

J. M. Cook *et al.,* "Old Smyrna, 1948-1951," *BSA* 53-54 (1958-59) 1-181; *ILN* 222 (1953) 328-29

R. M. Dawkins *et al.,* "Excavations at Sparta," *BSA* 12 (1905-06) 277-479; 13 (1906-07) 1-218; 14 (1907-08) 1-158; 15 (1908-09) 1-157; 16 (1909-10) 1-67; *id., Artemis Orthia* (London 1929)

V. R. d'A. Desborough, *Protogeometric Pottery* (Oxford 1952)

P. Dikaios, *op. cit.* supra, Ch. 2

H. Ephron, "The Jeson Tablet of Enkomi," *HSCP* 65 (1961) 39-107

A. Furumark, "The Settlement at Ialysos," *OpusArch* 6 (1950) 150-271

E. H. Hall, *Excavations in Eastern Crete: Vrocastro* (Philadelphia 1914)

L. B. Holland, "The Strong House of Erechtheus," *AJA* 28 (1924) 142-169

W. Kraiker, K. Kübler, *Kerameikos: Ergebnisse der Ausgrabungen* I (Berlin 1939)

Sp. Marinatos, "Le temple géometrique de Dréros," *BCH* 60 (1936) 214-285

W. R. Paton, "Excavations in Caria," *JHS* 8 (1887) 64-82

H. Payne *et al., Perachora* I (Oxford 1940)

J. D. S. Pendlebury *et al.,* "Excavations in the Plain of Lasithi III, i: Karphi," *BSA* 38 (1937-38) 57-145

K. Rhomaios, "Ek tou prohistorikou Thermou," *Delt* 1 (1915) 225-279

C. F. E. Schaeffer, "Enkomi," *AJA* 52 (1948) 165-171

———, *Enkomi-Alasia* (Paris 1952)

C. G. Starr, *The Origins of Greek Civilization, 1100-650* B.C. (New York 1961)

E. D. Townsend, "A Mycenaean Chamber Tomb under the Temple of Ares," *Hesp* 24 (1955) 187-219

J. Travlos, *Poleodomike Exelexis ton Athenon* (Athens 1960) 19-32. Eng. tr. forthcoming.

G. Welter, "Vom Nikepyrgos," *AA* 54 (1939) 2-22

S. Wide, "Gräberfunde aus Salamis," *AM* 35 (1910) 17-36

CHAPTER 4: *The Lyric Age*

P. Amandry, "La Colonne des Naxiens et le Portique des Athéniens," *FdD* II, ii (Paris 1953)

G. Ardaillon, *Les mines de Laurion dans l'antiquité* (Paris 1897)

E. Bethe, "Das archaische Delos," *Die Antike* 14 (1938) 81-119

R. M. Cook, *Greek Painted Pottery* (London 1960)

G. Dickins, *Catalogue of the Acropolis Museum* I (Cambridge 1912)

W. Dörpfeld, *Alt-Olympia,* 2 vols. (Berlin 1935)

Sir J. G. Frazer, *Pausanias* 2 (London 1898) 433 ff. (Marathon mound)

A. Furtwängler, *Aegina: das Heiligtum der Aphaia,* 2 vols. (Munich 1906)

H. Gallet de Santerre, *Délos primitive et archaique* (Paris 1958)

E. Ghislanzoni, "Cirene," *EI* (1931)

R. Hampe, "Die neuen deutschen Ausgrabungen in Olympia," *Die Antike* 14 (1938) 243-248

I. T. Hill, *The Ancient City of Athens* (Cambridge, Mass. 1953), ch. 14 (Pre-Periclean Acropolis)

Fr. Hiller von Gaertringen, *Thera,* 4 vols. (Berlin 1899-1904)

R. Horn, "Kyrene," *Die Antike* 19 (1943) 163-213

J. Hulot, G. Fougères, *Sélinonte: ville, acropole, temples* (Paris 1910)

P. Kavvadias, G. Kawerau, *Die Ausgrabung der Acropolis, 1885-1890* (Athens 1908)

F. Krauss, *Paestum: die griechischen Tempel* (Berlin 1941)

P. de La Coste-Messelière, G. de Miré, *Delphes* (Paris 1943)

G. E. Mylonas, "The Cemeteries of Eleusis and Mycenae," *Proc-PhilSoc* 99 (1955) 57-67

J. V. Noble, "The Technique of Attic Vase-Painting," *AJA* 64 (1960) 307-318

H. Payne, G. M. Young, *Archaic Sculpture from the Acropolis* (London 1936)

G. Rodenwaldt, *Korkyra: archaische Bauten und Bildwerke I: Der Artemistempel: Architektur, Dachterrakotten, Inschriften* (Berlin 1940); II, *Die Bildwerke des Artemistempels* (ib. 1939)

C. T. Seltman, *Athens: its History and Coinage before the Persian Invasion* (Cambridge 1924)

C. P. Sestieri, *Paestum* [4] (*Itinerari dei Musei e Monumenti d'Italia,* Rome 1956)

T. L. Shear, H. A. Thompson, annual reports on excavations in the Athenian Agora (see infra, Ch. 8)

J. Travlos, *op. cit.* supra, Ch. 3, 33-46 (Archaic Athens)

G. Welter, *Aegina* (Berlin 1940)

P. Zancani-Montuoro, U. Zanotti-Bianco, *Heraion alla Foce del Sele,* 2 vols. text, 2 vols. plates (Rome 1951-54)

CHAPTER 5: *The Classical Age*

W. R. Agard, "What is 'Classical' Sculpture?," *CJ* 49 (1954) 341-349

N. Balanos, *Les monuments de l'acropole: relèvement et conservation,* 2 vols. (Paris 1938)

J. A. Bundgaard, *Mnesicles: A Greek Architect at Work* (Copenhagen 1957)

Rhys Carpenter, *The Sculpture of the Nike Temple Parapet* (Cambridge, Mass. 1929)

J. Chamoux, "L'aurige," *FdD* IV.5 (Paris 1955)

E. Curtius, F. Adler, *Olympia: Ergebnisse der Ausgrabung* I (Berlin 1897)

W. B. Dinsmoor, *op. cit.* supra, Ch. 2

———, "Observations on the Hephaisteion," *Hesp* Suppl 5 (1941)

———, "The Temple of Apollo at Bassae," *MMS* 4 (1933) 204-226

———, "The Sculptured Frieze from Bassae: A Revised Sequence," *AJA* 60 (1956) 401-452

E. N. Gardner, *Olympia, its History and Remains* (Oxford 1925)

R. Hampe, U. Jentzen, W. Wrede, *Bericht über die Ausgrabungen in Olympia* I (Berlin 1937)

I. T. Hill, *op. cit.* supra, Ch. 4, Chs. 9, 15, 16

M. B. Jameson, "A Decree of Themistocles from Troizen," *Hesp* 29 (1960) 198-223

Chr. Karouzos, "Ho Poseidon tou Artemisiou," *Delt* 13 (1930/31) 41-104

H. Kenner, *Die Fries des Tempels von Bassae-Phigalia* (Vienna 1946)

R. Koldewey, O. Puchstein, *Die griechischen Tempel in Unteritalien und Sizilien* (Berlin 1899)

F. Krauss, *op. cit.* supra. Ch. 4.

E. Kunze, H. Schleif, *II-VI Berichte über die Ausgrabungen in Olympia* (Berlin 1938-58)

B. D. Meritt, H. T. Wade-Gery, M. F. McGregor, *The Athenian Tribute Lists,* 4 vols. (Cambridge, Mass. 1939-53)

J. Papadimitriou, "Anaskaphai en Brauroni tes Attikes," *Prakt* 1945/8, 81-90; 1949, 75-90; 1950, 173-187. See also *Erg* 1956, 25-31; 1957, 20-25; 1958, 30-39; 1960, 21-30.

J. M. Paton *et al., The Erechtheum,* 2 vols. (Cambridge, Mass. 1927)

F. C. Penrose, *An Investigation of the Principles of Athenian Architecture*[2] (London 1888)

T. L. Shear, H. A. Thompson, *loc. cit.* infra, Ch. 8

A. H. Smith, "Lord Elgin and his Collection," *JHS* 36 (1916) 163-370

D. B. Thompson, "The House of Simon the Shoemaker," *Arch* 13 (1960) 239-240

J. Travlos, *op. cit.* supra, Ch. 3. Ch. 3

F. Villard, *Sicile grecque* (Paris 1955)

T. B. L. Webster, *Greek Art and Literature 530-400* B.C. (Oxford 1939)

CHAPTER 6: *The Fourth Century*

O. Benndorf, R. Heberdey, W. Wilberg, J. Keil, *Forschungen in Ephesus,* 4 vols. (Vienna 1906-23)

C. W. Blegen, "The December Excavations at Nemea," *Art and Archaeology* 22 (1926) 127-134

——, *"Excavations at Nemea, 1926,"* *AJA* 31 (1927) 421-440

E. Bourguet, *Les ruines de Delphes* (Paris 1914)

O. Broneer, "Excavations at Isthmia," *Hesp* 22 (1953) 182-195; 24 (1955) 110-141; 27 (1958) 1-37; 28 (1959) 298-343

H. C. Butler, *Sardis* I, i, II. i (Leyden, 1922-25)

A. Defrasse, H. Lechat, *Epidaure, restauration et description des principaux monuments du sanctuaire d'Asclèpios* (Paris 1895)

W. Dörpfeld, "Die Skeuothek des Philon," *AM* 8 (1883) 147-164

G. Fougères, *Mantinée et l'Arcadie orientale* (Paris 1898)

E. A. Gardner *et al.,* "Excavations at Megalopolis, 1890-91," *SPHS Suppl. Papers* I (London 1892)

D. G. Hogarth, *British Museum Excavations at Ephesus: the Archaic Artemisia* (London 1908)

P. Kavvadias, *To hieron tou Asklepiou en Epidauroi* (Athens 1900)

H. Knackfuss, *Didyma* I, 3 vols. (Berlin 1941)

E. Kunze, "Neue Ausgrabungen in Olympia," *NDA* 263-310

M. Mayer, "Miletos," *RE* (1932), esp. Sp. 1622-1655

C. T. Newton, *A History of the Discoveries at Halicarnassus* (London 1862)

A. N. Orlandos, reports on excavation at Messene, *Erg.* 1956-60, esp. 1957, 75-80; 1958, 142-148; 1959, 110-117; 1960, 159-167

A. W. Pickard-Cambridge, *The Theater of Dionysus in Athens* (Oxford 1946)

A. Rehm, *Didyma* II (Berlin 1958) 321 ff.

G. M. A. Richter, "A Tanagra Statuette," *BMMA* 26 (1931) 18-20

D. M. Robinson, J. W. Graham, "The Hellenic House," *Excavations at Olynthus* VIII (Baltimore 1938)

E. G. S. Robinson, "The Coins from the Ephesian Artemision Reconsidered," *JHS* 71 (1951) 156-167

H. A. Thompson, R. L. Scranton, "Stoas and City Walls on the Pnyx," *Hesp* 12 (1943) 269-383

E. Vanderpool, "News Letter from Athens," *AJA* 64 (1960) 265-267 (Piraeus finds)

T. Wiegand, H. Schrader, *Priene: Ergebnisse der Ausgrabungen 1895-8* (Berlin 1904)

J. Wiesner, "Olympia," *RE* (1939) Sp. 75-174

J. T. Wood, *Discoveries at Ephesus* (London 1877)

CHAPTER 7: *The Hellenistic Age*

B. Ashmole, "Hellenistic Art," *CAH* 8 (1930) 668-708

Chr. Blinkenberg, K. F. Kinch, E. Dyggve, *Lindos, fouilles et recherches 1902-1914*, 1952, 3 vols. in 4 (Berlin and Copenhagen 1931, 1942, 1960)

E. Boehringer, "Pergamon," *NDA* 121-151 (Asklepieion)

J. Bradford, "Aerial Discoveries in Rhodes," *AntJ* 36 (1956) 57-69

E. Breccia, *Alexandrea ad Aegyptum* (Bergamo 1922)

E. Dusenbery, "A Samothracian Necropolis," *Arch* 12 (1959) 163-170

E. M. Forster, *Pharos and Pharillon* (London 1918)

———, *Alexandria: a Guide*[2] (New York 1961)

A. Gabriel, "La construction, l'attitude, et l'emplacement du Colosse de Rhodes," *BCH* 56 (1932) 331-359

L. Heuzey, H. Daumet, *Mission archéologique de Macédoine*, 2 vols. (Paris 1876). I, 175-226: Palatitsa

H. Kähler, *Der grosse Fries von Pergamon* (Berlin 1948)

J. D. Kondis, "Anaskaphikai ereunai eis ten polin tes Rhodou," *Prakt* 1951, 224-245; 1952, 547-591; 1953, 275-287; 1954, 340-360; 1955, 267-283

D. I. Lazarides, *Thasos* (Salonika 1958)

K. Lehmann, "Excavations in Samothrace," *AJA* 43 (1939) 133-145; 44 (1940) 328-358; *Hesp* 19 (1950) 1-20; 20 (1951) 1-30; 21 (1952) 19-43; 22 (1953) 1-24; *Arch* 6 (1953) 30-35; 7 (1954) 91-95

———, *Samothrace* [2] (Locust Valley 1960)

R. Martin, "L'agora," *Études thasiennes* 6 (1959)

M. Mellink, "Archaeology in Asia Minor." *AJA* 59 (1955) 236-37; 60 (1956) 381-82; 62 (1958) 98-99; 63 (1959) 83-84; 64 (1960) 66; 65 (1961) 48-49 (Claros)

L. Morricone, "Scavi e ricerche a Coo, 1935-43," *BdA* 35 (1950) 54-75, 219-246, 316-331

P. Petsas, "New Discoveries at Pella," *Arch* 11 (1958) 246-254

K. A. Rhomaios, "To anaktoron tes Palatitsas," *ArchEph* 1953/54 (1955) 141-150

P. Roussel, *Délos* (Paris 1925)

A. Rowe, "Excavations at Pompey's Pillar," *BSRAA* 35 (1942) 124-161

――――, "Excavations at Kôm-el-Shukafa," *ib.* 3-45

P. Schazmann, *Kos* I, i: *Asklepieion* (Berlin 1932)

J. Schramm, "Der grosse Altar," *Altertümer von Pergamon* III. i (Berlin 1906)

E. Schulte, *Der Pergamon-Altar, entdeckt, beschrieben, und gezeichnet von Carl Humann* (Dortmund 1960)

E. Sjöqvist, R. Stilwell, "Excavations at Morgantina (Serra Orlando)," *AJA* 61 (1957) 151-159; 62 (1958) 158-164; 63 (1959) 169-173; 64 (1960) 125-135; 65 (1961) 277-281; 66 (1962) 135-143

H. A. Thompson, "Stoa of Attalus," *Arch* 2 (1949) 124-130; see also *Hesp* 23 (1954) 55-57; 24 (1955) 59-61; 25 (1956) 66-68; 26 (1957) 103-107

R. Vallois, *L'architecture hellénique et hellénistique à Delos* (Paris 1944)

H. Winnefeld, "Die Friese der grossen Altars," *Alt. von Perg.* III. ii (Berlin 1910)

W. Zschietzschmann, "Pergamon," *RE* (1937) Sp. 1235-1266

CHAPTER 8: *The Greek World under Roman Sway*

E. Bacon, *Digging up History* (London 1960) 80-84 (Athenian Agora)

O. Broneer, "Terracotta Lamps," *Corinth* IV. ii (Cambridge, Mass. 1930)

――――, *A Guide to the Excavations of Ancient Corinth* [4] (Athens 1947)

F. Dörner, "Die Entdeckung vom Arsameia am Nymphenfluss und die Ausgrabungen im Hierothesion des Mithradates Kallinikos von Kommagene," *NDA* 71-88

T. Goell, "The Excavation of the 'Hierothesion' of Antiochus I of Commagene on Nemrud Dagh (1953-56)," *BASOR* 147 (Oct., 1957) 4-22

P. Graindor, *Athènes sous Auguste* (Cairo 1927)

――――, *Athènes sous Hadrien* (Cairo 1934)

――――, *Un milliardaire antique: Hérode Atticus et sa famille* (Cairo 1930)

E. Honigmann, "Kommagene" *RE* Supplbd 4 (1924) Sp. 978-990

R. Horn, *loc. cit.* supra, Ch. 4

C. Humann, O. Puchstein, *Reisen in Kleinasien und Nordsyrien* (Berlin 1890). Nemrud Dagh.

G. Karo, "Archäologische Funde," *AA* 1931, 224-227. Piraeus plaques.

C. Kraeling, *Gerasa* (New Haven 1938)

M. Lang, C. W. J. Eliot, *The Athenian Agora: A Guide to the Excavations* (Athens 1954) New ed. in preparation by H. A. Thompson.

————, "The Athenian Citizen," *APB* 4 (Princeton 1960). Kleroteria.

D. Levi, "Missioni in Levante," *ASAtene* n.s. 19/20 (1957/58) 398-401. Cyrene

F. Miltner, *Ephesos* (Vienna 1958)

F. von Oppeln-Bronikowsky, *Archäologische Entdeckungen im 20. Jahrhundert* (Berlin 1931). Piraeus plaques.

H. Plommer, *Ancient and Classical Architecture* (London 1956)

D. M. Robinson, *Baalbek and Palmyra* (New York 1946)

H. S. Robinson, "The Tower of the Winds and the Roman Market-Place," *AJA* 47 (1943) 291-305

M. Rostovtzeff, *Caravan Cities* (Oxford 1932). Palmyra and Dura.

————, *Dura-Europus and Its Art* (Oxford 1938)

G. Roux, *Pausanias en Corinthe* (Paris 1958)

H. C. Rutledge, "Herodes Atticus, the Greek Citizen of the World," *CJ* 56 (1960/61) 97-109

H. Schrader, "Archäologische Funde," *AA* 1931, 287-293. Piraeus plaques

R. L. Scranton, "The Lower Agora," *Corinth* I. iii (Cambridge, Mass. 1951)

T. L. Shear, annual reports on excavations in the Athenian Agora, *Hesp* 2 (1933); 4-10 (1935-41)

M. A. Sisson, "The Stoa of Hadrian at Athens," *BSR* 11 (1929) 50-72

H. A. Thompson, annual reports on excavations in the Athenian Agora, *Hesp* 16 (1947)-29 (1960)

————, "Buildings on the West Side of the Agora," *ib.* 6 (1937) 1-226

————, "The Odeion in the Athenian Agora," *ib.* 19 (1950) 31-141

————, "The Athenian Agora (A Sketch of the Evolution of its Plan)," *Acta Congressi Madvigiani* 1 (Copenhagen 1958) 341-352

C. Watzinger, "Palmyra," *RE* (1949) Sp. 262-277

S. S. Weinberg, "The Southeast Building; the Twin Basilicas," *Corinth* I. v (Princeton 1960) 35-109

T. Wiegand, *Baalbek*, 3 vols. (Berlin 1921-25)

————, *Palmyra: Ergebnisse der Expeditionen von 1902 und 1917*, 2 vols. (Berlin 1932)

INDEX

INDEX
OF PROPER NAMES

Other MENTOR Books on Ancient Greek
and Roman Civilization

THE GREEK EXPERIENCE   by C. M. Bowra

An extraordinary study of Greek culture, its achievements and philosophy. Forty-eight pages of photographs.

(#MP349—60¢)

THE WORLD OF ROME   by Michael Grant

A brilliant survey of the conquest and culture of the Romans from 133 B.C. to A.D. 217. Profusely illustrated with photographs, line drawings and maps.

(#MT351—75¢)

BULFINCH'S MYTHOLOGY: Volume I, The Age of Fable

A retelling of the myths of ancient Greece and Rome, with Introduction by Palmer Bovie.   (#MP449—60¢)

MYTHS OF THE GREEKS AND ROMANS
by Michael Grant

Taking full advantage of contemporary scholarship, Dr. Grant presents the ancient myths in engrossing fashion.

(#MQ562—95¢)

THE ANCIENT MYTHS   by Norma Lorre Goodrich

A vivid retelling of the great myths of Greece, Egypt, India, Persia, Crete, Sumer, and Rome. (#MP528—60¢)

THE METAMORPHOSES   by Ovid, translated and
with an Introduction by Horace Gregory

Ovid's magnificent collection of legends and myths, translated into vital modern poetry.   (#MQ579—95¢)

GREEK HISTORICAL THOUGHT
edited by Arnold J. Toynbee

The eminent historian's brilliant translations of Greek historical experience from Homer to the age of Heraclius —a stimulating guide for our own times.

(#MP431—60¢)

The Literature and Thought of Classical Civilization in a Wide Selection of MENTOR Books

THE ILIAD OF HOMER   **translated by W.H.D. Rouse**
A brilliant prose translation of Homer's great epic of the Trojan War, by a noted English scholar.
(#MT650—60¢)

THE ODYSSEY OF HOMER   **translated by W.H.D. Rouse**
A modern prose translation of the world's greatest adventure story, the travels of Ulysses. (#MT677—75¢)

THE AENEID   **by Vergil, translated by Patric Dickinson**
The great Roman epic of adventure, war, and love, in a brilliant new verse translation by a noted English poet and classical scholar.   (#MT348—75¢)

THE OEDIPUS PLAYS OF SOPHOCLES
                                                translated by Paul Roche
A dramatic and forceful new verse translation of "Oedipus the King," "Oedipus at Colonus," and "Antigone," suitable for both acting and reading. (#MT238—75¢)

PROMETHEUS BOUND   **by Aeschylus**
                                                translated by Paul Roche
A brilliant new translation by a noted British classical scholar and poet of the great classical drama of man's striving for progress and enlightenment.
(#MP561—60¢)

THREE GREAT PLAYS OF EURIPIDES
                                                translated by Rex Warner
The tragedies of "Medea," "Hippolytus," and "Helen" in a new verse translation.   (#MT241—75¢)

THE LOVE POEMS OF OVID
                                        translated by Horace Gregory
New verse translations by a distinguished poet, of selections from Ovid's famous *Amores, The Art of Love,* and *The Cures of Love.*   (#MP578—60¢)

To Our Readers: If your dealer does not have the Signet and Mentor books you want, you may order them by mail enclosing the list price plus 10¢ a copy to cover mailing. (New York City residents add 5% Sales Tax. Other New York State residents add 2% plus any local sales or use taxes.) If you would like our free catalog, please request it by postcard. The New American Library, Inc., P. O. Box 2310, Grand Central Station, New York, N. Y. 10017.